T0320077

MEASURING UP

SOCIAL SCIENCE HISTORY

Edited by

Stephen Haber and David W. Brady

MEASURING UP

A History of Living Standards in Mexico, 1850–1950

MORAMAY LÓPEZ-ALONSO

STANFORD UNIVERSITY PRESS

Stanford, California

Stanford University Press
Stanford, California

This book has been published with the assistance of the
Dean of Humanities at Rice University.

Library of Congress Cataloging-in-Publication Data

López-Alonso, Moramay, author.
  Measuring up : a history of living standards in Mexico,
1850-1950 / Moramay López-Alonso.
    pages cm.—(Social science history)
  Includes bibliographical references and index.
  ISBN 978-0-8047-7316-4 (cloth : alk. paper)
  1. Cost and standard of living—Mexico—History.
2. Stature—Mexico—History. 3. Diet—Mexico—
History. 4. Public health—Mexico—History. 5. Public
welfare—Mexico—History. 6. Poverty—Mexico—
History. I. Title. II. Series: Social science history.
  HD6996.L658 2012
  339.4'7097209034—dc23
                                              2012010625

Typeset by Newgen in 10.5/13 Bembo

Para mis padres, Angélica Esmeralda Alonso Zepeda y Carlos Eduardo López Lara

For Bill

CONTENTS

Tables

Figures

Photographs

ACKNOWLEDGMENTS

Research for this study was done in two stages. The first was completed at the Department of History at Stanford University and was supported handsomely by the Consejo Nacional de Ciencia y Tecnología and the Centro de Investigación y Docencia Económica in Mexico, a Graduate Research Opportunity Grant at Stanford University, and a Mellon Foundation Summer Research Grant. I conducted the second stage of my research while I was head of the Dirección de Estudios Financieros Internacionales at the Secretaría de Hacienda y Crédito Público in Mexico.

Research in Mexico was carried out at the Dirección General de Archivo e Historia at Secretaría de la Defensa Nacional, the Dirección General de Delegaciones at Secretaría de Relaciones Exteriores, the Archivo General de la Nación, the Biblioteca del Instituto Nacional de Antropología e Historia, and the Hemeroteca Nacional. I would like to express my appreciation to the directors and staff of all these institutions for their efficiency, expertise, and patience, especially at those archives that were not open to the public. I would also like to thank my wonderful research team at the Hacienda. Raúl Porras Condey, Manuel del Monte, Rogelio Sandoval, and Emmanuel Vargas, with the assistance of a number of *servicio social* students, enthusiastically combined research in the public finances with data gathering and the construction of height databases, for which they had to learn more anthropometric history than they ever anticipated. Without their help I would not have been able to complete the second stage of archival research. A word of thanks goes to Jean Niswonger at Rice University's GIS Data Center, who helped me prepare the maps.

The initial writing of this book was done at the Center for U.S.–Mexican Studies at the University of California, San Diego, where I was a visiting research fellow in 2004–2005. A Richard Gilder Fellowship at the Humanities Research Center at Rice University in 2007–2009 enabled me to develop my arguments. I would like to thank the Department of History at Rice University for granting me leave to make final revisions to the manuscript.

Stephen H. Haber made this work possible in all sorts of ways. I thank him for his unwavering support and for encouraging me to delve into a topic barely studied in the economic history of Mexico. To him I owe an immense debt of gratitude. Herbert Klein helped open doors in the field of anthropometric history. Richard Steckel and John Komlos have given me the benefit of their time and expertise since my days as a graduate student; they welcomed me to the anthropometric history group. Without their counsel, analyzing height data would have been a daunting task. Catherine Mansell Mayo has been a source of courage, inspiration, and strength throughout.

I appreciate the comments on the living standards/anthropometric history portions of this study provided by Joerg Baten, Antonio D. Cámara Hueso, Amílcar Challú, Tim Cuff, Zephyr Frank, Jorge Gelman, Kris Inwood, Lyman Johnson, José Miguel Martínez-Carrión, Adolfo Meisel, Alexander Moradi, Ricardo Salvatore, Daniel Santilli, Marco Sunder, and Virginia Vitzthum. Carl Caldwell read and provided extremely useful comments on two versions of Section 1.

John H. Coatsworth, Eric Van Young, the late Paul Vanderwood, and John Womack Jr. provided sage advice on Latin American and economic history. A special word of thanks goes to Richard Salvucci, who read the entire manuscript with care and penetrating insight and whose own work on Mexican economic history serves as an example to all scholars.

In Mexico several researchers shared their time and expertise. Lourdes Márquez Morfín gave me direction on how to undertake interdisciplinary research combining physical anthropology and history. Doctor Francisco Gómez Pérez from Instituto Nacional de Nutrición was generous with his time and in sharing documents with me that do not circulate frequently outside of the medical community. Conversations with him gave me a better understanding of the synergies between health and nutrition in the Mexican population. With his assistance I was also able to bring together the knowledge I had acquired on human biology and archival information about health with the current health status of the Mexican population. Hugo López Gatell and Arantxa Colchero were kind to spend time talking to me about the relationship between nutrition and pathologies of the Mexican population and how they relate to public health problems in contemporary Mexico. Through our dialogue I was able to shape my argument on the link between public health policies and the needs of the population. Laura Cházaro García shared her work and gave me time, both of which were valuable in helping me construct the argument on the history of science and medicine in Mexico. Luisa Gabayet, the late Carmen Casta-ñeda, Sandra Kuntz, Graciela Márquez, Aurora Gómez-Galvarriato, Luis Jáuregui, and Antonio Ibarra gave me the opportunity to present my work in different academic fora. The comments and reactions of the audiences were crucial in the writing process.

Many colleagues discussed the ideas in this study with me. My conversations with Edward Beatty, Yovanna Pineda, William Suárez-Potts, William Summerhill, and Mauricio Tenorio-Trillo were especially valuable; I treasure their friendship and support.

Many colleagues and friends at Rice University have contributed in different ways to the preparation of this book. In particular, the help and support of Carl Caldwell, Caroline Levander, Aysha Pollnitz, Allison Snider, Kerry Ward, and Lora Wildenthal have been and are much valued and appreciated.

Anthony G. Lozano read, revised, and critiqued the entire manuscript twice and revised my translations. With endless patience, my uncle Tony has been helping me overcome the Hispanic baroque tendencies in my use of the English language.

Earlier versions of some of the arguments I present in Section 2 were published in "The Ups and Downs of Mexican Economic Growth: The Biological Standard of Living and Inequality, 1870–1950," *Economics and Human Biology* 1, no. 2 (2003): 169–86, and "Growth and Inequality: Standards of Living in Mexico, 1850–1950," *Journal of Latin American Studies* 39 (2007): 81–105. I am grateful to these journals for giving me the opportunity to publish; the book has benefited from the feedback I received from the reviewers of those articles.

Among the many to whom I owe gratitude, three people stand out: my parents, Angélica Esmeralda Alonso Zepeda and Carlos Eduardo López Lara, and my husband, Bill. My parents provided me with unconditional love and have supported in every way they can all my endeavors. My husband, Bill, has endured the enjoyment and the hardships of writing this book. For all their help, love, and support, I dedicate this book to them.

AGN	Archivo General de la Nación
CIESAS	Centro de Investigaciones y Estudios Superiores en Antropología Social
COLMEX	El Colegio de México
CONASUPO	National Food Support Program
COPLAMAR	Program for Depressed Regions and Marginalized Groups
DMR	Diminishing marginal returns
DSP	Departamento de Salud Pública
ENAH	Escuela Nacional de Antropología e Historia
HR	Height requirement
IMSS	Instituto Mexicano del Seguro Social
INAH	Instituto Nacional de Antropología e Historia
INEGI	Instituto Nacional de Estadística Geografía e Informática
INNSZ	Instituto Nacional de Nutrición Salvador Zubirán
ISSSTE	Instituto de Seguridad y Servicios Sociales de los Trabajadores del Estado
K&K	Komlos-Kim test
NCHS	National Center for Health Statistics
OLS	Ordinary least square regression
PEM	Protein energy malnutrition
PRI	Partido Revolucionario Institucional
PRONASOL	Programa Nacional de Solidaridad
RFIHD	Rockefeller Foundation International Health Division
SAM	Mexican Agrarian System
SDN	Secretaría de la Defensa Nacional
SRE	Secretaría de Relaciones Exteriores
SSA	Secretaría de Salubridad y Asistencia
TOLS	Truncated ordinary least square regression
TR	Truncated Regression
UNAM	Universidad Nacional Autónoma de México

MEASURING UP

Introduction

In twenty-first-century Mexico, politicians of the new democratic era are not shy about openly stating that poverty and inequality are the root causes of the old and new social problems the country suffers. During electoral campaigns, politicians of all levels (federal, state, and municipal) and of all parties repeatedly promise they will enact poverty-alleviation programs more effectively than their predecessors. This political rhetoric has become commonplace since the Partido Revolucionario Institucional (PRI) lost the presidential elections for the first time in 2000. Whereas studies of poverty have certainly commented about its contemporary extent, historical overviews of antipoverty policies and their impact on the population are as novel as the ubiquity of poverty-alleviation promises in electoral campaigns is common. Existing studies on poverty in Mexico reveal limitations not only in scope, but also in analyzing the effectiveness of past government policies. Moreover, most studies fail to contextualize these issues in terms of national, world, and scientific events. Electoral speeches can be taken as recognition of the state of affairs of poverty and inequality in Mexico at the beginning of the twenty-first century. *Measuring Up* shows how new research tools and an interdisciplinary perspective enable us to delve more deeply into the roles that governmental policies have played in connection with nutrition, health, and poverty, as well as how these various elements intersect, in the century between 1850 and 1950.

Although today it is acceptable to acknowledge the degree of poverty and inequality prevailing in Mexico and blame former administrations for it, it is important to recall that each administration in turn established programs to combat the conditions leading to poverty. For example, on December 12, 1988, at the beginning of his presidential administration, Carlos Salinas de Gortari created the National Solidarity Program (PRONASOL), which was designed to foster social development.[1]

At the time, the economic crisis that had hit Mexico hard throughout the 1980s had substantially decreased the real wages of the working classes, the number of people falling into extreme poverty was rapidly increasing,

1

and the resulting social discontent was reaching worrisome levels. In addition to the difficult economic circumstances, the controversial and contested 1988 presidential elections made Carlos Salinas de Gortari politically vulnerable. Maintaining political stability hinged upon the capacity to take prompt action to offer solutions to social problems. But the origins of poverty and inequality did not form part of the economic crisis of the 1980s, nor was PRONASOL the first program launched to address these issues.[2] Since the 1960s, the falling contribution of agriculture to gross domestic product (GDP) has been a warning of a potential crisis of the rural sector, and it has necessitated the government's creation of programs to reverse the decline in agricultural production and the pauperization of the rural population.[3] This is how programs such as the National Food Support Program (CONASUPO) in the 1960s, the Mexican Agrarian System (SAM) in the 1970s, and the National Program for Depressed Regions and Marginalized Groups (COPLAMAR) in the early 1980s were created. Poverty, however, was not a mid-twentieth-century phenomenon, and government policies were not able to eradicate it.

As far back as 1937, President Lázaro Cárdenas established that it was the government's responsibility to assist the poor beyond the provision of basic needs and medical assistance.[4] The objective behind this initiative was to integrate the poor into the labor force so that they could earn their own living and contribute to Mexico's economic growth. This was the first time in the history of modern Mexico that a president stated that assisting the poor was the responsibility of the state—nearly two decades after the revolution had ended.[5] Interestingly enough, social assistance programs were launched at the national level in 1940 only after land and labor reforms were completed, and only when a critical mass of workers and peasants had been sufficiently co-opted by the ruling party to ensure political stability.

By the time Lázaro Cárdenas announced that it was the government's responsibility to assist the poor, Mexico had been an independent nation for nearly 120 years. For much of this time, different governments had worked to eliminate institutions that represented the colonial order. One of the fiercest battles was fought against the Catholic Church and all this institution represented. National governments divested the Catholic Church of its wealth, its privileges, and its powers. This process was slow because it was challenged by different social groups at different times. Sometimes the challenges resulted in violent confrontations. Significantly, the Church lost control over resources to assist the needy. In 1861, the liberal government issued a decree to secularize the remaining ecclesiastical welfare institutions and proceeded to confiscate their assets. Only in 1937, when Lázaro

Cárdenas announced the principle that the government was to be responsible for assisting the poor and took concrete measures to address this matter, did these welfare institutions emerge from a form of legal and institutional limbo. Between 1861 and 1937, the government did not want the Church's interference in state affairs, including charity and welfare; yet it was not certain what to do with the poor.

The rise of capitalism and the philosophical beliefs that endorsed it explained poverty in a way that challenged the traditional religious notions that it was inherent to all societies.[6] In Mexico, the bourgeoisie that formed out of the modernization of the economy, industrialization, and export-led growth during the second half of the nineteenth and early twentieth centuries favored liberal ideas. The secularization of society was a foundation of the liberal revolution. This meant promising equality before the law for all citizens, a rejection of Catholic religion and its privileges, and the rejection of any form of corporate property in favor of the principle of private property. With the rise of anticlericalism came the demise of charitable donations to the Church as an increasing proportion of the oligarchy stopped believing that it was necessary to share part of their wealth with the poor to secure their place in the kingdom of heaven. Although new modes of production created more wealth, capitalists in particular were less willing to engage in charitable enterprises. Moreover, popular social Darwinist ideas, holding that the poor were poor because they were less fit for survival, reinforced the notion that it was useless to give charity to individuals that society had labeled as undesirable. It should be stressed that the oligarchy that emerged after the 1910 Mexican Revolution were even fit generous than their predecessors. The government's anticlerical policies along with its failure to define a welfare program for the lower classes combined with the already declining interest of the oligarchy in sharing their wealth with the poor. Inevitably, this was not conducive to a more equitable society. This trend would guarantee that in spite of the sociopolitical and economic transformation that took place in Mexico during the period 1850–1950, the number of people living in poverty would continue to rise. Astonishingly, historians have focused very little attention on how this central fact of life in Mexican society took place.

The Mexican government launched emergency poverty-alleviation programs even in the midst of the period of sustained economic growth known as the Mexican Miracle (1940–1970). This raises the questions: Were levels of poverty and inequality among the Mexican population ever not a critical issue? Was there a "golden era" of equality that politicians so readily promised? Based on the extant historiography it is hard to know what happened prior to the 1950s. There is substantial literature on the history of government welfare policies and on the programs devoted to fighting poverty since 1950, as if poverty and inequality were both phenomena that emerged in the 1950s, but this is not the case. Moreover, it would be hard to write a history of poverty and inequality without knowing the evolution of living standards. Unfortunately, the history of living standards is a subject that social, political, and economic historians have marginalized.

Of course, there is no period in the history of Mexico as a modern nation in which poverty and inequality were not issues, and no scholar denies their importance. Still, the traditional historiography that covers the period 1850–1950 addresses these topics tangentially. Much of this early historiography was written to justify and extol the 1910 Mexican Revolution. Later scholars tended to present facts from a Marxist perspective, trying to highlight the damage that capitalist development inflicted on peasants and workers. The deterioration in the standards of living and its implications for levels of poverty and inequality are constantly mentioned both as consequences of government policies and causes of political instability. To substantiate their assertions, historians have relied mainly on anecdotal information.

The general argument has been that the reforms of the mid-nineteenth century incorporated into the Constitution of 1857 mandated the privatization of lands, permitting their seizure by wealthy landowners with the government's consent.[7] The reform laws and related government policies were implemented differently throughout the country.[8] Wealthy landowners with government connections who were seeking to expand their commercial agricultural operations took advantage of this new legislation to seize peasants' communal and private lands that were near their properties. Peasants were deprived of their land and hence became dependent on wage labor for the large haciendas. Consequently, by becoming dependent on wages, peasants also became more vulnerable to changes in the price of basic foodstuffs.[9]

For small landholders, land seizure occurred somewhat differently. Most small landholders were ranchers who had obtained the title to their land from the government as a reward for their willingness to emigrate north to colonize the region and defend it from foreign invasions and indigenous attacks. The construction of the railroads that linked the north to the rest of the Mexico and to the United States, along with heavy foreign investments to industrialize the regions, increased the value of land as well as the incentive to expropriate it. Land seizures were undertaken by local oligarchies of landholders while the government made no attempt to respond to the complaints of the colonists and of the indigenous tribes of the region.[10]

Scholars writing in the decades after the revolution used emotionally charged anecdotal evidence to substantiate their argument that living standards in the countryside deteriorated as a result of land privatization and concentration of ownership in the nineteenth century. Jesús Silva Herzog describes "unhappy populations with no fire in their homes, no shoes and empty stomachs."[11] Luis González writes about peasants who lived semi-enslaved in the haciendas and workers who, "being victims of an uncertain life, preferred to be drunk half of their lives."[12] In brief, traditional historiography treats land seizures and dependency on wage labor as synonymous with deterioration in the standard of living of the bulk of the rural population.[13]

With regard to the urban and industrial proletariat, the traditional argument is that discontent started circa 1900. Prior to 1900, investments in industry created jobs that paid reasonably well. The downsides of industrialization came later. As early as the 1930s scholars were supporting this argument. In 1934 Marjorie Ruth Clark wrote, "As industrialization of the country proceeded, the cost of living rose rapidly while wages, generally speaking, remained almost stationary. The already miserable standard of living fell even lower."[14] Compared to the peasant population, industrial and urban workers represented a minority of the working class. However, they represented the labor force in the most dynamic sector, and their protests also created trouble in the cities for the government authorities.

The decline in real wages was a quintessential example of the decline in living standards of the urban working classes prior to the 1910 Revolution. Traditional historiography presents the strikes of Cananea (1906) and Río Blanco (1907) for higher wages as the origins of the revolution. Through Charles Cumberland's work on the Mexican Revolution we learn that, according to early twentieth-century estimates, the laborer's average wage ranged between twenty-five and fifty cents. By way of contrast, the price of basic commodities had increased during the same period.[15] Frank Tannenbaum explains, "Industrialization was paralleled by a rapid increase in the cost of living without a corresponding rise in the wages of the masses."[16] Pioneering traditional Mexican historians of the revolution, like Alfonso Teja Zabre, argued along the same lines.[17] Decades later, Friedrich Katz still uses the same wage argument in his explanations of the causes that led the working classes to join the revolutionary movements as he writes, "The most immediate cause of worker dissatisfaction was the sharp decline in living standards between 1900 and 1910. Even in the period up to 1907 real wages were eroded by inflation."[18]

Most of the statistical information to support these arguments of the decline in living standards based on rising prices and stagnant wages is very limited. These sources are not very reliable as they have two problems: first, they are very limited as to the years and the places they cover; second, it is not clear how the data were gathered. In the case of peasants, the simple assertion that land seizures provoked a decline in living standards does not offer a tangible comparison of how standards of living declined.

For the postrevolutionary period, what we know about living standards is told indirectly. The historiography is very explicit in describing all investments that were made to modernize the country. One underlying assumption is that modernization was meant to improve the living standards of the population. The efforts translated into social reforms aimed at improving the working conditions and the property rights of the laboring classes, for example, through the land reforms (Article 27) and the labor reforms (Article 123) of the 1917 Constitution.[19] These reforms, however, are described as slow and limited: "Historians who point to the paucity of reform in the 1920s and the conservatism of the regime are right. . . . Formal policies— the doings of the state and the political elite—were not co-terminus with social reality, and things often changed (or refused to change) in defiance of governmental wishes."[20] Elite reluctance about change did not go as far as dismissing these reforms altogether because there was a constant threat of popular revolt. Through the unionization of the working class, laborers gained, at least to a certain extent, some bargaining power over their working conditions and wage levels. Land redistribution, on the other hand, is described by Alan Knight as a positive policy for living standards: "In the short term, it not only enhanced peasant living standards and self-esteem but also shifted the political balance."[21]

Nowhere in the literature do we find compelling evidence on exactly how the standards of living improved. There is no attempt to actually measure the living standards to draw a comparison with the Porfirio Díaz regime and—to the degree that quantitative evidence is brought to bear—the analysis is not based on substantial systematic evidence.[22] There is, however, a constant mention of the need to decrease inequality and alleviate poverty. As early as 1947, the leading historian of the Colegio de México, Daniel Cosío Villegas, asserted that the revolutionary government had failed to diminish inequality, commenting: "Instead of being distributed equally among the most numerous groups and those in greatest need of moving up the social scale, the new wealth was allowed to fall into the hands of a few who of course had no special merit of any kind."[23] In writing on Mexico's economic development, a leading economic historian of the mid-twentieth century, Fernando Rosenzweig, points out the poor distribution of income as one of the problems of contemporary Mexico. He bases his assertion on the data obtained in the first measurement of income distribution in 1957. He exposes the improvement of living standards as one of the tasks that need to be fulfilled by the postrevolutionary government.[24] Interestingly, he makes no attempt to explain why this had not already been addressed.

In the past decades cultural historians of Mexico—in Mexico and abroad—have been increasingly interested in writing the histories of the lower strata of the population with regard to both urban and rural individuals. Today the historiography on modern Mexico is rife with studies on the activities, values, yearnings, troubles, frustrations, and projects of marginalized members of society. These studies emphasize the "history from below" perspective. In contrast, almost no studies have been written on the history of poverty and inequality as sociopolitical and economic phenomena for the national period prior to 1950. Two exceptions in this historiographical lacuna are Moisés González Navarro's *La pobreza en México*, written in 1985, and Silvia Marina Arrom's *Containing the Poor*, published in 2000.

Judging by the scholarship produced in the fields of social, political, and economic history of Mexico in recent decades, it appears that the study of living standards has failed to awaken an interest among these scholars. There are, however, some exceptions to this apparent marginalization of the subject, such as the price series for foodstuffs created by the Colegio de México (COLMEX) group, as well as works by John Coatsworth, Aurora Gómez Galvarriato, and Jeffrey Bortz. The COLMEX group undertook the first attempt to build data series on basic food prices and wages, and then inferred the living standards of the working classes by trying to estimate their purchasing power. Nonetheless, they did not take into account the fact that a substantial portion of the population operated outside the monetized economy.[25] The works of Coatsworth, Gómez Galvarriato, and Bortz look at the evolution of living standards with a systematic analysis of wages and food price data, but their works only concentrate on a specific region or a specific sector at some point in time in the nineteenth or twentieth century.

Coatsworth's essay, "La producción de alimentos durante el Porfiriato," shows that food production for domestic consumption increased at the same rate as population growth. He thus rejects the traditional hypothesis that developmental policies favoring industry and the export sector were detrimental to agricultural production for domestic consumption. His findings, in the aggregate, suggest that Mexicans were not eating less.[26] Coatsworth, however, does not venture to say anything about how this food production was distributed among the different strata of the population, leaving the effects of distribution as a subject for further study.[27]

Bortz's work focuses on industrial wages in Mexico City from 1939 to 1975. The data series produced by the government for that time period resulted from different methodologies and changes in the definitions of some of the industries. Bortz circumvents this problem by constructing a data series using firm-level data. He finds that real wages in Mexican industry fell sharply after 1939, reached a low point in 1946, remained exceedingly low until 1952, and did not recover their 1939 levels until 1968.[28] Bortz's recent essay with Marco Aguila, "Earning a Living: A History of Real Wage Studies in Twentieth-Century Mexico," concludes: "It is not clear that any generation of Mexican industrial workers can experience modernization of supply and demand for labor—under conditions of sustained underdevelopment."[29] In other words, in spite of heavy modernization during World War II, wages remained at an underdeveloped level.

Aurora Gómez-Galvarriato's work on the evolution of prices and wages from the Porfiriato (1876–1910) to the decade following the outbreak of the 1910 Revolution also offers an interesting analysis of the living standards of industrial textile workers in Orizaba. She shows that real wages declined only toward the end of the Porfiriato, by 18 percent between 1907 and 1910.[30] However, she has also noted on the basis of other works that in certain respects, in contrast to agricultural workers, industrial workers were relatively privileged.[31] A recent historiographical essay by Gómez-Galvarriato and Mauricio Tenorio Trillo, which reviews studies on the economic history of the Porfiriato, suggests that very little of this literature addresses the evolution of living standards across Mexico.[32] Since the 1970s Coatsworth has been concerned with the evolution of living standards in Latin America and, up to this day, he continues to highlight the importance of studying living standards in a long-run perspective. Coatsworth has recently mentioned the possibility of using trends in stature as a tool to measure the biological standards of living.[33] Nevertheless, except for the work of Coatsworth, Bortz, and Gómez-Galvarriato, there has been no attempt to measure living standards over a long period.

Thus, apart from González Navarro's *La pobreza en México*, there have been no long-term studies on any of these three subjects. It is surprising that this void actually exists given the fact that living standards are better understood when analyzed in a long-term perspective. Poverty and inequality cannot be altered in a short period of time unless there are radical social, political, and economic changes, such as a sustained revolutionary transformation as was the case with Cuba and Russia. Mexico had a revolution in 1910, but its effectiveness in improving the quality of living standards of the masses is uncertain. Government documents argued one thing; the results told a different story. Indeed, one example of the uncertainty of the effects of the revolution is the fact that there is no consensus with regard to how long it lasted. To this day, scholars still debate when the Mexican Revolution actually ended.[34]

By focusing on factors of height and biological well-being, this book can contrast fluctuations in the biological and material standard of living with government policies and historiographical assertions about such policies or political and economic changes. A national approach to the evolution of living standards facilitates comparisons across regions and social classes. *Measuring Up* therefore offers the first national examination of the evolution of poverty and inequality over the hundred-year period from 1850 to 1950.

The concept of "living standards" itself differs significantly across disciplines. This study takes into account the multifaceted nature of the subject. Hence, living standards will be examined from the perspectives of politics, economics, demography, scientific advances in the field of medicine and nutrition, and technological innovation applied to public health. History is used as a bridge across these disciplines. The aim is to present an integral study of the history of living standards over a hundred-year period in Mexico. I should also clarify that the scope of this book does not address the evolution of spiritual and emotional living standards of the Mexican population. These aspects of well-being fall outside the scope of this study.

The period 1850–1950 is fundamental in the history of Mexico because of profound transformations that took place both in Mexico and worldwide. Over this century, Mexico went from being a mainly rural, preindustrial country to a modern, industrialized economy full of the contrasts and disparities we recognize today. Political upheaval, a foreign invasion, and civil wars also made their mark in this time period. These events inevitably had an impact on the living standards of the population. There were global changes that had impacted Mexico's population. Research findings in the natural sciences made it possible to learn about the causes of the most deadly infectious diseases, their prevention, and eventually, their treatment and cure. Technological innovations in civil engineering allowed the building of effective sanitary infrastructure in cities at a time when populations were becoming increasingly urbanized as a result of industrialization and economic modernization. Science and technology made it possible to improve public health, leading to what Richard Easterlin has called a "Mortality Revolution."[35] These transformations reached Mexico during this period and had significant repercussions in the living standards of the population.

The dearth of long-term studies on poverty and inequality in Mexico before 1950 is partly due to the lack of relevant databases to analyze the evolution of standards of living from a long-term perspective using the same methodologies employed to measure living standards in post-1950s studies. This does not mean that it is impossible to study the history of living standards before 1950. Rather, it is necessary to find alternative methods to measure living standards. In particular, recent advances in the field of human biology allow a better understanding of the determinants of human growth. These findings have been used by economists, who have shown that human measurements can be used as a welfare measure.[36]

The interest in auxology (the study of human growth) goes back much further, to the seventeenth and eighteenth centuries. In these centuries, a few individuals recorded human heights. More extensive progress in the field of auxology came in the late nineteenth century.[37] But the deplorable use of human measurements in Hitler's Germany for racialist purposes in the 1930s and 1940s undermined the credibility of this methodology. This led to work by scholars who were interested in developing a national accounting system and in measuring welfare to avoid the use of human stature as an indicator of health and nutritional status. This culminated in the 1950s when the United Nations set standards of developing indicators to measure global living standards.[38]

Only since the 1960s have economic historians of Europe and the United States used heights to assess the impact of industrialization on the living standards of the populations, in a field that came to be known as "historical anthropometry." Most of these studies deal with the eighteenth and nineteenth centuries, when institutions like the military, prisons, and schools began to gather these data in a systematic way. However, as more scholarly research has been produced in this field, the use of heights as a measurement of living standards has been criticized by some scholars on the basis that "height is an excellent indicator of the nutritional status of children, but it has deficiencies as a more general measure of nutritional status of the whole population."[39] In this debate, other scholars have argued in favor of its use, stating, "Carefully handled, measurements of the height of adults can be excellent indicators of the nutritional status of those adults as they grow older."[40] In addition, some scholars have defended the use of height data to examine the evolution of living standards in cases in which it is the only reliable data available, as is the case of subsistence-based economies, cash economies, "and economies where the government's administrative apparatus is very weak, [and] may suffer from very poor and incomplete data collection."[41] Researchers also argue that adult heights remain relevant to study "in countries whose income levels have not reached those of the West."[42] The case of Mexico in the period 1850–1950 is one in which the use of adult heights as a measure of living standards is pertinent.

Living standards are not only affected by economic and political events; health and nutrition, too, have an impact on the quality of life. This is why Richard Steckel, a leading scholar in the field of anthropometric history, suggests that in analyzing the trends in heights in a particular country "one should take into account three equally important elements: first, the timing of industrialization relative to the recognition of germ theory of disease and public health principles; second, the extent of urbanization; and third, diet."[43] *Measuring Up* applied all these factors to the case of Mexico.

In keeping with the multidisciplinary nature of this study, the chapters of this book are organized thematically while following a chronological order within each chapter. Because this study is intended for an audience with varying interests, very technical aspects are presented in the endnotes or in the Appendix. This allows the reader to follow the argument without having to focus on quantitative analyses or on technical knowledge of welfare legislation or on the nutrients a balanced diet should include and the pathologies resulting from nutritional deficiencies.

Section 1 traces the origins of poverty alleviation, including social welfare programs from the mid-nineteenth century until 1950. It explains from a long-term perspective how the issues of poverty and the needs of those at the bottom of the social scale were addressed by the authorities in power. It includes a survey on the evolution of ideologies and objectives that informed the design of policies concerning welfare. The politics behind the provision of welfare and the design of welfare institution are also discussed.

I argue that nineteenth-century liberal reforms affected the living standards of the popular classes by reducing assistance given through religious institutions. The banning of religious corporations of lay members and the disentailment of communal property undermined local communities' ability to organize. Private welfare institutions created during the Díaz administration (1877–1911) were limited in number and extent in great part because of the absence of laws that would support and protect them. In Mexico, social legislation came late and with a certain lack of detail that allowed for the perpetuation of inequality. The labor law that emerged from the 1917 Constitution covered a small proportion of the working classes. This in turn established strong foundations for the growth of the informal economy. After many delays, the government finally established a poverty-relief agenda in the late 1930s. Although a unionized working class was eventually protected by social legislation—and this was reflected positively in their standards of living—the great majority of the working classes remained marginalized, especially those living in the countryside.

Section 2 analyzes the evolution of standards of living. It is possible to evaluate whether the evolution of welfare institutions favored the perpetuation of inequality across social classes. The first chapter presents the methods and sources employed in the analysis and discusses the subject of well-being and living standards. It goes from the philosophical question of what it means to "live well" to the more practical questions of how we measure living standards and income inequality, then to why adult heights are the best way to study the evolution of biological standards of living in Mexico. It presents a road map pointing out where to obtain height information, how to build databases, and how to organize information to analyze trends in height.

The second chapter tests the relevance of political events and policies discussed in Section 1 for the population's well-being. I compare the trends in heights of the upper and lower strata of the population as well as trends across regions. An advantage of this long-term study is that we can observe if there is a convergence over time. I also test if there the was a structural break in the trends in heights for people who were born after the enactment of the liberal reforms in the nineteenth century and after the 1910 Revolution. The timing of industrialization relative to the recognition of the germ theory of disease and public health, and the extent of urbanization and diet, are all taken into consideration. I argue that the different trajectories of heights in our samples reflect living standards of the different sectors of the population as well as the effects of welfare policies on the people's well-being. Upper classes display a tendency similar to that of the evolution of GDP per capita. The working classes inserted in the formal economy are shorter in height than the upper classes, but there is a converging trend with the wealthy. By way of contrast, the heights of people belonging to the classes who received little or no assistance to overcome poverty suffered a decline during the nineteenth century, evidence that their standards of living deteriorated during the Díaz administration and the years of the revolution. Their biological standards of living decline and do not start to recover until the 1930s. After this period recovery is relatively fast, and cohorts born in 1950 have the average stature of their ancestors born in 1850.

To complete the height analysis, I compare the case of Mexico with other countries and with respect to modern-day standards. This way it is possible to put the Mexican case in a global context. In 1850 Mexicans are not the shortest in the sample, but by 1950 they do fall to the lowest rank.

In Section 3, I will show that health and nutrition influenced the trends in heights presented in the previous section. The first chapter presents a narrative of the history of health and nutrition during the years studied. Through the examination of the health and demographic history of Mexico, as well as the evolution of dietary habits of its population, this chapter will delve into the ways in which health and nutrition influenced the evolution of the biological standards of living of the population. I argue that the unequal provision of health services, dietary habits that perpetuated nutritional deficiencies among the popular classes, and unchanging fertility patterns all played a crucial role in creating the evolution and perpetuation of unequal living standards among the Mexican population. Poor health status affected the evolution of biological standards of living of the popular classes for cohorts born between 1850 and 1950. Although some figures on health status improved over time, such as life expectancy, there were others, such as average stature of the population, for which there was no sign of improvement by the mid-twentieth century. Ongoing economic, social, and political changes would have suggested otherwise. Innovations in medicine, along with government's investments in public health and public works, were able to control the spread of infectious diseases, but there was little improvement in nutrition. Government investments were a good start to improve public health but insufficient to service a population with very rapid demographic growth. On the issue of nutrition, I will argue two things: the dietary habits of the majority of the population barely changed during this time, and there were sharp contrasts in diet across social classes. The second chapter of the section will continue to look into the synergies between health and nutrition by way of the analysis of the quantitative evidence available.

This book thus synthesizes different strands of evidence to create an integral framework for understanding the evolution of living standards of Mexico's population between 1850 and 1950. It starts to fill the historiographical lacunae on living standards. It seeks to shed light on the past, leaving food for thought on the present and future of living standards. Accordingly, it makes a contribution from the field of history for scholars of the present interested in formulating policies to alleviate poverty in countries such as Mexico that are rich but unequal.

Institutions and Living Standards

The problem of poverty all but defines modern Mexican history. This section therefore traces the origins of poverty alleviation, including social welfare programs from the mid-nineteenth century until 1950, from the time, that is, when Mexico was a preindustrial and rural nation to a period of rapid industrialization and urbanization. During the same period, Mexico underwent deep social and political transformations due to civil wars, foreign invasions, and a thirty-five-year dictatorship, among other significant events (see Table 1).

The purpose of this section is to answer one of the questions posed in the Introduction of this book: how efficient institutions in charge of social welfare were in fulfilling their mission statement over time. It does so by explaining from a long-term perspective how the issues of poverty and the needs of those at the bottom of the social scale were addressed by the authorities in power. To tackle this goal we need to survey the evolution of ideas, mentalities, and objectives that informed the design of policies concerning welfare and then assess how they were adopted in Mexico.

As industrialization gained importance in the growth and development of the Mexican economy, so did the role of the industrial proletariat in the design of welfare institutions. Concomitant to the process of industrialization and changes in the productive process were the ongoing debates around what welfare provision entailed and who should provide it. We could even talk about a distinction between welfare as charity and welfare

TABLE I
Chronology of main events and relevant presidencies,
1855–1952

Event/presidency	Years
Liberal period	1855–1876
Benito Juárez	1858–1872
Maximilian Von Hapsburg (Second Empire)	1864–1867
Porfiriato	1876–1911
Revolution	1910–1920
Francisco I. Madero	1911–1913
Postrevolutionary era	1920–1950
Álvaro Obregón	1920–1924
Plutarco Elías Calles	1924–1928
Lázaro Cárdenas	1934–1940
Manuel Avila Camacho	1940–1946
Miguel Alemán Valdés	1946–1952

as the services that the laboring classes were entitled to as part of their remuneration. Since both forms of welfare have an impact on living standards, both will be discussed in this section.

It is also important to take into consideration the role that politics played in welfare provision. During this period, politics defined the role the state would play as welfare provider and to what extent the state was going to allow or even encourage the participation of the Church and civil society in this part of the nation's life. Welfare institutions and welfare provision would be affected by the conflictive relationship between the state and the Catholic Church from the promulgation of the Reform Laws and the 1857 Constitution until the late 1930s, when a new equilibrium in Church–state relations was established and the state took a more proactive role in the provision of welfare.

Politics remained relevant after 1910, because the state's participation in welfare provision initiatives was defined to benefit groups that the ruling party viewed as allies. These initiatives were the antecedents of poverty-alleviation programs that became ubiquitous after 1950. As we will see in this section, the betterment of the living standards of the population at large and the potential gains that this improvement could bring to Mexico as a nation were part of the political rhetoric; the reality, however, was one of persistent inequality.

The argument of this section is threefold. First, in Mexico the design of welfare institutions was shaped by social and political events taking place during this period as much as by ideas on welfare developing in countries of the Western world as understood by Mexican intellectuals.

Second, the role of the Catholic Church, the most important welfare institution since the colonial period, dramatically reduced its capabilities of serving the needy during the period 1850–1950. With the triumph of liberals and the drafting of a new constitution in 1857, the state managed to establish a legal framework that undermined the power and wealth of the Catholic Church such that it diminished the size and scope of its welfare institutions. Although some secular private welfare institutions emerged during the second half of the nineteenth century, they did not fill the void left by Catholic charitable enterprises as they ceased to exist. Secular welfare institutions barely grew in number and size during the first half of the twentieth century, in large part because the state bureaucracy hindered their creation and the government did not grant them legal personality until the late 1940s.[1] In the postrevolutionary period, the limited growth of these institutions was also the result of the new centralizing and paternalistic state rhetoric that took responsibility for the people's welfare. This discourse did not favor the development of a sense of social responsibility among the upper strata of the population to inspire them to "give back," in the way it evolved in other countries of the Western world.

The third part of the argument of this section is that in Mexico, the foundations of a welfare state did not begin to take a clear shape until the late 1930s, during the Lázaro Cárdenas presidency. During the second half of the nineteenth century, politicians and intellectuals reflected extensively on the role that the state should play as a welfare provider and continued to support the idea that it was not the responsibility of the state to care for the poor. There were a few laws and policies developed around that time that had some impact on welfare. Still, the incentive behind their creation usually had to do with the need to meet the requirements of economic modernization. In the early years of the postrevolutionary era there were some glimpses of intent to establish a legal and institutional framework that could help improve the well-being of the population; after all, in the consolidation of the new revolutionary state it was important to gain the support of groups that could serve as political allies. These glimpses can be seen in the reforms made to the 1917 Constitution pertaining to labor rights. Nonetheless, the actual enforcement of the new legislation was very slow and tended to favor only a limited segment of the population, namely, those groups that the government needed as allies to guarantee political stability and, after 1929, to guarantee permanence of the ruling political party in power.

The following section is organized into three chapters. The first chapter presents the different philosophical, political, and economic ideas that informed and influenced decision makers in Mexico on the subject of welfare.

This chapter will overview debates on how the poor should be considered an undeniable part of society, if they should or should not receive any form of help, and, if so, who should be responsible for providing such assistance, the state or civil society. This chapter will also examine the different discussions around the social question that stemmed from changes in patron–client relations as a by-product of the transformation in productive processes and the rise of capitalist modes of production. In general, Mexicans emulated the Western world model, but the different countries of this group each had its own way of addressing the different aspects of welfare provision; Mexicans did not follow the example of one particular country. Instead, they borrowed ideas from different countries that they deemed feasible to adopt in Mexico, then designed and implemented their welfare institutions à la mexicaine.

The second chapter will present an overview of the evolution of charitable institutions during this time period, but will also provide a brief background on the colonial era. The purpose of this chapter is to explain how the Catholic Church went from having a monopoly in the provision of welfare through different entities such as convents, hospitals, schools for the poor, and hospices, in close collaboration with civil society at large, to being gradually dispossessed of its wealth and attributions. We will explain how the Church continued to assist those in need, even under the persecution of the state, and how new nonreligious charitable institutions emerged despite the legal and bureaucratic obstacles posed by the government.

The third chapter will cover the evolution of welfare as a public policy. For most of the nineteenth century there was recognition from a good number of people in power that there was widespread poverty, but there was no direct commitment to alleviate it. Instead, they sought to modernize the nation and to foster economic growth, assuming that as a result there would be fewer poor people. Although governments at times took concrete actions to rid society of social problems that poverty provoked, such as vagrancy in the cities, the results were not necessarily successful over the long run, since they did not address the root causes. I will also explain how changes in the modes of production as a by-product of the rise of capitalism required a revision in patron–client relations. In this chapter I will show how at the end of the Porfiriato, attempts to modernize the organization and operation of the government brought changes in the institutions that provided some form of welfare assistance. A distinction emerged between welfare assistance to the poor and welfare as a means to enhance social development. In addition, by the late 1930s the postrevolutionary government made a commitment to care for those in need. Institutional changes to establish a strong welfare state were promising, but the actual reach of the new institutions was disappointingly small.

Chapter 1

The Ideas Behind the Making
of Welfare Institutions

The Catholic Church of the nineteenth century viewed poverty as inherent to human society and hence ineradicable. The biblical foundation of these assertions, rooted in the readings of Matthew 26:8–11, among other texts, gave the basis for accepting poverty in the Western world as well as for proclaiming the Catholic Church the mother of the poor and hence the institution responsible for assisting them. In general terms, this is how in the history of the Western world the terms *Catholic Church, poverty*, and *charity* became closely intertwined. In this chapter I will discuss the ideas that shaped concepts and policies on welfare, poverty, and charity as they evolved in the Western world and as they were adopted in Mexico.

Prior to the mid-nineteenth century it was, in fact, basically impossible to eliminate poverty from societies.[1] This was because all societies during the preindustrial era—and even during the first phases of the Industrial Revolution—were still economies whose growth was bounded by physical restrictions inherent to traditional modes of production, especially in agriculture. Agriculture required that the greatest portion of laboring people made use of extant production techniques; the constant threat of potentially adverse climatic conditions such as droughts or frosts made societies vulnerable to crop failures, and these failures forced people into poverty.

Three classical economists of the late eighteenth and early nineteenth centuries described and explained these limitations: Adam Smith, David Ricardo, and Thomas Malthus. Although Smith and Ricardo had a great optimism about the benefits of industrialization, they recognized the limits imposed on economic growth by agricultural production. In his *Wealth of Nations* (1776), Adam Smith declares his enthusiasm for the effectiveness of the division of labor. In his famous parable of the production of nails, he explains the gains to be made from this innovation in the organization of production. Still, he recognizes that the division of labor as introduced in industrial production could not be applied in agriculture.[2] In the early nineteenth century, David Ricardo, in his *On the Principles of Political Economy and Taxation*, presents the different angles of diminishing marginal returns (DMRs), which offers an additional explanation of the limits of agriculture production to the one posed by Smith.[3] Ricardo assumes a fixed method of agricultural production, such that the condition of the land becomes the key variable in value.[4] Ricardo explains that DMRs were among the causes that inhibited the further growth of economies at the time, and that DMRs also held true not only for food production, but for all sectors of the economy. He reasons that nearly all branches of production were based mainly on animal and vegetable raw materials that were a part of agriculture. Thomas Malthus's argument of human demographic behavior (ca. 1803) was another compelling explanation, contending that traditional societies would always have poor people.[5] In times of plenty, better nutrition would decrease mortality and, lustful as human beings were, they would raise fertility rates and eventually the additional labor supply would force wages back to the minimum subsistence level.

Decades later, the ideas of these three classical economists were put into question by technological innovations in agricultural production that would free economies from such barriers. The introduction of these innovations increased the production of agricultural goods while it required fewer people working in the fields. Fewer people working in the fields meant more people available to work in other sectors of the economy, such as the nascent industries. These changes resulted in a steady rise in real incomes for the economy in general. More wealth was created. Changes in the productivity of the economy resulted from innovations in agricultural technology and industrialization as much as from research and innovations in the fields of physics, chemistry, and biology that made it possible to develop technologies that increased the supply of energy available for production.[6] In addition, despite the growing prosperity in the economy, fertility tended to decline in most Western societies. Alas, Malthus did not live long enough to see that the evolution of populations in the industrializing world did not match his argument on human demographic behavior.

Karl Marx was one of the contemporary observers of the mid-nineteenth century who realized that the new modes of production created more wealth, and he understood the depth of transformation that the rise of capitalism would bring to Western economies. Marx feared that, in the new capitalist economy, workers would not receive a fair remuneration for their labor and the poor would not have any part in the distribution of the new wealth created.[7] He noted that the scale of economic growth taking place in the mid-nineteenth century was such that enough wealth was being created to eliminate poverty. From that time on, if poverty existed, it was no longer the fault of weather calamities producing poor harvests or lack of land to put to work, but rather a lack of political will to provide the lower strata of the population with sufficient remuneration from labor to acquire adequate food, fuel, housing, and clothing. Malthus, in other words, had been refuted by the capitalist mode of production. Thus, Marx insisted, if poverty existed in an industrialized society, it was because of the unequal distribution of wealth. From this point onward, industrializing economies had the potential to create sufficient resources from growth, and, for the first time in the history of humankind, the abolition of poverty was a possibility. Henceforth, Western societies had to modify their ideas on poverty. New modes of production also required a modification of labor relations as a rising number of people began to depend solely on their wages to earn their living.

It is important to define what we understand by the word *poor* as well as by the concept of poverty, both of which took on different meanings in the century this study examines. People could be poor in a definitive way, such as the elderly who had no one to care for them, those with incurable diseases, those with a physical or mental disability, or those who were so malnourished that they did not have the energy to work and make a living. Others could be poor due to unfortunate circumstances that could be described as temporary, for instance, those who were out of work or lost their crops and thus were not able to feed themselves and their families. The poor could also be pregnant single mothers or widows who had no one to look after them, or orphan children. These poor people were also defined as the able-bodied. Some poor people were lifetime urban dwellers; others were rural dwellers who in times of harsh conditions in the countryside migrated to the cities in search of work. Some scholars have drawn a distinction between those who are poor and those who are marginalized.[8] The argument for this distinction is that poor people have an income, albeit insufficient to make a living; they are inserted in the economy. The marginalized are individuals alienated from the economy. Just as there were different reasons why someone could fall into poverty, it is reasonable to assert that each type of poverty requires different kinds of assistance. The Catholic Church decided its duty was to help both the poor and the marginalized according to the needs of each group. For the poor it was help to endure their condition (illness, old age), normally by giving them room and board. To the marginalized, it was helping them acquire skills that would integrate them into society as productive people. The definitions just described can be generalized to any preindustrial society or any society in the process of industrialization. What cannot be generalized is the way each society reacted to this phenomenon.

When trying to determine who is poor, we should also keep in mind that although some of the basic definitions of poverty are universal, poverty is very much shaped by cultural values and norms in each society and that these evolve over time. The same holds true about the way people deal with poverty at the individual, family, and community levels and as a society at large. This point is particularly important to stress in this study given that Mexico as a country underwent significant changes between 1850 and 1950 while retaining many of its cultural values and traditions. Changes were mainly social, political, technological, scientific, and demographic; all have to be taken into account when assessing welfare provision policies. In the case of Mexico, most cultural values, however, remained the same or barely changed, and this had an impact on the way people adapted to the many social, political, and economic transformations taking place.

In deciding who should receive help, experts on this topic in the Western world made the distinction between those who were poor and those who were marginalized, as part of what was understood as a "moral economy." The able-bodied were often considered vagrants because, although able to work, they were not employed; they were thus categorized as "nondeserving." Those who had some physical impediment, such as being crippled, elderly, or mentally ill, who begged for alms because they could not work, were categorized as "deserving." Western societies of the Enlightenment era believed that it was not good for society to support (through almsgiving) vagrants and "professional beggars," as they were believed to disdain work and feign their disabilities because of their corrupt nature. The able-bodied poor were thus not eligible to receive charity, whereas the marginalized were. Moreover, the able-bodied were to be punished for their ill nature and forced to work. Men were conscripted; women were put to work as servants. Young orphans and street children were also eligible for charity, but fell into a different category of charity because they could still be taught to be good citizens, productive workers, and obedient servants, depending on the age at which they could be put to work. The advent of modern industrialized capitalist economies created new and different kinds of social needs. Labor market, public health, and plain poverty issues required that each be treated separately. During the second half of the nineteenth century industrializing states underwent an institutional transformation that led to the emergence of the modern welfare state.[9] The notion of deserving and nondeserving poor in the social policies narrative prevails to this day.

All throughout the period 1850–1950, Mexican extended families were, for the most part, the social networks that supported the needy. It was not until the 1940s that a European-style welfare system developed. The prevalence and preponderance of the extended family's assistance contrasts with countries such as England where, as early as the sixteenth century, people expected the government to care for the elderly and the sick.[10] In Mexico, extended families traditionally have taken care, in one way or another, of members who were in need. Family ties encompassed relatives of the second and third degree as well as ties created through a religious commitment known as *compadrazgo* (fictive kin). This way godchildren and *compadres* became members of the extended family. The heads of the household frequently had daughters who were single mothers; their illegitimate offspring were also included in the household as members of the extended family.[11] The fact is that in Mexico the social fabric was woven in such way that people were more likely to have someone who would care for them in the world than in other societies with state-run social institutions.

The family economy in Mexico was and still is a strategy of survival for extended families.[12] How the family economy is organized in precise terms is unique to each family in each time period. A number of factors determine the different arrangements of family economies, namely, the number of members in the household, the gender, the ages, whether they were rural or urban, the level of schooling of the members, their material living conditions, and the desired level of consumption. Over time the number and variety of consumption goods desired by members of a household significantly changed.[13]

Communities also play a relevant role in the provision of welfare for individuals. They can create networks of help that facilitate assistance to individuals or families that fall into poverty or become destitute due to unfortunate circumstances such as death or illness of one of the family members, especially when this member is one of the household breadwinners. Just as with the families, the nature and strength of the arrangements created are unique to each community. A number of factors determine these arrangements, namely, the wealth of the community members, the level of participation of members in the arrangements created, and the level of congeniality in a community, to name a few.

Different priorities bring communities together in different cultures and times. In English communities members would contribute to a fund to help those in need in semirural communities; at the end of the nineteenth century, Americans would contribute to create a hospital or a clinic in growing cities. In Mexico communities would be more likely to help pay for the proper burial of a member of the community or to embellish the town church for the feast of the patron saint rather than create a fund to help community members who fell ill or to ensure against a harvest failure.[14] The drawing of comparisons among Mexico, England, and the United States is not an attempt to say that one case is better than another, but rather highlights the relevance of cultural values in defining the patterns of behavior and decision making. Moreover, we should keep in mind the timelines of each nation: Mexico remained an economy bounded by traditional modes of production for much longer than England or North America.

Institutions also play a role in the provision of welfare. Welfare institutions were administered by the Church, the state, or private individuals. The efficiency with which welfare institutions operate depends on the same variables with which other institutions work. One must address how adequately designed the rules of operation are for the needs of the community, whether their rules are enforceable, or if community members are willing to participate.[15] Moreover, it is important to take into account whether there is state intervention or not and, if there is, whether this is positive or not. The latter is relevant to understanding the scale of action of the institution.[16]

An example of efficient welfare institutional operation is England at the time of the enactment of the Elizabethan Poor Law in 1598 and 1601. Given the increase in the number of poor and in an effort to centralize political power in England and Wales, Elizabeth I established a mandatory publically financed system of poor relief. The parish was assigned to be the local unit of poor law administration and taxation. This basic administrative framework was efficient enough to persist largely unchanged for nearly two centuries. Social, political, and economic conditions at the time contributed to making this administrative framework functional.[17] Similar initiatives took shape in Mexico, in which the Catholic Church played a leading role in providing assistance to the needy with the government's approval. They were not, however, as effective as the English system.

In Mexico, institutions evolved at a different pace and rhythm. Nineteenth-century Mexican institutions were defined by the prevailing social, political, and economic circumstances of the new nation. Financial distress, political instability, and social disparities colored the picture. As previously mentioned, there were profound institutional transformations between 1850 and 1950. In deciding how to implement these changes, Mexican policy makers and intellectuals sought models already developed in Europe, which they hoped to adapt to Mexican circumstances. The following discussion is divided into three periods: liberalism (1850–1876), Porfiriato (1876–1910), and postrevolution (1911–1950).

The political reforms of the second half of the nineteenth century were inspired by a transformation in attitudes and by Natural Law philosophers. The state no longer sought to restrain the market as it did during the colonial period, but rather to use the market's revenues for economic development.[18] The new constitutional order had as its model a community of free male citizens based on property rights. It sought to grant economic freedom to reduce transaction costs and to grant political freedom to promote an active and responsible citizenry. This order was established through the creation of a legal framework that would respect property rights in the same fashion as the United States of America. A regulatory framework was launched with the idea that the state should favor the development of the market, as this facilitated economic growth. The state would interact with the market through the federal budget. By favoring this new political and economic order, the liberal state tried to gain legitimacy, something that had been missing in all the years of political instability that followed independence from Spain in 1821.

The adoption of Western liberal ideas in the organization of the political and economic life of Mexico brought changes that failed to reflect the reality and needs of the country. Mexican liberals were overly optimistic with regard to the benefits that a private property system could bring to the economy. They entertained the idea that, by a mere change of the law, they could transform the prevailing land tenure system into a private property system nationwide. Along those lines, the 1856 Lerdo Law ordered the disentailment of urban and rural property of the Church as well as communal lands, a law incorporated in the new Constitution of 1857. Contrary to their expectations, these legal initiatives failed to establish a private property system as envisioned by liberals or to bring economic prosperity to the population at large. What ended up happening was that the enforcement of this legislation took away the wealth of the Church while enriching the oligarchy, without bettering the livelihood of those at the bottom of the social scale. These legal changes also affected the existence and operation of welfare institutions managed by the Catholic Church, with negative consequences for those who received their assistance.

Welfare was addressed tangentially by the 1857 Constitution. Its focus on the rights of individuals overlooked the transformation of institutions that would care for those in need. It ignored the poor as an existing segment of society. While overlooking the need to create legal mechanisms to provide relief, the 1857 Constitution did not omit the measures that were to be taken against vagrants and criminals. With regard to vagrancy and criminality, it was specified that the state would punish as delinquents those who did not live according to the Constitution's mandate, meaning making a living "honestly," and those who offended the rights of others or of society in general. This definition left much room for interpretation of what was good or bad, and implicitly assumed that everyone had to work in trades and professions acceptable to the government aside from behaving with "decency."[19] Moreover, those who did not have a full-time job would risk becoming delinquent in the eyes of the state. The state could punish those who did not want or could not make a living according to the status quo. The cultural history of Mexico is rife with studies that cover in detail the treatment of vagrants, criminals, and other subaltern members of society.[20] From these studies, we can learn at length about the life and deeds of the subaltern. For the purpose of this book suffice it to say that following Western thought, the Mexican government labeled the poor as "good" or "bad," *deserving* or *nondeserving*. A moral judgment underlay the categories; a social Darwinism influenced by Herbert Spencer informed its implementation. The "good" still had hope of being integrated into society. Provided they received adequate training, the able-bodied could be turned into hardworking, decent, obedient workers free of vices, like some sort of efficient working machines. If they were not able-bodied, they deserved to receive assistance. The "bad" were beyond redemption, the scum of society who should be prevented from reproducing. Because of their inferior condition, if they were able-bodied, they deserved to be put into forced labor or be conscripted into the army to keep them away from their vicious ways of living and from inflicting further damage on society. Those who were not able-bodied should be put away so that they could end their existence without the risk of contaminating the rest of society. These views prevailed in Mexico from the liberal period to the end of the Porfiriato.

Mexican authorities could not decide whether the poor should or should not be given help since some thought that help might give them a sense of entitlement and would make it impossible to turn them into good citizens.[21] This point of view was consistent with liberal ideas that were against state intervention on social matters including that men were free and thus it was not dignified to receive charity.[22] Moreover, they could not decide whether the poor were poor due to racial inferiority or due to environmental causes. Some opinion leaders like Pablo Macedo, Guillermo Prieto, and Manuel Sánchez thought that Mexican Indians—to use their term—were flawed by nature. Hence, they were against welfare provision by the government because it would only perpetuate their ill nature and idleness at the expense of society. Other intellectuals, like José María del Castillo Velasco, Francisco Zarco, and Francisco Pimentel, considered Indians an obstacle to modernization, but thought that the problem could be solved by giving Indians education and the possibility of having title to their own land in the form of private property.[23] These liberal politicians and intellectuals were influenced by positivist thinking. De facto, Porfirian government authorities carried on with the notion that the government should not be a charity provider, especially for the *nondeserving* poor.

Catholics, by contrast, had their own views on charity and welfare, very much influenced by Leon XIII's *Rerum Novarum* and as a response to the enactment of the Reform Laws. By the time the Porfirian regime was well established, a new generation of priests, ordained after the triumph of the Reform Laws and focused on social justice, had gradually organized and gained a significant following of laypeople. In 1903, 1904, 1906, and 1909 the Church held four congresses in some of the country's major cities (Guadalajara, Puebla, Morelia, and Oaxaca) during which the Church's focus on social justice became apparent.[24] The social agenda of the Catholic Church was discussed during the conferences, although discussion of politics was forbidden. The social agenda was deemed necessary because Catholic leaders believed that, if no alternative was created for the popular classes, it would be easy for the populace to succumb to socialist, communist, or atheistic ideas.

During the first congress in 1903 in Puebla, the topics of discussion were the living conditions of the working classes and of indigenous populations. In more detail, the subject of Christian syndicalism and savings alternatives for small rural landholders was discussed.[25] The participants understood Christian syndicalism as "respectful obedience and Christian submission to the authorities."[26] A lay member presented the German cooperative system, funded in Germany in 1854 by Friedrich Raiffeisen, as a way to help small farmers. Eventually this system was effectively launched by the Operarios Guadalupanos in Guadalajara under the direction of José Refugio Galindo, a Catholic lay activist. Early on, it was agreed that working-class and indigenous issues had many similarities and required a comprehensive solution: one that included economic, social, educational, and political components.

During the second congress in 1904 in Morelia, discussions centered on employment, economic and cultural assistance for the working classes, the need to fight alcoholism among the people, the promotion of indigenous groups, public assistance, and child vaccination campaigns. The third congress was held in Guadalajara in 1906, during which delegates addressed the moral responsibilities of both workers and employers, while emphasizing for the first time the need for employers to act with a sense of social justice; it called upon employers to treat workers as men, granting them a day of rest on Sunday and paying a wage. Nicolás Leaño, one of the lay participants, stated that "it was fair that a worker would receive in exchange for his productive labor a recompense that would be sufficient to support him and his family."[27]

When the fourth congress took place in Oaxaca in 1909, a city with a large indigenous population, the problems of the indigenous communities were singled out as one of the main topics of discussion. Moreover, the Círculo de Obreros Católicos (Catholic Workers Circle) had been established and was growing in numbers. Its members considered that, given the possibility that Porfirio Díaz would be stepping down from the presidency in the coming elections in 1910, it was time to reconsider including politics in the agenda. The Círculo had in mind the funding of a political party similar to the German Catholic Party, that is, as a Christian democratic party. After all, *Rerum Novarum* mandated that Catholics participate in politics. It is not surprising that when Díaz announced his retirement in an interview, this group joined the cause of Francisco I. Madero. Jean Meyer points out that, although traditional historiography makes little mention of these Catholic congresses, the social agenda established by the Catholic Church considered the needs of the popular classes many years before the 1910 Revolution. Politics or no politics involved, the Catholic Church was a pioneer in addressing social justice issues.

Journalist Trinidad Sánchez Santos was an active participant in these congresses; he argued that social evils among the poor were the end result of insufficient remuneration paid to the laboring classes.[28] He warned that pauperism, which should not be confused with poverty, was a problem that could cause social dissolution: "Pauperism is not the absence of work or economic means to support oneself but rather their absorption by vices; it is the poor man shocked by the rich man and craving his pleasures."[29] To Catholics, all poor people deserved charity, and they had a series of ideas on how charity should be provided in order to eliminate pauperism from society.[30] Theirs was an alternative solution to address social problems, in part as a reaction to the *social question* discussed by groups of socialists.

It became necessary to revise labor relations everywhere in the civilized world where there were new modes of production, and Mexico was not an exception to this phenomenon. At the ideological level, Mexican legislators were debating about the need "to supplement the civil law with political economy and sociological theory."[31] On one hand, political economy could serve to justify an argument against state intervention in labor relations; on the other hand, it could facilitate the development of a critique of a formal individualistic doctrine.[32] Those who criticized the status quo argued that the notion of freedom of labor gave license to employers to exploit and abuse their workers.[33] The new times required new legislation. In Chapter 3 of this section we will overview the action taken by authorities to regulate labor and how this included new institutions and organizations in charge of providing workers with the benefits necessary to guarantee their well-being.

Despite the growing Catholic movement for social justice and the first appearances of a more social political economy, the start of the twentieth century found the Mexican nation somewhat unprepared for the ongoing social and economic changes. It was as though Mexico was maturing unevenly as a nation; there were major reforming laws set in place while Mexico continued to be a traditional society. Economically, Mexico was on a path of growth and modernization that could potentially turn it into a player within the group of rich industrialized nations. Industrialists were establishing factories, and inflows of capital—both national and foreign—were being poured into different sectors of the economy. In contrast, for the most part, Mexico still resembled a traditional preindustrial society; the great majority of the population worked in agriculture and lived in poverty in the same conditions they had been living in for centuries.[34]

The Mexican political, social, and economic elites kept up with news from the civilized world and tried to emulate their ways of living. Interestingly, they made a selective emulation of the civilized world model: they wanted the amenities that resulted from technological and scientific innovations and they wanted a government that would rule a civilized society. In this they embraced modernity, but they overlooked the efforts of these civilized societies to provide free education to all of their population and to create poverty-relief institutions that worked efficiently. Elites did, however, gain an interest in participating in charitable organizations like the elites of the Western world. As we will see in the following chapter, the institutional framework for these organizations was an obstacle to the proliferation of these entities.

The outbreak of the 1910 Revolution was a reality check for the government and the oligarchy, who discovered the widespread dissatisfaction of the masses excluded from the prosperity brought by the new modern economy. Revolutionary leaders used the slogan of social justice for the poor in their fight. Articles 27 and 123 of the 1917 Constitution present the agenda on welfare proposed by the postrevolutionary governments. These articles concern land tenure and labor, respectively. It became clear that in the post-1910 era there would be a distinction between welfare as charity and welfare pertaining to the benefits workers were entitled to. How to address the needs of those unable to work was less clear.

The governments of the post-1910 period—that is, the postrevolutionary era—were influenced by the rise of the welfare state in the Western world. Mexican authorities, like many of their Latin American counterparts, became enthralled with the idea of launching a centralized paternalistic welfare state.[35] In the specific case of Mexico this was consistent with the rhetoric of the revolution and was an efficient way to buy allies for the cause while assuring the stability and permanence of the political party in power. The following chapters will show how this strategy was successfully applied as the same political party managed to stay in power for seventy years.

Chapter 2

Welfare as Charity

In Mexico, during the second half of the nineteenth century, the debates on welfare focused on who should help the poor, public or private institutions; to what extent they should be helped; and who was worthy of receiving help. These questions were framed from both economic and moral points of view. Furthermore, the role of the Catholic Church in ministering to the poor was a major issue. Although the Bourbon reforms had attempted to secularize welfare institutions since the late eighteenth century, while Mexico was still a colony of Spain, the reforms failed due to the lack of resources to take over charitable activities. By the mid-nineteenth century, the Mexican government was still attempting to secularize welfare institutions.

As we will see in this chapter, welfare as charity provision got caught between the state and Catholic Church conflict of the mid-nineteenth century, which lasted until well into the twentieth century. I will show how the state authorities, blinded by their anticlerical animosities, failed to see the negative side effects of diminishing charity provision by forcing the Catholic Church to sell its assets, namely, the government not filling the void in assistance to the needy left by Catholic charitable institutions.

The 1856 Lerdo Law and the 1857 Constitution had negative repercussions for the relationship between the Catholic Church and the government and for the country in general. Naturally, Catholics protested against these laws, presenting different complaints. A leader like Bishop Munguía

31

protested against the expropriation of Church property, arguing that the Church was the "only mother of the poor."[1]

Who would assist the needy if the Church was despoiled of their means to help? Enforcing these laws was going to be a difficult task since, as Jean Meyer asserts in his classic study on the Cristero War, the Catholic Church was an institution that had three hundred years of solid establishment. The state could not override it from one day to the next.[2] The disputes between liberals and conservatives over these issues triggered a civil war known as the War of Reform or Three Year War (1858–1861).

Catholics were distressed by the Reform Laws, as they hindered their ability to make charitable donations that would secure grace, that is, entry into heaven. Defying the liberal legislation, Catholics persisted in their donations to the Church. This is why it was not uncommon that in their wills, people would still leave money or properties to the Church for charity or in return for masses said for their salvation. The donations could be given in the form of land grants or real estate where the clergy could house their charity projects or the return for the usufruct of land.[3]

The liberal triumph in the War of Reform allowed federal authorities to resume their attacks against the Catholic Church. As part of this agenda, in 1861 the government issued a decree ordering the secularization of welfare institutions.[4] The liberal government wanted to take the legal possibility of offering charitable services away from the Catholic Church, not because they wanted to take over those services, as they did not deem it was their duty to do so, but to undermine the power of the Catholic Church. Liberals thought that charity should be given through private institutions, the way they were organized in the Western world. In particular, they had the model of the United States in mind. However, the principles and motivations by which charitable organizations operated in the Western world belonged to a different reality. This kind of community culture did not exist in Mexico. The notion of communal help did exist in the form of communities with brotherhoods (cofradías), but these organizations were declared illegal by the 1857 Constitution under the pretext of defending freedom of religion and the need to promote private property as the optimal form of property ownership. The Constitution also made illegal the indigenous communities' forms of organization. For the most part, these communities lived isolated from the political, economic, and social transformations that were taking place at the time.

By overlooking the need to create an institutional framework that would replace the charity services the Catholic Church had normally provided, welfare was left in a legal limbo by the state. This legal limbo was partly a reflection of the lack of consensus on whether welfare services should be given or not. After the disentailment of Church property that started in 1856, and later with the secularization of welfare institutions, bureaucratic obstacles made it difficult to undertake any charitable enterprise or establish a welfare institution. The government authorities were in principle committed to secularizing all activities that had traditionally been a part of the Catholic Church domain. As part of their liberal project, they believed that welfare and charity initiatives could emerge from the lay population provided there was a strong middle class, but Mexico had a small middle class during the second half of the nineteenth century. Moreover, as we will see later, the economic, political, and social circumstances were not favorable for the emergence of a strong, large middle class. As Jan Bazant's classic study on the disentailment of Catholic Church property concludes, the ideas of the liberal reforms to transform property ownership were not irrational or poorly designed; they had worked successfully in other countries.[5] However, the timing and circumstances under which such liberal reforms were undertaken could not have been worse. In practical terms, liberals were in need of cash to overcome budgetary pressures and wage the war against the French army that lasted from 1862 to 1867.

Not only were the Lerdo Law and the secularization decree enacted at a bad time given the prevailing political circumstances, but they also had several flaws that led to disappointing outcomes for both the government and the Church. For the government, they were disappointing because they failed to promote a private property system as liberals had envisioned or to make land more productive. For the Church, they were disappointing, among many other things, because their assets went to enrich the emerging anticlerical liberal elite. The sale of the Church's assets promoted a redistribution of wealth, but one that did not include those at the bottom of the social scale.

There were many irregularities in the enforcement of the Lerdo Law and the secularization decree that left the recipients of charitable services in a state of neglect while it made some politicians wealthy. For example, even before the promulgation of the secularization decree, as a result of the 1856 Lerdo Law, many of the buildings that housed these institutions were already in the government's possession; thus they could dispose of them as they saw fit, usually to get cash to meet financial obligations. The government sold a good number of the buildings where the Church had provided welfare and charity services, such as hospitals and schools, giving nothing in return to the needy. To add a bitter note, national emergencies forced the government to sell these properties at a price lower than their market value.[6]

There was little government involvement in charitable institutions unless there were rents to extract from them. This meant that as long as there was no property to expropriate, the government authorities would not meddle in welfare institutions' everyday operations. Silvia M. Arrom's study of the history of the Mexico City Poor House is a good study of this lack of government involvement in welfare issues.[7] She looks at the history of this lay institution, which operated from 1774 to 1871 with the goal of eliminating vagrancy in the city as well as disciplining the poor. The mission of this institution was consistent with the state views on poverty in vogue at the time. Not only was this institution unique in Mexico, but it also failed to fulfill its initial goal and ended up serving primarily middle-class people who had suffered some calamity forcing them into poverty; in its last years it was an asylum for destitute orphans.[8] One of the main conclusions of Arrom's work is that changes in political and economic circumstances that took place during the nearly one hundred years that the poorhouse existed had little impact on the way the institution was managed, and that the government would not be involved with institutions when there was nothing to expropriate.

Brotherhoods (*cofradías* and *archicofradías*) had assets used for charitable activities; these too were expropriated as part of the Reform Laws. Many of these corporations supported schools, many of which were closed and their buildings sold as a result of the Reform Laws; some were spared by the gracious intervention of a well-connected politician. The money from the sale of school buildings confiscated from the brotherhoods was used to pay the wages of government employees and to compensate different people for services rendered to the nation.[9] The fate of the schools belonging to these corporations that survived the Reform Laws exemplifies how secularization was good business for liberal politicians but added nothing to social reform.

One example of these irregularities is the case of the Colegio de San Ignacio de Loyola Vizcaínas, which was founded in 1723 by the Brotherhood of Our Lady of Aránzazu, organized by merchants from Navarra. In 1861, after the secularization decree, the Colegio de las Vizcaínas was to be closed and put up for sale. Melchor Ocampo, a close collaborator of President Benito Juárez, used his political leverage to prevent the sale of the school. Arguing that it had defended itself from intrusions from ecclesiastical authorities, the corporation renamed the *patronato* a "board of directors" to be in compliance with the new times. Although the Colegio de las Vizcaínas survived (and continues to exist to this day), in 1862 an official from the Spanish government reported that many of the properties that belonged to the school's endowment had been sold; interestingly, they were purchased by Francisco Zarco, the minister of the interior and a Frenchman who bought properties on behalf of the president for a tenth of their market value. It was the very same Francisco Zarco who signed the secularization decree.

Another formal irregularity in the enactment of the Reform Laws involved secular charitable institutions that were lay institutions the government mistakenly counted as religious, as was the case with the Hospital de Jesús founded in the sixteenth century by Hernán Cortés. Cortés's motivation for the foundation of this hospital was to compensate all indigenous people who had served him and who had been treated as slaves. During the enforcement of the Reform Laws in 1856, liberal authorities were in such haste to get cash that they sold part of the properties of Hospital de Jesús. Later they realized that this institution had been a secular one all along, so the sale of their properties was illegal. In 1861, the government again unlawfully sold a house belonging to the hospital to the family who had been renting it; this was the family of none other than Miguel Lerdo de Tejada, the author of the Reform Laws. Upon his death the government decided to sell the house, at a price, of course, lower than its market value. The patrons of the hospital complained, but the property was never returned to the hospital.[10]

The government did not eliminate Catholic charitable institutions completely after the enactment of the Lerdo Law and the secularization decree despite the expeditious enforcement of these pieces of legislation. Some institutions were able to survive thanks to the intervention of politicians, as was the case with the Colegio de las Vizcaínas just described. Others were able to reinvent themselves to survive the changes and relabeled their organizations "secular," like the St. Vincent de Paul's Sisters of Charity. This institution's board, which included reputable members of Mexican society, promptly recognized its dependence on the Mexican government.[11] The reports of the activities of this institution show that the government did not conduct a thorough surveillance to ensure that their activities were not guided by the Catholic Church. This apparent lack of surveillance is not a surprise given that it was not long after the rapid enforcement of the secularization decree that the French invasion interrupted Benito Juárez's presidency. In 1865, Maximilian of Habsburg, emperor of Mexico from 1864 to 1867, founded the Junta Protectora de las Clases Menesterosas, which among other obligations was charged with assisting the poor.[12] The creation of this board came in response to a report made in 1863 on the physical and financial state of welfare institutions operating at the time, by Joaquín García Izcabalceta, a well-known philologist and historian who happened to be the director of the Mexican chapter of St. Vincent de Paul's society.[13] The report stated that these institutions faced financial difficulties, and the assistance they provided was insufficient to help the number of needy.[14] A brief look at the simple financial statements presented at the end of the report provides examples of the irregularities in the enforcement of the Reform Laws and the secularization decree.[15] The board continued operating after the French were expelled from Mexico in 1867.

In addition to the adverse political circumstances during the Juárez administration, Catholic charitable institutions did not disappear because there were structural changes within the Catholic Church. The Church turned to the countryside, to the rural Mexico that had been utterly neglected by the liberal reforms. This turned out to be a rebirth of the Church, now a new Church that focused its efforts on peasants and the rural communities, with a new sense of social justice. Later these initiatives would be reinforced by Pope Leo XIII's *Rerum Novarum* of 1891. The lack of enforcement of the Reform Laws after the late 1860s allowed the flourishing of vocations and parishes in the countryside. Between the late 1860s and 1917, the number of ordained priests increased and many churches were built and rebuilt. The *Rerum Novarum* called for the application of Christian principles to patron and worker relations, peasants and landowners, capital and labor. A new generation of priests and laypeople proved willing to give a new dynamism to social Catholicism. The triumph of the liberal revolution brought with it a clear antagonism between political liberalism and Mexican Catholicism. In reality, anticlericals were only a minority of the population, but they happened to be the minority in power. Beyond the political battle fought with the liberal government, Catholics had an idea of who should receive charity and how the new laws would constrain their activities. Catholics believed charity should be provided to the needy, and although some poor people were harder to redeem than others, all individuals were the subject of redemption. They, in principle, agreed that charity should be given without making it appear as an entitlement and that help should be conducive to teaching the poor to help themselves, always under the assumption that everyone deserved a chance.

On one point, however, liberals, conservatives, the Catholic Church, and the new bourgeoisie agreed: their concern over the spread of socialist and communist ideas. Mexicans were utterly impressed by the events of La Commune in France in 1871, fearful that such events would spread around their own country. They believed that social unrest must be avoided. They regarded the destitute and the discontented laboring classes as a social threat that had to be contained and controlled. There was more concern for the urban poor than for their rural counterparts, as they represented more of a threat to the social order. This is one additional reason that explains why even though for many decades there was not a consensus with regard to welfare provision, charitable enterprises and welfare institutions did not disappear altogether. Fear of socialism and communism was hardly a noble reason for not completely abandoning the poorest of the poor, but it did motivate the upper sectors of society to do something for them.

Porfirian government authorities (1876–1911) carried on with the notion that charity should be a private virtue rather than a Church function, but the government institution in charge of overseeing welfare activities was reorganized and renamed. In January 1877 the Junta Protectora was transformed into the Junta de Beneficencia Pública (Board of Public Welfare); this was the government's response to the evident need to assist the poor. Schools, hospitals, and asylums were the three types of institutions that the Junta was charged with overseeing. The board was supposed to be integrated with honorable and outstanding members of society. Some women of the oligarchy were allowed to participate in this initiative; this was the only honorable venue at the time in which women could participate in public life. Notwithstanding all of the institutional limitations set by legislation, the Church continued to provide charitable services to the best of their capacity. The priests in small towns isolated from the government's surveillance continued to teach catechism and the alphabet to children. Porfirio Díaz did not attempt to change or annul any of the Reform Laws launched before his time, but he did not try to enforce them either. By looking the other way, the Díaz administration enabled the Catholic Church to transform itself into a different kind of institution and to gain strength from this transformation.[16]

As we mentioned earlier, Porfirian authorities did not consider charity desirable because it was a way of perpetuating the vagrants' mode of living. With new capitalist ideas, the notion of charity had become outdated. Wealth was a sign of success while poverty was a sign of weakness and failure. The capitalist bourgeoisie disdained the poor. Still, something had to be done to purge the cities of indigent people. The government authorities thought that welfare should be provided naturally by private individuals; however, during the last decades of the nineteenth century the extant help coming from private institutions was insufficient, so the government reluctantly had to allocate resources to welfare provision.

At the same time a separation emerged between charity provision and hospital services. The change occurred rather gradually and it responded to changes that were taking place inside and outside of Mexico. At the national level, changes were related to the ongoing rearrangement of the government's budget and the decision to allocate resources to social spending. At the international level, changes were the result of transformations in the medical profession. Social security and the provision of medical treatment began to stand as two different issues: the first was linked to labor and the second to health. The creation of public health institutions will be covered in further detail in Section 3.

During the Porfiriato many laypeople undertook charitable enterprises. Several members of the Porfirian oligarchy funded private welfare institutions of different kinds. These institutions assisted the elderly, orphans, poor children, the sick. For instance, in 1877, Porfirio Díaz's wife, Carmen Romero Rubio, provided the funds to establish the Casa Amiga de la Obrera, which was the first child care institution for working women in Mexico City. José Y. Limantour, secretary of the treasury, also funded welfare institutions; in 1910 he established the Casa del Estudiante (Student House) for low-income students. Moreover, he gave scholarships to poor students who showed promise to succeed. In 1879 Francisco Díaz de León, a well-to-do typographer, established public dormitories for the indigent. Toward the end of the nineteenth century, Luz Saviñón established a school for poor children, as did Concepción Gual y Cuevas. Many of these welfare institutions were short-lived due to multiple obstacles that were imposed by government restrictions. Such obstacles resulted from the absence of legislation for these kinds of institutions. It was easier to fund a private welfare institution than to turn it into a sustainable enterprise. The absence of legislation for establishing these institutions made them vulnerable to the whims of state authorities. Officials would grant legal personality and withdraw it as they saw fit, especially because it was often the case that these initiatives were not completely divorced from the hand of the Church. This was true in the case of Doña Luz Saviñón, who first attempted to establish a school as a Catholic seminary in Tacubaya. The government would not grant her permission to establish it unless she gave up her idea of its being a Catholic seminary. The lack of legal personality up until the early 1900s turned welfare institutions into easy prey for government expropriation. Since there was no legislation that allowed these institutions to own property, there were no property rights to defend. To make matters worse, the resulting distrust in the government made potential donors lose their incentive to make further donations to support these institutions.

In 1899, Porfirio Díaz decided to present an initiative to Congress that would grant legal personality to private welfare institutions. He realized that private welfare would be insufficient as long as there wasn't a legal

Photograph 1 Mexico City—in line for Red Cross soup. Photograph by Bain News Services. Courtesy Library of Congress.

mechanism that would require institutions to have well-supervised management. Moreover, it would be easier to guarantee respect for these institutions' property rights against fiscal attacks. In 1900, Article 27 of the Constitution was reformed so that private welfare institutions could legally purchase real estate. It was not until 1904 that this initiative was promulgated as a decree.[17] The decree also included the obligation of the Junta de Beneficencia to supervise the cleanliness and adequacy of the facilities as well as the proper management of the institutions. Between 1904 and 1906 the amount of resources devoted to private welfare increased, but the money went more into establishing new institutions rather than supporting existing ones.

During this period private and government ventures became more and more frequent. The joint collaborations would be formed for different reasons. It was often the case that a private individual would start a welfare institution and, when he or she ran out of funds to continue supporting it, the state or the municipality would contribute or assume the expenses. This was the case with one of Francisco Díaz de León's initiatives; as mentioned earlier, he was a well-to-do typographer with a high sense of social responsibility. He started out with public dormitories for the indigent of Mexico

City in 1879. In 1880 he opened an asylum for beggars, namely, children and the elderly. Soon thereafter he needed the help of the city government to finance the asylum. The asylum eventually required less help from the government as Díaz de León found ways to finance it. By the end of the nineteenth century he could no longer support the public dormitory and he again asked the municipality to take over the expenses of one of his welfare initiatives. These forms of arrangements were common in different states of the Mexican Republic.

In other cases a welfare institution would be established by a prominent politician with money out of his own pocket, but then the government would assist it, such as by letting the institution use a government building. Private welfare institutions, as mentioned earlier, could not purchase real estate until 1900. This was the case of the Asylum for Beggars in Yucatán in 1891 and three asylums funded in Mexico City by Benito Juárez. It is worth mentioning that the joint collaborations were undertaken at all levels of government, including the federal or state government and the municipalities. It was also the case that a welfare project might be founded by a state government and later it would be passed into the administration of the municipal government. One such example is that of the poorhouse in the city of Oaxaca, which was first founded in 1874 through a joint collaboration between private people and the state government; in 1880 the poorhouse was taken over by the municipality.[18]

Immigrant organizations also created their own institutions to help their members. They were funded with donations from within the immigrant community as early as the 1840s. The Spanish and French were the two most important groups. They created cemeteries, hospitals, and mutual societies. The motivation was to create institutions that would serve their communities, like hospitals and cemeteries, and would help members who might have any trouble, especially those who had migrated recently, as they were usually living under precarious circumstances. The Caja de Socorros Mutuos, funded by the Spanish community, was one of the first mutual aid societies established in Mexico. The welfare institutions established by groups of immigrants were prosperous and long-lived for two basic reasons: first, they had a constant flow of funds from well-to-do members of these prosperous communities; second, they tended to be on good terms with government authorities (in many cases they were business partners with the political class).

The outbreak of the 1910 Revolution did not have a direct impact on the fate of charitable institutions other than the evident need to assist the population affected by the calamities caused by warfare. The first years of the postrevolutionary period went by without significant changes to or attacks upon private welfare institutions as they became organized during the Porfiriato. The issues involved with lack of legal personality persisted. It seems that in welfare-related matters, the Porfirian status quo prevailed until Plutarco Elías Calles became president (1924–1928). In August of 1926, Calles decided to shut down all private welfare institutions for their alleged links with the Catholic Church. This sudden decision adhered more to Calles's anticlerical whims than to a well-thought-out policy. At the time, public welfare institutions did not have the resources or the infrastructure to assume the duties that private welfare institutions had handled until then. Moreover, Calles's decision meant that the government would deny private individuals the opportunity to manifest any philanthropic gesture regardless of their religious affiliation. This presidential decree was linked to Calles's assault upon the Catholic Church, which provoked the Cristero Rebellion that lasted from 1926 to 1929. Little did it matter that, aside from religious teachings, many Catholic organizations had been assisting the poor in areas where the government had failed. The frequent lack of enforcement or lack of full enforcement of government decisions also applied to Calles's determination to shut down private welfare institutions; in the end this initiative was not put into action.

During the postrevolutionary period most of the private welfare institutions continued to be in Mexico City. Still, other major cities in the country also had their own.[19] In general, private welfare institutions were not able to keep up with the rising number of urban poor.[20] The Junta de Beneficencia's reports show that there was continuity in operations of many private welfare institutions from the 1890s until 1940. These institutions did not grow in numbers, nor was there a rise in philanthropy among the Mexican oligarchy. These institutions continued assisting the needy while facing the same problems they had faced since the time of the Porfiriato. It was easier to obtain initial funding than ongoing support. There was a constant lack of funds to support everyday expenses; some of these institutions were overpopulated, and there were frequent abuses and corruption on the part of staff who worked in them. The quality of service was often low. For those institutions that started out well, it was common that within a few years, the quality of service would decline due to the impossibility of maintaining the facilities adequately. As for the recipients of assistance, they frequently failed to abide by the applicable rules. For instance, orphans would run away from hospices, while other residents refused to leave at the age of majority or when their education ended. One of the complaints of the Junta de Beneficencia was that board members of these institutions would often hide financial information out of fear that the government would seize their property. Regardless of who was the head of the government, there did not appear to be a tangible commitment to facilitate the emergence or growth of private welfare institutions.

In 1942, as part of the effort to have the private sector participate in assistance provision, President Manuel Ávila Camacho (1940–1946) issued a decree granting fiscal benefits to those who wanted to make donations to private welfare institutions. Donations became exempted from taxation. Moreover, legal personality would automatically be granted to foundations who wanted to fund private welfare institutions.[21] Private welfare institutions grew in number and their budgets expanded, but not to the same extent that new fortunes were built during the Mexican Miracle. In spite of fiscal and legal incentives for private welfare institutions, these institutions did not prosper. Over time, public welfare/assistance institutions became the main help providers in twentieth-century Mexico. It seems as though the Porfirian oligarchy was more generous and philanthropic than the post-revolutionary one.

Despite these important changes in secular provisioning of welfare, the Catholic Church did not stop helping the poor and did not disappear as a charitable institution. It continued working through formal and informal venues, depending on the times. The Church continued its mission to assist the needy with whatever resources were available. Anticlerical legal and governmental provisions and the lack of an institutional basis for private welfare dwarfed the extent of help they could provide. Looking at the evolution of welfare as charity during the period 1850–1950, one cannot help but wonder about the impact of the government's anticlerical policies on the well-being of the lower-income strata of the population. Leaving aside the ideological motivation for these policies, it seems as if the radical attitude of the different governments toward the Catholic Church did a disservice to the poor.

Chapter 3

Welfare as Public Policy

Welfare policies as we know them today did not exist in 1850. Politicians of the mid-nineteenth century were interested in attaining political stability that would create the adequate environment to foster growth and development. This required addressing social problems that got in the way of the modernizing project, such as cleaning cities and public spaces from vagrants and criminals as well as preventing protests that could arise from unhappy constituencies. Over the one-hundred-year period covered in this study, the profound demographic and economic changes that took place forced politicians to act—at times willingly and at times reluctantly—in response to the needs of the people.

The purpose of this chapter is to trace the transformations that took place in Mexico's social, political, and economic life that influenced the way government authorities thought and acted with respect to welfare provision. During the years of liberal reforms and until the onset of the Porfiriato (approximately 1850 to 1876) there was no explicit legislation or policies channeled to welfare provision. However, during the Porfiriato (1876–1911) a clear division began to exist between welfare as charity and welfare as a social policy. This distinction required that the government's administration adapt its institutional framework to better reflect the new needs of the modernizing nation. Post-1910 governments continued this line of action, but it was not until the Lázaro Cárdenas presidency (1934–1940) that the government explicitly committed to establishing the welfare state as we know it today. The changes implemented throughout this period were inspired by the models successfully implemented in other countries, but they were also launched in response to local events such as the 1910 Revolution. This chapter will analyze the emergence of welfare from a public policy perspective. The study will give particular attention to two aspects of welfare that occupied government authorities of the time: policies concerning the poor and policies set in place to meet workers' needs. This chapter will present an overview of changes in chronological order.

During the 1850s, "liberal reformers" lacked an explicit welfare agenda. The 1857 Constitution and legislation promulgated in the years that followed addressed welfare in a tangential way. This was done by creating laws that were meant to transform social and economic factors such as education, vagrancy, and labor. The implementation of these laws would be conducive to improving the living standards of the population. Still, there was no explicit mention or intent to redistribute wealth.[1]

Liberal politicians of that time were perhaps overly optimistic that, with the enforcement of new legislation, things would follow the order they envisioned on their own. This order included the improvement of living conditions of the population at large. But on many key subjects, this failed to happen.

Education was one key subject that clearly exemplifies the nature of liberal policies vis-à-vis welfare-related matters. Liberal intellectuals of the second half of the twentieth century believed that the country would prosper if the masses could receive an education. The 1857 Constitution defined education as free, but it did not specify that people had a right to education or that it was the government's duty to provide it. The government wanted to ensure that education was provided free of charge because at that time a good number of schools were run by the Catholic Church, and these schools charged for their services. The Constitution reserved the right to decide which credentials were necessary for the exercise of each profession so that the government could control who could teach.[2] As the result of Article 3, several religious schools were closed, and many of these schools served poor children. At the time, and in the decades that followed, the government did not have the resources to invest in public education to meet the needs of the population. Illiteracy rates among the adult population remained above 70 percent up until the 1930s. The liberal government overlooked the fact that the closing of religious schools was going to decrease the supply of schooling services at a time when the country was in great need of massive education campaigns.

The 1857 Constitution did not contemplate the provision of poor relief of any sort. Politicians of the Benito Juárez era (1855–1872) were, however, concerned with problems stemming from the vagrancy and criminal activity so ubiquitous in cities and roads at the time. They did draft penal codes that were meant to control those "unworthy" members of society. The penal codes of that time criminalized vagrancy and allowed authorities to force these people to join the army or be employed as laborers in the construction of public infrastructure works. Government authorities believed that forced labor would cure unworthy people of the ills of their flawed nature. They did not view beggary and vagrancy as a consequence of poverty and marginalization.

Liberal politicians of the second half of the nineteenth century also pondered the issue of labor. The modernization of the economy brought new modes of production and with them new needs from laborers as a rising number of them began to work for a wage and to depend solely on it for their subsistence. Still, there was no specific commitment in the 1857 Constitution to regulate labor. Interestingly, it was during the French intervention (1864–1867) that there began to be some form of labor regulation. In spite of being a monarchic ruler, Maximilian of Habsburg had liberal ideas that were in many respects more progressive than those advanced by Juárez's group. In 1865 Maximilian issued a decree that abolished the obligation of peasants and laborers to be tied to a certain landholder or factory or workshop patron, and it set limitations on child labor.[3] This decree marked the beginning of the end of Mexico as a preindustrial quasi-feudal system.

The freedom of labor required under this decree was an achievement for laboring classes. However, this new freedom made workers more vulnerable to hazards outside of their control, such as illness, unemployment, or accidents, as this new freedom came with workers relying solely on their wages to subsist. The vulnerability resulting from freedom of labor was a common result in societies that embraced forms of government that were inspired by liberal ideologies, but these societies (industrialized economies in Western Europe for the most part) had developed social mechanisms to assist workers who found themselves in a precarious situation. In these societies, workers had some form of social safety net granted by the state or community-based organizations through poor relief legislation. In Mexico, freedom of labor came with no form of social legislation to help workers should a hazard befall them.

The fact that there was no labor regulation initiative from the government did not preclude laborers from organizing to find ways to help each other, such as mutual aid societies. The emergence of these societies would later influence politicians' actions on welfare-related matters. The first mutual aid societies, *mutualistas*, appeared in the mid-nineteenth century and operated in the English style through voluntary cooperation and without government intervention. Some guilds of artisans created mutual aid societies as safety nets for difficult times. *Cofradías* were banned by the 1857 Constitution, but the same Magna Carta had established the right of free association. Aside from the guilds of artisans, there were other groups among the laboring classes that came together to establish mutual aid societies; these were workers in the service sector or industrial workers. The main purpose of most *mutualistas* established by the laboring classes was to create funds to assist members in case of illness, work-related accidents, or death. Those workers who wished to belong to mutual societies had to pay their membership fee and make a weekly contribution to the savings of the society. Moreover, they had to provide a medical certificate stating that they did not suffer from a chronic illness at the time of application to enter the societies. They also had to prove that they were honest and decent people. Membership entitled them to receive a stipend during the time of their convalescence while ill, and they could receive an indemnity in case of an accident that would prevent them from working. An indemnity would also be paid to widows of workers who died in a work-related accident, and the *mutualista* would cover the funerary expenses. *Mutualistas* could also extend short-term loans to members who were current on their fees to meet exceptional expenses, for instance, when a relative was sick.[4]

Still, only a small minority of the laboring classes belonged to a *mutualista*. During the Porfiriato the number of *mutualistas* proliferated: in 1882 there were approximately fifteen *mutualistas*; in 1894 there were fifty-four *mutualistas* in Mexico City and twenty-eight more throughout the republic; and, by 1906, there were 428. Although the majority of these associations were based in Mexico City, most cities of relative importance had at least one mutual aid society. It should be pointed out that, unlike private welfare institutions, *mutualistas* did have a legal personality as they were created under the protection of the law that established the right of free association.

Some intellectuals of the time had a favorable opinion of *mutualistas* because they thought they were the first stage of the social organization process. Eventually mutual societies would become cooperatives, which would be an optimal solution to the "social question." Moreover, these institutions did not receive help from the government and had very few donations from the oligarchy, although it was often the case that a member of the well-to-do and/or the political class would be on the board of directors.[5] *Mutualistas* did not become a major form of workers' organization because workers "could not keep up with the membership fees, did not have enough of class conscience and did not display a consistent capacity to organize themselves." Hence, they lost importance after the Porfiriato and were subsequently replaced by cooperatives and unions.[6]

Major players in the political sphere during the Porfiriato pondered extensively the importance of drafting social legislation and the extent to which the state should intervene in welfare provision. Western countries that were industrialized went through the same process, but these countries had different traditions. If Mexico were going to emulate one of these countries, then the issue became which model would be best for the country, one in which the state would have minor intervention, as was the case of England, or one in which there would be strong state intervention, as was the case of Germany.[7] The extensive consideration of these matters did not lead to any concrete progress because the prevailing consensus was that the state was not responsible for welfare provision; the liberals deemed private welfare to be the most natural means of assisting the needy.[8] The few policies and legislation on welfare pertained to the regulation and supervision of private welfare organizations covered in the previous chapter and the provision of health services, which will be studied in detail in Section 3.

Although intellectuals and politicians of the Porfiriato continued to believe that the state should not be in charge of welfare provision, they did recognize that the process of modernization required reforms to institutions that would be more attuned to new modes of production. These reforms included the rearrangement of public finances so that social spending could be included in the national budget. These reforms were administrative for the most part, and they did not indicate changing views of the government authorities on charity and welfare. They were motivated by the imperative to provide some sort of assistance to rid the cities of indigents.

The Porfirian government transformed the Junta Protectora de las Clases Menesterosas into the Junta de Beneficencia Pública, now more attuned to the new government organization. However, this board had a very narrow scope of action and a very small budget allocation. Its very existence was repeatedly contested; as early as the 1880s the group in Congress in charge of the budget wanted to eliminate it, arguing that it yielded too meager results to justify its existence.[9] In 1910, 2 percent of the federal budget was allocated to welfare; this percentage would vary among the different states of the republic.

There were some policies that were not directly related to welfare provision but did benefit the living conditions of certain segments of the laboring classes. Porfirian politicians realized the importance of investing in transportation and public goods to favor the economic growth, development, and modernization they yearned for. Therefore, they approved policies targeted at the development of transportation and public utilities in urban centers. The development of transportation facilitated the mobilization of workers to places where new job opportunities emerged. They considered that a larger supply of public goods would foster the material and cultural progress of society; it would help insert citizens into the capitalistic economy and thus would create a more productive labor force. In theory, by improving the living conditions of the population at large, the working population would be apt to work better for longer hours. These investments were concentrated in the largest cities of the country (Mexico City, Guadalajara, and Monterrey) as well as in localities that were important due to their strategic location for the development of the transportation network. The people who happened to live in these places benefited from these policies, but they represented a minority of the total working population.

Several things can explain the lack of will to develop social legislation during the Díaz administration. One reason was that Mexican elites and decision makers resisted change. For decades Mexican lawyers knew that similar changes were taking place in other countries that were industrialized or were in the process of industrialization. Mexican lawyers knew of the new social legislation drafted in places like Italy and France. Countries with the same legal tradition as Mexico were thus able to adopt a similar model without major changes to the legal system. In spite of the diffusion of the works of European lawyers on social legislation in Mexican law journals, Mexican lawyers and politicians were reluctant to draft new social or labor legislation under the pretext that in doing so they would go against natural laws of political economy.[10]

Another reason was that Mexicans did not perceive the need to act in haste. The labor force and economic activity were not changing very rapidly. During the Porfiriato and the two decades that followed the outbreak of the 1910 Revolution, agriculture remained the sector employing the largest number of workers. In fact, during this period the percentage of agricultural workers slightly expanded as there were no major technological innovations in agricultural production outside of certain areas devoted to export production. Agricultural production continued to be labor intensive for the most part. Indeed, Mexico was industrializing, but the size of the industrial labor force remained rather small. This trend was exacerbated by the fact that new labor technologies tended to be labor saving.[11] Laborers that were forced out of certain preindustrial trades such as traditional transportation and handicraft industries therefore tended to find employment in the service sector.[12] Thus, whereas there were substantial changes in the labor structure during the Porfiriato, they did not lead to a rise in the number of industrial workers. Furthermore, politicians favored the liberal notion that wages should be set by supply and demand and that the state's role was to ensure, through social policies, that labor input would be in optimal conditions. In the absence of well-organized, large-scale groups of workers, the use of force to put down protests demanding better working conditions remained a better option than the promulgation of social legislation. It was not until after the Díaz administration that the government saw a real need to develop social legislation that would allow the creation of a welfare state.

As early as 1911, the government that replaced Porfirio Díaz sent a welfare legislation initiative to Congress. This initiative contemplated both public and private welfare institutions. The approach on how welfare should be administered did not differ from the Díaz administration: public welfare would exist with the extant resources to help indigents and the handicapped. It was necessary to endow public and private welfare with a legal basis to sustain this initiative. The narrative of legislation initiatives and of public opinion continued to include notions of religion, morality, and the need for the poor to remain aware of their place in society so typical of nineteenth-century discourse. In these years, more emphasis was given to child assistance for nutrition, shelter, and education. There were also attempts to improve the quality of care given in hospitals.[13] The children of the working classes in urban areas were particularly privileged in these initiatives.[14] Unfortunately, the fights between the different political factions that ensued shortly thereafter brought this attempt to a halt.[15]

The worst years of armed conflict (1914–1917) and their resulting destruction caused a rise in the prices of basic commodities, food shortages, and the spread of diseases and epidemics. The urban poor were hit the hardest by these consequences of the war.[16] The federal and state governments launched campaigns to relieve hunger and disease among the people to avoid chaos and social unrest. But these were mere palliative measures. Help was given under warfare conditions, not with the idea of setting the foundations for a poor relief system. The relief campaigns included food distribution and the establishment of price controls for basic commodities to prevent the spread of famines and disease.[17] Notwithstanding, famine, disease, and epidemics including typhus, yellow fever, and Spanish influenza killed more people than the war itself.[18] Approximately one million people died during the decade of the 1910s. The highest rate of death was among the lower strata of the population.

In the end, Venustiano Carranza's faction prevailed over its challengers, and his victory put an end to the years of civil war. It was under his auspices

that the new constitution was drafted between 1916 and 1917. In view of
the participation of industrial workers in his coalition, it is no surprise that
urban workers had a powerful lobby in the constitutional convention.[19]
The 1917 Constitution was drafted over a two-month period. The group
of legislators was not as educated as their predecessors who wrote the 1857
Constitution. Nonetheless, the new Magna Carta was more in tune with
the new times. Articles 27 and 123 reflected the spirit of the demands of
the winning factions of the revolution. Article 27 granted the state the exclusive right of eminent domain, which provided for the expropriation of
private property in the public interest. The right to underground minerals
(including oil and hydrocarbons) was reserved to the nation. Article 123
formulated the main demands of the working classes; it was the legal en-
dorsement necessary to draft a labor law suitable for a modern industrialized
economy. On the subject of social development, Article 3 finally made the
provision of education mandatory. The constitutional drafters of this time
were aware that it was imperative to educate the people in order to integrate them into the new social, political, and economic order. If the 1857
Constitution was labeled as liberal, this new version was considered liberal-
democratic.[20] One of the main objectives of the new constitution was to
establish equilibrium between the people and the elite; it was the legal foundation on which the "new" Mexican state was built from 1920 to 1940.[21]

A revolution and a new constitution including the demands of the
revolutionaries could make one think that this phenomenon of building
a new state was unique to Mexico, but it was not. What was different
about Mexico was how the process occurred.[22] Other Latin American nations were undergoing similar changes where "there was an acceleration of
industrialization and related 'modernization' processes, including the dra-
matic growth of urban centers, a broadening of economic opportunities,
and a partial reordering of society."[23] In the case of Mexico this coincided
with the outbreak of the 1910 Revolution, an extended civil war, and the
drafting of the new constitution in 1917. In Mexico there was an armed
rebellion as a result of political circumstances at the end of the nineteenth
century, and there was a new constitution, because the one written in 1857
had to be updated to meet the needs of the new times.[24] The new reforms in the 1917 Constitution laid the foundation for the launching of
a welfare state, which took place during the Lázaro Cárdenas presidency
(1934–1940).

The governments that followed the promulgation of the 1917 Constitution did little to enforce social legislation or develop welfare policies on a
wide scale.[25] Mexico was not a pioneer in the introduction and expansion

Photograph 2   Policy makers of the Álvaro Obregón administration. Photographer unknown. Courtesy IISUE/UNAM/Fondo Octavio y Gildardo Magaña. Doc. 1018.

of a welfare system in Latin America.[26] It cannot even be considered as a nation that devoted a substantial effort to improving the well-being of its population, at least over the first half of the twentieth century. From a comparative perspective, the case of Mexico falls in the category of high development with low welfare effort.[27] The evolution of its politics explains the slow development of welfare policies.

Although civil war had ended, by 1920 there was still political instability, and this placed the establishment of a welfare system on hold. There were some policies set in motion, however, that improved the well-being of the population, such as the literacy campaigns and increased education spending during the Álvaro Obregón presidency, as well as the reorganization of health services, which will be discussed further in Section 3.[28] Some progress was also made in the development of labor law. Article 123 of the Constitution granted workers the right to form a union; established a minimum wage; limited the workday to eight hours; provided the right to have a day of rest for every six days of work; placed limits on female and child labor; restricted labor on behalf of pregnant women; guaranteed postpartum leave, rest, and employment; granted equal pay for the same work regardless of sex or nationality; mandated the payment of wages in legal currency; and granted the right for housing provision at a minimum rent, among other things.[29] The 1931 Federal Labor Law concretized certain aspects of Article 123 that mandated collective labor contracts, the legal recognition of unions, and decisions concerning the legality of a strike. This would be handled by the recently created Federal Labor Department. Having a labor law was no guarantee that it would actually be enforced for all workers in the nation. A substantial number of workers were not covered by the law and remained part of the informal economy.

During the post-1910 era, government authorities and public opinion all agreed that there was widespread poverty in the country and that this was a social problem. Still, certain perceptions and opinions from the previous era lingered. Well into the 1920s the positivist notions of the origins of poverty inspired by Spencer, Darwin, and Lamarck remained valid in tandem with the notion that civilized nations were so because of their racial superiority.[30] During the 1920s, ideas of racial prejudice and social equality were both discussed in public venues, but no consensus was reached with regard to the best policy to assist those who were considered "socially weak."

The lingering question of whether the state should provide charity remained as well: Was welfare charity? Some state governments said it was not. For instance, the federal district government argued that it provided welfare as a social service, not as charity. Discussions especially focused on whether the help—under whatever label governments used—should or should not be considered a state obligation.[31] No one questioned the fact that poverty was widespread in the country and that help had to be given to those who could not support themselves. Nonetheless, government authorities feared the possibility that the poor might come to think that they were entitled to receive help from the government and thus would have no motivation to ever try to work for a living. Once again public authorities conveniently decided to overlook the fact that in the civilized nations they so much admired, poor relief mechanisms had existed for centuries and, over time, poverty had declined. In those countries initiatives to alleviate poverty were both public and private. There the governments and their corresponding ruling groups believed it was a social responsibility to assist the poor.

The debate on charity, welfare, and social assistance at the government level came to an end during the Lázaro Cárdenas presidency (1934–1940). In 1935 and 1936, the federal government announced it would adopt the notion, widely accepted in civilized countries, that every individual had the right to be assisted when, due to involuntary circumstances, he or she did not have the means to support him- or herself or face an illness. The government in Mexico City discarded the old notion of welfare being humiliating to the recipients and announced that assisting the poor was one of the most elevated forms of social justice. In 1937, President Cárdenas sent a bill to Congress proposing changing the term *welfare* (*beneficencia*) to *public assistance* (*asistencia pública*). Moreover, the assistance the government would provide went beyond mere help to satisfy basic subsistence needs or medical treatment. In the future the government would also try to integrate individuals into society by making them "useful to the collectivity."[32] The reasons behind government assistance were completely detached from any religious premise. The motivation was to foster the well-being of society. The idea behind this legal initiative was that the government would formulate a policy to integrate the marginalized into the economy. One other relevant feature of Cárdenas's views on social assistance was the will to collaborate with the private sector. By 1940, tensions between the government and private welfare had ceased.[33]

The change in the government's position toward welfare and assistance to those in need at a time when the corporate state was being consolidated required some adjustments to include this policy in the government's organizational structure as well as in the budget. In 1939, a presidential decree made the Secretaría de Salubridad y Asistencia (SSA) the institution in charge of providing assistance to the needy. The federal budget heretofore allocated to assistance increased, albeit not consistently. With this increase came the expansion and diversification of services. In 1940, the National University (UNAM) founded the School of Social Work to prepare social workers to better understand the needs of the lower strata of the population. In order to better target help, the government defined six main categories of social assistance: (1) health (hospitals, health clinics, maternity clinics, mental asylums); (2) education for poor and handicapped children; (3) asylums for children and the elderly; (4) orphanages for abandoned babies; (5) miscellaneous (dormitories for indigents, eateries for indigents, public showers, day care centers, food and clothing distribution centers; (6) *Montes de Piedad* (pawnshops).

In 1942, too, Ávila Camacho issued a decree to create the Social Security Institute (Instituto Mexicano del Seguro Social, hereafter IMSS). This initiative was far from being innovative. All European countries and most countries on the American continent already had a social security system. The project was presented as a way for workers to create an entitlement

for the services they were going to receive in return for their contributions. The social assistance that the needy received was not an entitlement;
social security was. The benefits for IMSS beneficiaries were greater than
those granted by the Federal Labor Law. The quotas were calculated as being 12 percent of the annual salary; 6 percent would be paid by employers,
3 percent by employees, and 3 percent by state governments. Affiliation
to the IMSS was compulsory for private enterprises, state enterprises, and
cooperatives, and optional for state employees, family businesses, agricultural workers, domestic workers, temporary workers, and for those self-
employed. It is imperative to note that this distinction was based on the
realization that it would not be feasible to enforce this law for the entire
working population. Eventually, the government created a social security
system for its own employees: the Instituto de Seguridad y Servicios Sociales de los Trabajadores del Estado (ISSSTE).[34] Those who had no social
security of any kind could still go to SSA for assistance. The basic services
provided by IMSS and ISSSTE are similar to those of industrialized countries, except for unemployment insurance, which neither Mexican institution provided. It was not clear if having two social security systems was
more efficient than having a single system or why the government opted
for this format. The coverage was still limited with respect to the size of
the working population. The categories for which affiliation was made
optional were those branches of economic activity in which the informal
economy grew explosively. By leaving the option of going to SSA for help
at no cost, the government—albeit unintentionally—favored a negative
pattern among the uninsured working population of receiving assistance
without the obligation to pay for it.

In spite of its belated adoption, the introduction of a social security system was not welcomed by unionized workers. They even protested against
the initiative. Workers were unwilling to give up a percentage of their salaries for social security contributions at a time when the cost of living was
rising because of World War II. These complaints did not prevent the enactment of the decree.[35] The reluctance to cooperate with this service was a
reflection of the distrust of the working classes toward government policies
and institutions. In England, Germany, and the United States, the working
classes had a long tradition of contributing to the well-being of their community, and the institutions that managed the services were trustworthy,
whether controlled by the government or not. As a result, the obligation
to pay a fee to gain the right to benefits did not feel like an arbitrary im-
position as it did to their Mexican counterparts. In other Latin American
countries like Argentina, Chile, and Uruguay, the launching of a welfare

system responded to an effort to co-opt the growing critical mass of workers in the industrial sector that threatened to create labor disturbances. By 1943 in Mexico, the working classes had already been largely co-opted by the state-organized hegemonic party. The Mexican working classes were not keen to give up a percentage of their salary for benefits they had yet to see. Unionized workers were also concerned that this benefit would be exchanged for their right to profit-sharing, a benefit about which employers were displeased. Despite their complaints and reluctance, unionized workers were left with no choice but to join the social security system while their right to profit-sharing was not taken away. Over time, these workers realized that social security was a benefit that placed them in a privileged situation vis-à-vis the rest of the laboring classes.

The concerns over charity and the distinctions between welfare and social assistance, along with the divide between workers covered by the labor law and those who were not, drew sharp distinctions among the popular classes. It was as though the new times also transformed the different forms of poverty or redefined the categories among the lower strata of the population. At the top, there were industrial workers who became the aristocracy of the popular classes, yet without achieving middle-class status or affluence. Industrial workers were followed by lucky peasants who did receive good-quality land through the agrarian reform. Next were the urban, nonunionized workers—those who operated in the informal sector. Then there were the peasants for whom things had not changed with the new state. And at the bottom were urban and rural indigents. The way in which the welfare state was put in place left a significant portion of the popular classes unattended and marginalized. The institutional inadequacies that resulted from the federal labor law and welfare system allowed for the number of poor people to grow. Social security and social assistance services had a minimal outreach in the rural areas. Peasants in need who did not receive assistance moved to cities or the United States searching for new opportunities.

· · ·

The period 1850–1950 was one of profound transformations for Mexico. The country went from being a rural, preindustrial society to being a mainly urban, industrialized society with a growing service sector. The overview of the evolution of institutions and policies that influenced living standards of the population suggests that the state lacked an agenda for poor relief for most of this period and that the periodization of traditional historiography does not necessarily apply to the evolution of welfare institutions. One thing is certain: the state's neglect of welfare institutions had negative repercussions in the evolution of living standards of the popular classes.

The Catholic Church was the institution that traditionally had been responsible for welfare provision to the popular classes. Liberal reforms began to undermine the power of the Catholic Church as early as the late eighteenth century as the Bourbon regime tried to take over welfare duties, but it was not until the late 1850s that liberal politicians acted effectively on this matter. The disentailment of the Catholic Church's property in 1856 and later the secularization of welfare institutions in 1861 sharply reduced its infrastructure, thus undermining its efforts in charitable enterprises. These anticlerical policies also affected those people who normally made charitable donations through the Church as a means of ensuring entry into the kingdom of heaven while on earth. The decline in welfare services provided through the Church was not replaced by any government initiative. The banning of religious corporations of lay members and the disentailment of communal property also affected the popular classes. The sum of all these reforms exacerbated social polarization during the second half of the nineteenth century.

Neither the Church nor private welfare disappeared altogether. During the Porfirio Díaz administration, Church and state tensions reached, in effect, a truce. Reform Laws were not abrogated, but Porfirian authorities looked the other way. The Catholic Church underwent a reform and turned its charitable efforts toward the poor in the countryside. A new generation of clergymen emerged, one that focused more on principles of social justice. The Church was prepared to act through formal as well as through informal venues. The Catholic Church regained strength as a welfare provider and the Díaz administration did nothing to stop it.

Private welfare institutions were created during the Porfiriato, but they were limited in number and extent when compared to their counterparts in industrialized countries. This was partly due to the lack of a welfare law that would back them up. Private welfare institutions were created, but without any guarantee that they would be recognized with legal personality at all or that their property rights would be respected. This allowed the government to decide on a discretionary basis which institutions would receive legal guarantees and which would not—which was an efficient way to exert control over these institutions. Such a degree of vulnerability naturally inhibited the growth of private welfare institutions.

The anticlerical spirit of liberal ideas was not the only feature that had a negative effect on welfare provision. Ideas concerning the causes of poverty in society and of the state's role in charity provision also had a negative impact. The rise of capitalism and the idea of economic success came to be in opposition to the idea that there would always be the poor and that charity was necessary in all societies. The poor came to be seen as social scum that had to be eliminated. Social Darwinist ideas embraced by some of the intellectuals of the time reinforced the notion that the needy were less fit for survival. Even though some of the members of the ruling class were influenced by positivist and capitalist ideas, the government did not define a position with regard to poor relief. Nonetheless, the fear of the spread of socialist and communist ideas was a reminder that the needy could not be left in oblivion.

The process of industrialization and the introduction of new forms of production changed labor–capital relations. An agricultural and industrial proletariat developed. By becoming dependent solely on the sale of their labor for subsistence, this segment of the laboring classes became more vulnerable. A labor law was necessary to redefine the relation between labor and capital, between workers and employers. But for the second half of the nineteenth century authorities and intellectuals only thought about the need to address the social question. In fact, the ruling class of the second half of the nineteenth century kept up with the modern and progressive ideas coming from the civilized world and tried to emulate them as much as possible, as long as they would be convenient to their interests. They wanted "civilized cities," modern forms of production, and modern forms of government as long as their privileges would not be altered.

Social legislation came late and with a certain lack of detail that allowed for the perpetuation of inequality. Labor demands were addressed by Article 123 of the 1917 Constitution, state legislation, and later in more detail by the 1931 Federal Labor Law. These laws addressing workers' and peasants' needs were enforced for those groups who pledged allegiance to the ruling political party. They became in a way the aristocracy of the proletariat. Most other working people were basically left to swell the ranks of the informal economy.

What took the Mexican government so long? Mexico was a latecomer in the introduction of a welfare state for at least two reasons: politics and institutional inertia. For decades, political instability forced government authorities to address the more pressing needs for the nation to function on a day-to-day basis. Establishing a poor relief system was the last thing on their agenda. Moreover, liberal ideas justified not paying much attention to the issue, especially when poverty was considered part of all societies. During the Porfirio Díaz administration, political stability was attained and the rates of economic growth and development would have made a poor relief system functional; nonetheless, institutional inertia won and it continued to be that way until well into the postrevolutionary era. At the time the poor did not represent an indispensable group to co-opt by the political party in power, so creating government programs to address their needs was put on hold.

The government did not establish a poor relief agenda until there was a defined position regarding welfare provision. It was not until the late 1930s that President Cárdenas stated that the needy had the right to be assisted by the government when they could not support themselves. Moreover, the state would create programs to help these people integrate themselves into the working population. A government institution, the SSA, would be in charge of providing the social assistance services. This institution was independent from those that served the working classes. Neither the Cárdenas group nor their successors fully realized the daunting task of establishing a poor relief system, with all the accumulated lags of a century of government neglect. The large and growing numbers of needy people were accustomed to government indifference as much as they were used to mistrusting government institutions. They had no confidence that such institutions would provide assistance of any kind or that these assistance institutions would stay in place for long. Having survived at the margins of society, they were not aware of the rights and obligations of citizenship. The incentive was high to enjoy social assistance as some form of free ride while it lasted. Although some did take advantage of social programs to acquire a form of education and training in order to have social mobility, many did not consider education important; thus many children of the lower classes kept working instead of going to school. A culture of poverty emerged, as Oscar Lewis has shown in his classic study *Five Families*, a culture that resisted the very goals of both liberal and progressive governments between 1850 and 1940.

Section 2

Anthropometric Evidence

Chapter 1

The Measure of Well-Being and Growth

Why and How Do We Use Heights to Understand Living Standards?

What does it mean to live well? This is a broad question that includes material as well as spiritual matters.[1] The path to happiness and spiritual and emotional well-being is unique to each individual; the same life experience will have different repercussions in the psyche of each human being. Neither history nor the other social sciences have the analytic tools and evidence necessary to adequately address issues of spiritual well-being. They do, however, have a set of tools adequate to address material well-being. Yet this question is a complicated one. It is difficult to define what the basic material needs (food, shelter, and clothing) are, given that they are heavily (but not solely) determined by culture, and this is relative to the social environment where we live. In short, there is no *perfect* way of defining or measuring people's material well-being. There are, instead, a series of conventions that we refer to as the standards of living.[2]

Let us examine these points from three perspectives. In the first place, there are different ways in which we can examine living standards. Certain methods of measurement and their applications need to be spelled out. The advantages and disadvantages of each method will be explained in this chapter. With regard to Mexico (1850–1950), the data available suggest height as the best measure of income distribution and of living standards. In the second place, I lay out the sources available, methods used, and unexpected challenges posed when working with these sources. In the third place, I frame my analysis as a statistical portrayal of people and places in our story. The last section of this chapter explains how the analysis of these sources will contribute to understanding the evolution of living standards, poverty, and inequality from a long-term macroperspective.

Human Well-Being and Income Distribution

There are several methods for measuring changes in living standards and income distribution over time. In general terms we can divide these methods into five categories: GDP *per capita*, wage series for workers, income distribution, demographic measures, and height and body mass.

1. *GDP per capita* is the ratio of a country's domestic product divided by the number of people living in that country. This method is used in studies to measure living standards, but it can be misleading if we do not have information on how wealth is distributed in the population. In societies characterized by evenly distributed incomes, GDP per capita is a good measure of living standards because it proxies the income of the average inhabitant of that country. In countries in which income is unequally divided—Mexico being an obvious case in point—GDP per capita is a less useful measure. One additional drawback of GDP per capita is that it does not capture the impact of investment in public goods, and, as I will show in this book, public goods such as sanitary infrastructure have significant repercussions in the living standards of any population, as is the case for Mexico.

2. *Wage series for workers.* The analysis of wages looks at the evolution of income based on the wages of the working class. If some conditions are met, this measurement can tell us a lot about the living standards of a society. Such conditions indicate that the wage series cover all sectors of the economy. They should also cover all the regions of the country and all occupations so that we have information on both skilled and unskilled workers. We should also have information on the basic features of the household, namely, the size and the ages of the household members that a worker's wage has to support. It is also necessary to know what the cost of living is in each place. If all these conditions are met, then wage series for workers can be used to study changes in the living standards of the population. These conditions, however, are rarely obtained. More often than not, we have fragmentary wage data and must draw inferences based on informed speculation. Indeed, there are some studies on economic history that show that wages are not a good way of calculating living standards.[3] Two classic works by Mokyr and O'Gráda and Nicholas and Steckel, on the evolution of the English and Irish prior to the 1845 famine, support this argument by

showing that although workers wages and per capita income of the English were higher than those of the Irish, disparities in the standards of living were not as stark as one would guess. The English had systematically higher wages than the Irish; however, by analyzing the evolution of variables such as stature, literacy, and tobacco consumption, they show that one could easily be inclined to think that the Irish had higher standards of living.[4] In addition, wages fail to capture the impact of investments in public goods.

In the case of Mexico, the quality and the quantity of the data available make it even more difficult to meet these requirements. It was not until the 1980s that the Census Bureau of Mexico began to refine the methods of data gathering to have enough information about the income and spending patterns of Mexican households.[5] In addition, the raw data we have on income by occupation are even more problematic. There are very few records of wages for workers available, and those that exist only cover certain periods and certain regions of the country. The data on workers' wages available for the period prior to the 1930s are for Mexico City and Veracruz.[6] The information they can provide may be very useful for regional studies but is rather limited for the purpose of making generalizations about living standards at the macro, that is, national, level over long periods of time.

3. *Income distribution: the Gini coefficient and Lorenz curve.* The index of inequality is a useful measure for studying living standards of a population, as it shows how wealth is distributed in a society. If we use this measure in conjunction with the GDP per capita, we end up with a reliable notion of the living standards of the population. There are several ways to measure income distribution. The two most commonly used are the Lorenz curve and the Gini coefficient.[7]

The Lorenz curve and the Gini coefficient are good measures of income distribution when we have complete information on income. It is extremely helpful if, in addition, we can learn about the changes in patterns of consumption in a given society. This means knowing what the wage levels are; what the compositions of the households (if they have children and if so how many) are; and how much households spend on food, clothing, transportation, education, medical care, savings, and recreation. By having this information on consumption patterns and wage levels, it is possible to have a good picture of the evolution of living standards of a population.

However, we should keep in mind that societies are constantly changing and with them the patterns of consumption. For this reason, there are some demographic changes over time that should be taken into account; for instance, in modern industrial societies there is a tendency toward a

growing number of unrelated individuals living together as a household
and a relative decline in families. In addition, more and more old people
live by themselves, and more children move away from their families as
soon as they receive an income sufficient to support their own expenses,
even if they are still single. As a result, there are more independent income
units (households) with lower average incomes. Another common problem that experts face when making an international comparison of well-
being standards and income distribution is that the data necessary to carry
out these estimations of Lorenz curves and Gini coefficients are generally
not available. Until relatively recent times, the cost—both financial and
computational—of gathering systematic data about household income and
expenditure was unaffordable. This meant that they only began to be gathered in the post–World War II era; hence, the use of these particular measures is almost impossible when working with historical data. For Mexico
there are insufficient data to estimate Gini coefficients and Lorenz curves
until 1957; it is then that we find the first measurement of income distribution with these methods.[8]

4. *Demographic measures.* Demographers are among the scholars who have
attempted to analyze the evolution of living standards the furthest back in
time. The kind of data they work with makes this possible. There are three
basic demographic measures that explain changes over time in the living
standards of a society: life expectancy, infant mortality, and rates of population growth. Most of the data demographers use to calculate these measures
come from population censuses and parish and town records.

    a. *Life expectancy.* This measure is the average number of years an in-
       dividual is expected to live in a certain society, calculated with the
       number of births, the number of deaths, and the ages of the deceased.
    b. *Infant mortality.* This figure shows the percentage of children who die
       before reaching age one. It is generally understood as an indicator of
       hygiene levels and the quality of nutrition because children are less
       resistant to diseases and malnutrition.[9]
    c. *Rates of population growth.* This figure basically shows how fast a pop-
       ulation is growing. It depends on the interaction of several demo-
       graphic variables, including the birthrate, infant mortality, mortality,
       age of marriage, age of mortality, and migration patterns.

Changes in these measures reflect changes in the living standards of the
population. A rise in life expectancy and rates of population growth along
with a decline in infant mortality indicates an improvement in the living
standards of a society. The investment in public utilities such as clean water,

sewers, and clean streets improves public hygiene and create a healthier environment in which people have a lower risk of disease and thus live longer.

It is important to understand, however, that demographic behavior is—at least partially—culture specific. The postulate that a couple can decide how many children to have is fairly recent. Although couples could hypothetically limit the number of births, they could not control infant mortality. It was not until the twentieth century that technological and scientific development made it possible to decrease infant mortality to present-day levels.[10] Even when infant mortality could be reduced, not all populations have reacted the same way at the same time since culture plays an important part. As I show later in this book, Mexico is a good example of this.[11] In understanding demographic behavior, one should take into account that different societies have different attitudes toward nonmarital fertility, birth control practices, and child labor; all these have repercussions in fertility rates, even under the assumption that infant mortality has been radically reduced. Another substantial problem that weakens the explanatory power of demographic variables is that they can lead to confusion if used jointly with wage and income levels. For instance, in some periods of the history of some developed nations, we find that demographic variables moved in the opposite direction of wage and GDP per capita, like most Western countries in earlier phases of industrialization. A compelling example of this is the rise in life expectancy among the U.S. population during the years of the Depression.[12] Still, with an adequate knowledge of the population studied, demographic variables are a powerful tool to understand the evolution of living standards.

5. *Height and body mass.* The evolution of height is another way of looking at the evolution of living standards and income distribution. Height can be used as a proxy of well-being because the final height of an adult is the result of the interaction of several variables, which are all related to income.[13] The logic behind this is as follows: if people have good nutrition, adequate clothing, reasonable shelter, and receive some schooling, they are more likely to grow taller than those people who, despite having the same genetic endowment, grow up under less favorable conditions. Not receiving one or several of these inputs puts an individual at a disadvantage in developing to his or her optimum. Thus, in a given society, people from the richer income strata would be taller than people from the poorer income strata. There are studies in the field of economic history and development economics that support this argument. The classic example of differences in heights across social classes is that of English boys in the late eighteenth and early nineteenth centuries; upper-class boys

attending a military academy were on average taller by seven centimeters than boys living in poorhouses.[14]

Three additional points give relevance to height as a measure of living standards and income distribution over measures such as GDP per capita or wages. First, in premonetized societies the use of statures is practically the only way of measuring the standard of living. In the case of agrarian societies where peasants receive their income in kind or in the consumption of their own produce, it is difficult if not impossible to calculate wage incomes. Second, heights measure results rather than inputs. Third, heights are observable in all societies, providing us an easier way to draw comparisons at the international level. Two classic works by Richard Steckel explain and exemplify these points.[15] Figure 1 presents the determinant of heights and the sources most commonly used to measure them.

There are some common problems of using height data. First, it is almost impossible to have a sample of an entire population. This problem is more accentuated when working with historical data. For historical data, one usually finds samples of a certain part of the population and only for scattered years. Ideally we would want to have information on men, women, and children, but usually most of the data refer to adult males.[16] Most of

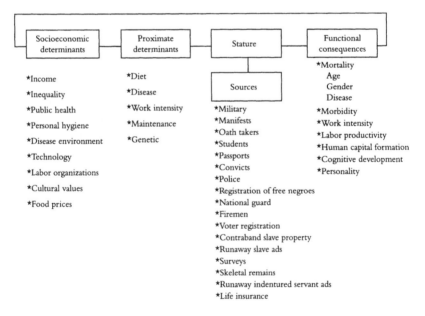

Figure 1   Relationships involving statures

SOURCE: Steckel, "Stature and the Standard of Living," 1908.

the available data sources on heights are from military, slave, or prisoner records, and the majority of these records are only for adult males, especially the military records that have been the most widely studied sources. Later in the chapter, I will discuss the quality and sources of data further.

Second, we do not always know the accuracy of these measurements because we know little about how individuals were measured and how measurements were rounded off. For example, we do not know if soldiers were consistently measured with or without shoes.[17] Doing it one way or the other does have an impact on the average height of the soldiers. If we compare a sample of soldiers measured with shoes to a sample of soldiers measured without shoes there is a bias of approximately half an inch more for the former. This is not a problem if the method of measurement is consistent over time, but it is a problem if the method changed.[18]

Third, the data typically record the height of an individual at a point in time. Beyond this, however, we want also to have longitudinal data (the height of the individual over time) as well as information on weight; we would also want the data to be fully cross-sectional (all measures of the population). The longitudinal data are useful to observe the growth process and thus make inferences about the health history of an individual, whereas the cross-sectional data give a better picture of the entire population. Unfortunately, when working with historical data we find very few studies that include any kind of longitudinal study. We also work with data on weight. Height and weight are both requisites for calculating body mass index, which has direct implications for the health of individuals.[19] Because the widespread use of weight scales did not start until the 1880s, we only have information on body mass for the turn of the century, and this is only from the places where it was first adopted.

In spite of all the limitations mentioned above, there are relevant things that can be learned from height data. The final stature of an individual is the outcome of having a certain diet and living in a certain environment. These two are the result of the income level that the person's family had when he/she was a child. Hence, final height is an output of the biological standards of living of the population. John Komlos, one of the experts in the field of anthropometric history, was the first to propose this term in 1985 to annotate the scope of living standards that human stature could explain.[20]

All the problems germane to working with height data make it an imperfect measure of well-being. However, in the absence of reliable data on income, wages, and prices at the national level for the period 1850–1950, this is a good alternative. In studying the evolution of income distribution and the history of living standards in Mexico, this is the best alternative and perhaps the only applicable method. Substantiating this assertion requires an assessment of the disadvantages of applying the methods just discussed to the study of Mexico. Let us now review these disadvantages.

The data on GDP per capita has two basic problems: it is incomplete for the period of study, and, in some cases, it is not clear how the series were constructed. For the nineteenth century, the GDP per capita is only available for a few years. The data to construct the series were drawn from different primary and secondary sources without explaining how the data were gathered.[21] The twentieth-century data come from the National Statistics Bureau (Instituto Nacional de Estadística Geografía e Informática, hereafter INEGI). However, INEGI does not provide the methods employed to construct the series. Without the methods and/or sources, it is impossible to replicate the results. What appears to have been done is the following. The first input–output matrices for national accounts were not constructed until 1950. The first industrial and agriculture censuses were not carried out until 1930. Researchers apparently took scattered observations about the output and exports of various commodities and plugged them into the 1950 input–output tables. The result is the product of controlled conjecture and informed speculation. How accurate they were is anyone's guess. In addition, GDP per capita could not say much about the evolution of living standards of Mexicans given that Mexico has experienced endemic inequality throughout its history. As mentioned above, the case of England in the early phases of industrialization is the classic example of a society with rising per capita incomes where the improvement in living standards was dubious because of the high inequality levels prevalent at the time.[22]

Using wage series for workers would also have its downsides. The quality of data does not meet all the requirements necessary to make it a reliable measure because there are no data available on price series as there are for industrialized nations. For wages, there are some samples for scattered years in some specific regions for some specific sectors like mining and the textile industry—especially the textile industry in Veracruz—but these are not representative of the Mexican population. For the Porfirian era there are some statistics available, but, as occurs with other statistical series, the absence of methods and sources utilized makes it impossible to replicate the results.[23] Since the 1930s, there were series on wages constructed by government agencies. In fact, there has been some debate on how the evolution of wages is correlated to the performance of the Mexican economy and the evolution of living standards since the mid-1930s. The debate is centered on whether the evolution of wages does or does not reflect an improvement in living standards since there are periods of the twentieth century for which it is argued that the distribution of income worsened at a time when wages were rising and the economy was growing.[24] Interestingly, this is the same kind of debate that we find in other historical studies of living standards that use data on wages.[25] Most of these studies raised the question of whether the Industrial Revolution had or had not enhanced the living standards of the laboring classes. There is no single answer to this question because the time and pace of industrialization were unique to each country.[26]

There are three basic problems with available information on wage series. First, they do not cover the entire 1850–1950 period; second, they focus on industrial wages, but I note that the industrial proletariat formed a relatively small fraction of the laboring classes;[27] and third, it does not take into account the people who did not work for a wage or were self-employed.

For the price of consumer goods, we find a similar problem. There are no detailed-enough data on what the prices of consumer goods were across Mexico. In most cases, the data available are unreliable for the same reason data on wages are, that is, results cannot be replicated. One exception to this dearth of studies is Gómez-Galvarriato and Mussachio's work on price series for Mexico City in the period 1886–1926. This study, however, covers only the country's capital over a forty-year period; therefore, it cannot be used to make generalizations about the country as a whole over a one-hundred-year period.[28] Neither is there any information on the consumption patterns of the population. Not knowing the consumption patterns of a population prevents us from making inferences about the living standards of the population under study.

One last argument against wages, prices, and income as measures of living standards for the case of Mexico is that until the twentieth century most of the people operated outside of the monetized economy. The majority of the population lived in rural areas and lived on subsistence agriculture. Barter was very common. Cash was only used for special transactions; thus, it was not part of everyday life. Financial services were not available to the majority of the population. Common people made investments and savings through nonmonetary means such as raising animals to sell or exchange later.

We cannot calculate the Lorenz curve and the Gini coefficient of Mexico for a period prior to the 1950s to study the evolution of living standards. The reason for this is that prior to the establishment of the Census and Statistics Bureau, the Mexican government did not obtain the information on wages and prices for all representative groups in the society, thus precluding calculations of these measures of inequality. The fact that inequality cannot be measured with conventional tools does not mean that there was no inequality, but it does mean that we cannot know exactly how unequal the society was with the help of such conventional tools.

Demographic measures available cannot be used because there were no real population censuses done for most of the nineteenth century. For the nineteenth century, there were two sources that kept information on the population: the civil registrar and the parish records. However, both of these institutions had their shortcomings. The civil registrar did not cover the whole nation, and even the people who lived in places covered by the civil registrar did not make use of it. Parishes and priests did not keep thorough records of the population. The Church had lost power to the government and was short of priests. Both of these problems made it impossible to service the whole population. Hence, the data available from these sources are insufficient to be used as a proxy of the living standards during the nineteenth century. In addition, the first population census for which we have information that we can refer to was not undertaken until 1895. Thus this method, that is, that of demographic measures, cannot be used to measure standards of living because the data series available do not cover the whole period we are studying.

It is imperative to point out that, just as with price and wage series, there are demographic history studies for the period under study that provide reliable results. These studies, however, only provide fragmented information for the big picture. Robert McCaa's works are perhaps the most complete. His work on the populating of Mexico from the prehistorical era to 1910 offers a general view of the evolution of the main demographic variables with extant information. In this work one can ascertain what has been done and what can and cannot be done with records available; it offers a road map of what remains to be done in the field of demographic history. McCaa's work does not cover the whole 1850–1950 period, but his findings will be used to complement the analysis of this book, particularly in Section 3.[29]

The Sources

The primary sources I work with are the recruitment files of inducted soldiers from the military archives of the Department of Defense (Secretaría de la Defensa Nacional, hereafter SDN), recruitment files of inducted soldiers from the rural militia (Cuerpos Rurales) of the Legajos de Gobernación at the 1821–1910 Public Administration section of the General Archives (Archivo General de la Nación, hereafter AGN), and the passport records from the

Department of Foreign Affairs (Secretaría de Relaciones Exteriores, hereafter SRE). The data include men and women except for the rural militia. The samples contain information on heights, occupation, literacy, place of birth, place of recruitment (for soldiers), and, for federal soldiers (*federales*), information on health status. This information allows us to undertake a systematic study of the evolution of heights, controlling for intervening variables.

THE MILITARY ARCHIVES

The military archives are not readily available to the public, and gaining access to them required personal contacts and patience. The lack of cataloging made it difficult to decide on a point of departure. This situation posed several challenges for my research. After several weeks of detective-like research, the unusual layout of the archives became clear. I discovered that they were organized into five main divisions: (1) the historical documents (Documentos Históricos); (2) the deserters and dismissed personnel (Sección de Cancelados); (3) the personnel who served until they retired and those who died while in service (Sección de Personal Extinto de Infantería, Caballería y Artillería); (4) the veterans from the revolution (Veteranos de la Revolución); and (5) the Health Department personnel (Personal de Sanidad).

While disentangling the puzzling organization of the archives, I immediately set to work spending endless hours gathering data in heights records. I started working in the Archivo de Cancelados because it was the section of the archive where height information was more readily available yet harder to organize. As I got more familiar with the archive, I moved to sections where the files were more complete.

The historical documents are divided into the colonial era and the nineteenth century. Most of the very famous historical documents in the military history of Mexico are there. Professional historians spend most of their time restoring these documents. The files of the veterans from the revolution (Veteranos de la Revolución) are in another separate and vast division; it is mainly files filled with accounts of people, both civilians and soldiers, justifying their participation in the revolution. Starting some two decades after the revolution and up until the mid-1960s, the government opened up a program in which all people who could prove that they had participated in the revolution were granted an emolument in compensation for their participation in the cause. The twentieth-century documents are in the Archivo de Concentración; this contains information on soldiers who are still alive (Sección de Personal Activo). I note that the Sección de Personal Activo, the Sección de Cancelados, and the Personal Extinto are generally closed to the public; if researchers want to consult them they have to have special permission.

Photograph 3 Federals at Torreón. Photograph by Bain News Services. Courtesy Library of Congress.

Photograph 4 Federal soldiers and rebels. Photographer unknown. Courtesy IISUE/UNAM/Fondo Octavio y Gildardo Magaña. Doc. 999.

Photograph 5   National Army. Photographer unknown. Courtesy IISUE/ UNAM/Fondo Octavio y Gildardo Magaña. Doc. 1013.

The Sección de Cancelados included the files of all deserters and dismissed personnel. By *deserters*, I mean all soldiers who illegally left the service. By *dismissed personnel*, I mean all those who left the army before they fulfilled the time of their contracts. Soldiers under these circumstances could request one of three types of leaves (*licencias*): the permanent leave (*licencia absoluta*), which meant they were completely quitting after a contract that usually lasted three years; the indefinite leave (*licencia ilimitada*), which meant they were quitting, but there was a chance they would return to service eventually; and the extraordinary leave (*licencia extraordinaria*), which was granted to people who were disabled by a wound or by a disease or because they had a family situation that forced them to leave the army. These individuals were not entitled to any retirement pension or indemnity, except for those disabled by wounds suffered while in service.

The Sección de Personal Extinto was the section that contained the files of the deceased. This section was also divided according to the regiment to which the soldiers had belonged. Personal Extinto included all soldiers who had served in the military and died while in service or retired and then died. Soldiers were granted a full pension if they retired after serving in the army for thirty years. If they had served from twenty to thirty years, they were entitled to a partial pension starting at 60 percent for those who served twenty years. In addition, all soldiers had to retire no later than age forty-six. In the event that they turned forty-six and had not served twenty years in the army, then they were entitled to a once-and-for-all payment as well as a discount on health services from military hospitals. If they were killed in combat, their widow and children received a retirement pension, calculated according to the number of years that the soldiers served in the army. In my saga to find information on health and on heights of women who had served in the military, I found out that there was still another division I had to visit: the Sección de Personal de Sanidad, which included nurses, doctors, and janitorial personnel.

Surprisingly, all of the personnel assigned to working in the archives knew how to put files in place, but no one understood the logic by which the archives were organized. The files are in boxes with numbers. However, the numbers do not correspond to a chronology. The boxes are arranged in alphabetical order. So in the same box one can find soldiers under the last name "García" who had served in the military in the first half of the century. This means that one could find files from the 1910s through the 1950s in the same box, with the same last name as the common denominator. One advantage to the chaotic way of organizing this archive is that it allows one to build a sample with a high degree of randomness.

Allowing for the limitations in the organization of these sources, I was able to gather data from most of the divisions I mentioned above. I constructed three basic samples: (1) the deserters and dismissed personnel (Archivo de Cancelados); (2) the nondeserters/nondismissed (Personal Extinto de Caballería, Infantería y Artillería), including soldiers who served and retired and others who were killed in action; and (3) women in the military (Personal Femenino-Archivo de Sanidad). Approximately 95 percent of the male soldiers were volunteers. I did not have a sample from the officers because, interestingly enough, the heights of the incoming cadet students in the Colegio Militar (the national military academy where future army officers are educated) were not systematically recorded; in fact, they were seldom recorded. Hence, I decided not to work with them.[30]

To give the reader an idea of potential systematic biases, the essential requirements to join the military are listed below; the instructions were that the inductee must:[31]

    I. Be at least 18 years old and not older than 45.
    II. Be Mexican by birth or by naturalization.
    III. Not be suspended from rights of citizenship.

IV. Not have any chronic or contagious diseases or any handicap that hinders the use of weapons.

V. Not have any physical defect "or monstrous or ridiculous appearance."

VI. Not be deaf, an idiot, or a monomaniac.

VII. Understand the Castilian language.

VIII. Be at least 1.60 meter in height.[32]

Judging from these requirements, we would expect to find a sample biased toward Mexican, healthy, adult, nonindigenous males. De facto, however, we do not find these biases in the sample. The reason for this is the low degree of enforceability of these requirements for most of the period of study. The analysis of the data from the recruitment files will show that height and health were the least enforced requirements, followed to a lesser extent by age and understanding of the Castilian language (Spanish). The lack of enforcement will show up more frequently in the sample drawn from the Cancelados section.

The recruitment files contain information on age, height, place of birth, place of recruitment, literacy, occupation before joining the military, and health status. Age is a self-described variable because birth certificates were not widely issued until the 1930s, and parishes did not issue copies of baptismal records. Heights were measured with the metric system, which was officially adopted in Mexico in the 1880s.[33] The samples are cross-sectional because soldiers were measured only at the time of recruitment. The heights were rounded off to the nearest centimeter. The place of birth is also self-described. The place of recruitment allows us to check if there are certain patterns of migration, the impact of the process of urbanization, and, most importantly, draw a comparison of the quality of life between rural and urban dwellers. There is a risk of overestimating the number of urban soldiers because it was often the case that if someone was from a very small town, community, or rancho near a city, this person would say he was from the nearby city.[34] This information enables one to see the regional composition of the sample and permits us to draw comparisons across regions. Literacy was based on whether or not the recruits could sign their names at the time of their recruitment. The military had programs to teach illiterate soldiers to read and write, so in theory all nondeserters eventually became literate.

By *health status*, I mean if soldiers had a disease and died of it, and if so at what age. I should clarify that under normal circumstances an individual is expected to die old (say, sixty-five or older) and of a degenerative disease. In this way I could classify the most common causes of death by disease in the population and draw a comparison between the incidence of epidemic and nonepidemic diseases. I could also study the most common causes for contracting nonepidemic diseases as well as infectious diseases. Moreover, I learned from the causes of death at different ages if there were any correlations between age and the cause of death. That way I could infer if the young died or did not die of the same diseases as the old. Using this information I could get an idea of the health status of the soldiers and see if it had any correlation with nutritional status. I should stress that I gathered all the information on health available in the records. However, as will be explained later, this information was not recorded as systematically as the rest of the variables.

The information on occupation before joining the army is the variable that allowed me to identify the social class of the soldiers. Literacy is also a relevant variable during this time, for it can be employed as a proxy for education. It also works as a good way to determine social class because the Mexican population showed high percentages of illiteracy up until the 1920s.[35] Unfortunately, not all the files had this information systematically recorded. The advantages and disadvantages of the quality and quantity of information contained in these samples are discussed below.

The Deserters and Dismissed Personnel. The sample of deserters is highly random. During the nineteenth century, there was a strong need for soldiers for several reasons. Over the period that this study covers, Mexico suffered several foreign invasions and internal political unrest was prevalent. Interestingly, there was no conscription. As a result, although there were certain legal restrictions regarding who could be inducted into the army, these regulations were not necessarily obeyed. I found several cases where soldiers were expelled from the army because they did not meet one of the requirements, yet they had already been admitted and served for a month or so! Since there was a continuous shortage of soldiers, one can expect that a sample of the heights of the soldiers from this source should not have a bias toward taller soldiers. Up until the first decades of the twentieth century, it is not clear how the minimum height requirement (HR) was set and if this changed over time. Since the 1930s, as the social and political environment in Mexico became more stable, the need for soldiers diminished. President Lázaro Cárdenas (1934–1940) deliberately reduced the size of the armed forces and the federal budget allocated to them. Soldier selection became more compliant with the requirements; thus, the minimum height prerequisite became strictly enforced. As a result, further into the twentieth century we no longer get records of soldiers shorter than 160 centimeters. In spite of the fact that the selection of soldiers became stricter, joining the military became a career option appealing to certain groups. We then find that for cohorts born during the last two decades of this study, the lower strata of the population tend to be overrepresented, and this might create a downward bias over time. The combination of these two features makes the sample biased toward shorter soldiers, but not shorter than the minimum HR.

There are two limitations concerning the deserters and dismissed personnel sample (*cancelados*). One is that the size of the sample is very small with respect to the total of this category. I have a sample of 2,600 deserters whereas there are 110,000 files of *cancelados*; this is for all cohorts born between 1870 and 1950.[36] The other is that it does not provide any information on health or information on length of life. The average length of stay of the deserters was just a few months. Most of the time the soldiers were not captured after they deserted, but if they were, they were imprisoned for a while and then were reintegrated into the service.[37]

The information on dismissed personnel is the same as the information on deserters. The permissions for dismissal most commonly requested were the ones to arrange family affairs. Even though the dismissed personnel served in the army for an average of three years, once they left the army there was no follow-up because they were not entitled to a retirement pension or to medical services. Thus the biases we encounter are the same for both the deserters and the dismissed personnel.

The Nondeserters. The sample of soldiers (Personal Extinto) who served and retired or were killed in action or died of disease is more complete because it provides information on the health status of soldiers and their life expectancy. It is the most similar sample to the ones used for studies in the United States and Europe. Hence, we can draw more information from it. There are twenty-five hundred soldiers in this sample, which constitutes approximately 40 percent of the total in the nondeserters category during this period (fifty-eight hundred soldiers).[38]

There are three basic shortcomings to this sample. The first is that there is no information on the weights of the soldiers, so it is not possible to calculate the body mass index, which is useful for drawing inferences on the health status of the soldiers.[39] The second is that the soldiers were only measured at the time of recruitment; therefore, if the soldiers were recruited before reaching their final adult height, the information we have for these soldiers is an underestimate. The third is that the information on the diseases the soldiers suffered while they were in service or when they retired

is incomplete. In the best recorded of these cases, the death certificate gives
a list of all the diseases the individual suffered at the time of death, even if
they were not all the causes of death.

Women in the Military. I also retrieved data on women. My sample of
women is an attempt to take into account all sectors of the population.
With the opening of the school for nurses in the second decade of the
twentieth century, women were officially included in the army. Unfortunately, during the first years of the school's existence, the admission files did
not record the stature of the recruits. It was not until the end of the 1930s
that statures began to be recorded on a systematic basis. At the same time,
women were recruited as soldiers to work as office clerks and in the cleaning and cooking services. The sample for the female population is therefore
reduced with respect to the male population. However, this sample covers
a wide spectrum of the society because it contains information on women
who came from the countryside but had no education, on women who
had some skills, and on women who were aiming to have a career. I reviewed 70 percent of all the files on female recruits since the beginning of
their official induction into the military. However, only 10 percent of all
those files had information on heights. I went through approximately three
thousand files on nurses of which only three hundred had information on
heights. Throughout this period there was no minimum HR for women.

The rate of dismissals among female recruits was very high. In the case
of student nurses, they provided a letter explaining why they were request-
ing a dismissal just as they needed a letter of permission from their parents
to join the military. There is no evidence that they were imprisoned for
deserting the way that males were. The most common causes of leaving the
military were that they were going to marry or that their parents and/or
families needed them at home. Even if they finished their studies, they did
not serve in the military for very long, not even long enough to qualify for
a pension. The nurses who served during the revolution served for the longest periods. They did qualify for retirement and they were also considered
veterans of war.[40] Unfortunately, the heights of the women who served
during the revolution were not recorded.

It is not possible to learn very much about the health history of women
in the sample. There is no information on the causes of death of female soldiers because none of them were in the army long enough to serve, retire,
and die, and those who did die were shot during the battles of the revolution. If they were ill, they would usually leave the military. It was possible

to find out which were the most common endemic diseases they suffered from. This we know through the letters they sent to the authorities to justify their absences to avoid getting arrested for not showing up for work.

Heights and Social Class. Until the 1930s, the heights of boys entering the school of officers (Colegio Militar) were not recorded. Once they graduated, their enrollment files did not record their height either. There is information only on their age, civil status, military rank, and place of birth. It was perhaps the case that, unlike draftees, the authorities feared the desertion of officers less. The absence of data on heights for the school of officers leaves the sample without information on the heights of the upper classes.

Race. The issue of racial composition is very hard to disentangle. There is no reliable way to differentiate race in Mexico for the military the way it is done for the nineteenth-century military of the United States. Most of the Mexican soldiers were mestizos. There likely was a significant number of indigenous recruits, but it is very hard to determine the percentage because this particular information was not recorded in the recruitment files. After independence from Spain was officially granted in 1821, one of the principles of the new nation was that the government would not make any distinction among citizens based on ethnic or racial origins. Race lost validity for legal purposes and thus ceased being recorded in administrative documents. Most of the files I worked with have pictures of the recruits, providing a rough idea of the racial origin of the soldiers. Not surprisingly, most appear to be mestizo. The recruitment requirement of understanding the Castilian language would work against the recruitment of indigenous males who were monolingual in their aboriginal language. However, although all soldiers spoke Spanish, we do not know if this was their first language or not. We cannot, therefore, determine the percentage of indigenous individuals through language distinction.[41] The desertion records, however, do make it possible to draw inferences about indigenous backgrounds. By analyzing the language that the captured deserters used or by reading the causes of desertion, we can infer if a soldier came from an urban or rural locale or if they came from an indigenous community. I found some cases of soldiers who belonged to seminomadic indigenous groups from the north in the state of Sonora. For example, a particular soldier with the last name "Ala Blanca" (White Feather) deserted because he felt "imprisoned." This kind of analysis is very useful, but could not be used systematically because not all records are so detailed.

Photograph 6   Rurales. Photographer unknown. Courtesy IISUE/UNAM/ Fondo Octavio y Gildardo Magaña. Doc. 990.

Photograph 7   Mexican *rurales*, dead *insurrectos*, and body of Edw. Lawton lying in pit with surrounding guard. Photograph by Photograph by Bain News Services. Courtesy Library of Congress.

THE RURAL MILITIA

The rural police (known as *rurales*) was created in the 1860s to guarantee public security in a period defined by economic stagnation, law and order deterioration, and the spread of banditry and smuggling in a time when contending political factions staged coups.[42] Juárez was facing the opposition of the conservatives first and of Maximilian and the monarchists later. Parallel to this, the country was full of bandit gangs who made a living from robbery and kidnappings on the roads as well as in the cities.[43] The government was under financial stress; thus, it could not afford to have a large army. As an alternative, Juárez decided to form a group of rural policemen.[44] There was no conscription for this group because it was thought to be a group of volunteers who would be loyal to the president. They were paid a higher wage than regular soldiers for the entire period this militia existed. However, during the Juárez presidency, recruits were expected to bring their own rifles and horses. Years later, during Porfirio Díaz's presidency, requirements changed, and instead of bringing their equipment, recruits had to pay for their weapons, their horses, and their uniforms. In the end, after the cost of these items was deducted from their wages, the higher pay did not reflect a higher income. This explains the high rates of desertion observed among the *rurales*. Many of the recruits were former bandits, and the authorities were fully aware of this fact.[45] The president had the twofold purpose of showing the public that the government was making a credible attempt to improve public security and of keeping bandits as allies who could eventually be of help in fighting the enemies of the regime.[46]

Porfirio Díaz continued to support and make use of the rural police force in the same spirit his predecessors did, with a strong emphasis on using them, and quite effectively, as a means to ensure political centralization.[47] He gave monetary rewards and political privileges to *rurales* who proved to be loyal to him, devoting a good part of the federal budget to this purpose. With the end of the Díaz administration, the rural police corps saw its organization diminished; many of the members eventually joined the different factions of revolutionary armies or went back to banditry.[48]

The data for rural soldiers are drawn from the Legajos de Gobernación at the 1821–1910 Public Administration section in the AGN. The sample covers all recruits between age twenty-three and fifty who served in the rural militia for whom there is a recorded numeric stature.[49] The data set has 6,820 soldiers. The recruits of this corps came mainly from the bajío (center/north), and less so from the central region of the country; very few of them came from the north. Recruitment changed over time and, toward the end of the Porfiriato, there were several detachments created in the northern states.[50] Half of them came from rural areas and the rest from small towns and cities.[51] More than half of the recruits were landless peasants, a third were artisans, and the rest were muleteers, petty merchants. This militia did not attract factory workers or miners.[52] The average age of recruitment was thirty. Half of them were illiterate. Once soldiers got tired, they deserted and could make some money selling their equipment. It is then not surprising to find that desertion rates were high in spite of the severe punishments for deserters.[53] Tracking down deserters was so expensive that superiors preferred to recruit new soldiers to replace those who left the service. This explains the high number of recruitment records as compared to the relatively small size of the corps.[54] Corruption was the rule in the management of this army, and discipline problems were constant and numerous.[55] Administrative reports constantly mention cases of soldiers stealing weapons and other equipment to resell it. These reports suggest that these men were mercenaries who took the rural militia as a temporary job from which they could extract rents until they found something better.[56] Their effectiveness in maintaining public security was doubtful if we judge by the number and types of complaints presented by the civil population.[57] They often abused their authority in towns where they were stationed. Sometimes they would ally with the local boss and then become a threat to the population.[58]

Given that the data obtained from the military archives provided too small a sample of the upper strata of the population, it was necessary to search for an alternative to fill out this missing part of the picture. The passport records were the solution. The SRE has microfilmed records of all passports issued since 1910. It should be pointed out that this archive is not a public repository either. Gaining access to this archive was fortuitous since the first two directors I requested permission from had been academics and understood the nature and relevance of the research I was conducting; unfortunately, once SRE changed directors to nonacademics I was denied access for good.

Assuming that people who requested passports were people who had the means to travel abroad for business, study, or leisure, we consider these records an appropriate source for gathering data on heights for the middle and upper classes. The data set has 22,500 observations, of which 16,612 include sufficient information for a regression analysis; the data set was built by examining all passport applications made from 1910 to 1942.[59] As with any historical data, these series present advantages and disadvantages.

On the one hand, these data sets have tremendous advantages. First, since these are records of all people who were going to travel at the time, the sample includes men, women, and children. Second, we can determine the social stratum an individual belonged to. For adult men we know their profession, which enables us to define where they were located on the social spectrum. We cannot do this for adult women because most Mexican women at the time did not have a profession. We can, however, infer their social class by searching in their birth certificates for the profession of their father. The same can be done for children, teenagers, and young adults who are listed as students. Therefore, for similar ages among students and schoolchildren and for adult women, we can draw comparisons of heights across social classes.

On the other hand, there are three basic disadvantages to working with these records. First, although the microfilms are available for the period starting in the 1910s, the heights were not recorded in numerical figures until the late 1910s and the change to numerical figures was gradual. Hence, what we have for height in the early part of the 1910s are descriptions like tall, medium, and short (*alta, mediana, baja*). This creates a problem of accuracy because there were no rules to specify how tall is tall or how short is short. It was not until circa 1923 that all statures were recorded in numbers. This was mainly in meters and centimeters, but from time to time one could find some heights given in feet and inches. Second, these figures are self-reported. Unlike the military, there was no independent verification. Third, these records reflect all the passports that the SRE issued but not all permits issued for people traveling abroad. Prior to the existence of regional delegations of the SRE, some states had the right to issue permits to travel to a specific place. These were those states of the republic that were too far away from Mexico City to make it practical to come to the capital just to have a passport issued. We have no record of these permits, which presumably are located in state archives. Thus, our sample perhaps undercounts people from the border states.

OTHER SOURCES

I worked with some data published by official sources. These sources were the population censuses published by INEGI, the national nutritional surveys of 1963 and 1979 (Encuestas Nutricionales de México), and an official nutrition and health report of 1993.[60] The nutrition surveys and the health and nutrition report were kindly given to me by Dr. Gómez Pérez, a researcher from the Instituto Nacional de Nutrición Salvador Zubirán (INNSZ); these documents do not have much diffusion outside of the medical research community. From these sources, we can find information on the diet and health of the population across regions and across social classes during the twentieth century. The population censuses are a useful source on the most common diseases during the period of study. From the data in the nutritional surveys, we can obtain an understanding of the synergy between nutrition and health of the Mexican population. The 1963 survey in particular has height measurements that we can compare to the samples from the military and the passport records. The 1993 health and nutrition report provides information on the health status and nutrition problems of the present time. All this information is useful for drawing a comparison with the data on the military and to see how health and nutrition have evolved over time, hence completing our tracing of the evolution of living standards in contemporary Mexican history.

However, these sources have disadvantages. The disadvantages of the INNSZ studies are that they are cross-sectional studies and they cover mainly the rural and lower strata of the population, so we have little information on the higher-income groups. The disadvantage of the INEGI data is that it only covers the information gathered by the national government's health institutions, and this leaves us without information on the important portion of the population who do not have access to health-care services.

The secondary sources I worked with were several works on the history of health in Mexico, some contemporary accounts of the health problems in Mexico, and works and articles on physical anthropology published by the Instituto Nacional de Antropología e Historia (INAH), Centro de Investigaciones y Estudios Superiores en Antropología Social (CIESAS), and UNAM. The works on the history of health in Mexico provide us with anecdotal evidence that is helpful for putting the data on diseases from the military samples in context. The articles in the journals give us the most recent findings in research in physical anthropology that is related to anthropometric studies. Although these studies usually cover specific groups at a point in time, they are also useful for drawing comparisons with our samples from the military and the passport records.

A Statistical Portrait of the People in Our Story

The territory that today comprises the Mexican Republic is diverse in its natural resource endowment; its central and southern regions constituted the heart of Mesoamerica. The benign climates and fertile valleys of these regions allowed for several civilizations to develop prior to the Spanish conquest. The northern part of the territory had a harsher climate and deserts; thus, the groups that populated this region were seminomadic and hunter-gatherers. Each group adapted to its natural environment, yielding different indigenous groups with different racial characteristics. These differences along with the miscegenation process that resulted from the Spanish conquest yielded an even wider spectrum of racial diversity. A vast literature on the field of physical anthropology illustrates such differences in depth.[61] Interestingly, during much of the nineteenth and twentieth centuries, the discourse of the Mexican government on the issue of race revolved around a notion of unity, a race that emerged from miscegenation. Many of its policies focused on the unification and homogeneity of the population. It is not until the early 1980s that the Mexican government acknowledged that Mexico is a nation of racial, cultural, and linguistic diversity.

Mexico is a nation of diversity as much as of disparities. On the economic performance of the different regions of Mexico, we can assert that there have been sharp differences as well. During the colonial period, regional development obeyed the needs of the colonial administration. Development occurred in those regions that had mining or labor resources.

Transportation was developed only to foster trade links between mining centers, Mexico City (the capital of the viceroyalty), and the port of Vera-cruz. In the nineteenth century, after independence, the regions of Mexico began to develop differently. In the mid-nineteenth century the government became interested in developing transportation to unify the country, and the north of Mexico emerged as a new pole of industrial development. Commercial interests of the northern states were focused on the U.S. markets.[62] Moreover, in this border area during the last quarter of the nineteenth century, there was a boom in the economy based on the export of raw materials.[63] The government then saw it was in its best interest to invest more heavily in the development of the transportation system.[64]

As a result, regional development obeyed the interests of certain natural resources and of industrial development. This meant a rising disparity between the southern and the northern regions of the country. This adds to the disparity across social classes that I discussed in Section 1.

How can we know that the data we have gathered are reliable? The research findings on the patterns of human growth indicate that, although mean heights may vary from population to population, they are normally distributed.[65] It is, however, common to find certain problems with heights because of the peculiarities of the sources from which they are drawn.[66] This is why before doing any height data analysis it is necessary to determine the basic characteristics of the samples. For instance, while constructing a data series with archival sampling it is important to be aware of potential problems. Sometimes small samples are not normally distributed due to the low number of observations. This is one potential problem with the samples we are working with in this study. It is important to have normally distributed samples so that we can estimate trends and cross-sectional patterns using ordinary least squares (OLS) linear regression analysis. Therefore, we need to check if the samples are normally distributed. If the samples do not pass the normality tests, it is necessary to determine the type of shortfall they have and then correct it. The following will present a description of the basic features of the data series constructed.

The Basic Features of the Data Series

As explained in the preceding, the sample from the military archives was gathered in different sections of the archives, and it contains the heights of soldiers born between 1870 and 1950. The sample of rural policemen was gathered at the Legajos de Gobernación at the AGN, and it contains the height of recruits born between 1850 and 1899. The sample gathered from the passport records contains all people who requested a passport from the SRE from 1918 to 1942. Heights in numeric values were not recorded prior to 1918. Because the archives were closed to any form of scholarly research, I had to stop the series in 1942. In order to draw comparisons across regions, across social classes, between literate and illiterate, and between men and women, we need to classify the data to create samples and subsamples.

The geographical and socio-occupational classification was established under the following conventions. The geographical classification was done dividing the country into four regions: north, bajío (center/north), center, and south (see Figure 2).[67] In Figure 2 we can see which states correspond to each region. The occupations were collapsed into four categories: unskilled workers, skilled manual laborers, skilled white-collar workers, and elite. The social class categories for the military were defined based on the soldier's occupation prior to recruitment. For the passport records, the definition was based on the occupation declared in the application form. Table 2 shows the most common occupations listed in both data sources and their categories.

To classify literacy I followed the UNESCO convention. This convention considers that any person who can sign his or her name is literate. Thus, for the military samples I counted as literate all those soldiers who

CENTER	SOUTH
19. Hidalgo	26. Guerrero
20. México	27. Oaxaca
21. Federal District	28. Chiapas
22. Morelos	29. Tabasco
23. Tlaxcala	30. Campeche
24. Puebla	31. Yucatán
25. Veracruz	32. Quintana Roo

NORTH
	BAJÍO	
1. Baja California		
2. Baja California Sur	9. Durango	
3. Sonora	10. Nayarit	
4. Sinaloa	11. Jalisco	
5. Chihuahua	12. Colima	
6. Coahuila	13. Michoacán	16. San Luis Potosí
7. Nuevo León	14. Zacatecas	17. Guanajuato
8. Tamaulipas	15. Aguascalientes	18. Querétaro

Figure 2   Four regions of Mexico

TABLE 2
Occupational distribution

Occupational groups	Occupational dummies
Labrador (farm worker/farmer)	Unskilled
Campesino (peasant)	Unskilled
Jornalero (laborer)	Unskilled
Obrero (worker)	Unskilled
Minero (miner)	Unskilled
Albañil (construction worker)	Unskilled
Zapatero (shoemaker)	Skilled manual laborer
Talabartero (saddler)	Skilled manual laborer
Tejedor (weaver)	Skilled manual laborer
Sastre (tailor)	Skilled manual laborer
Operario (machine operator)	Skilled manual laborer
Herrero (blacksmith)	Skilled manual laborer
Carpintero (carpenter)	Skilled manual laborer
Curtidor (tanner)	Skilled manual laborer
Comerciante (merchant)	Skilled manual laborer
Panadero (baker)	Skilled manual laborer
Chofer (chauffeur)	Skilled manual laborer
Filarmónico (musician)	Skilled white-collar
Mecanógrafo (typist)	Skilled white-collar
Profesor de instruction primaria (schoolteacher)	Skilled white-collar
Tenedor de libros (bookkeeper)	Skilled white-collar
Empleado federal (federal employee)	Skilled white-collar
Propietario (landowner)	Elite
Médico (physician)	Elite
Abogado (lawyer)	Elite
Ingeniero (engineer)	Elite
Estudiante (student)	Students were assigned a social class according to what their parents' occupations were.

signed their recruitment file. If a soldier could not sign his name, the space was filled by the legend *no sabe firmar* (does not know how to sign). When the space was left blank, it was hard to determine whether the file had not been filled out properly or whether the soldier did not know how to sign. More often than not, this information was missing in the *cancelados* section. As a result, we do not have the information on literacy for all the soldiers in our sample. In the *rurales* sample, literacy was not systematically recorded; thus, I decided not to include it as a variable of study in this particular sample. All files I reviewed in the passport records had a signature of the applicant; therefore, I assumed 100 percent literacy in this sample.

The quality of data on urbanization provided by the historical statistics is very imprecise and is only available for scattered years. In addition, in the military samples the urban/rural origin was hard to infer because the place of birth was self-reported. To establish a reference for classification

I counted as urban those soldiers whose place of birth was a city that was listed as having more than fifteen thousand inhabitants in the figures provided by INEGI for the years 1878 and 1900.[68] For the passport records, all the birth certificates were issued in cities; thus I assume that they were all urban.

For the purpose of this analysis we only use adult heights; this means heights of males and females twenty-three years and older.[69] We do so because previous works in anthropometric research show that in studying long-term trends, it is more reliable to work with adult heights. The reason for this is that the pace of growth of children and teenagers is not very uniform and can be temporarily altered by factors like disease, differences in climate, and differences in nutrition. Thus, by working with adult heights we eliminate the effects of temporary distortions.[70] Previous studies of historical heights have shown that, prior to the twentieth century, the populations reached their final height in their twenties; today the final height of the same populations is reached at an earlier age. The explanation for this phenomenon is the improvement in health and nutrition. The research in medical science has also stressed that the velocity and timing of the growth spurt and the attainment of final height may change across populations.[71] This suggests that populations living under different climatic conditions and different diets can have different patterns of growth spurt. By looking at the distribution of heights of different age ranges, we can check how distributions change for ages beyond eighteen years. Figure 3 shows height distributions for the different samples; a visual inspection led us to assume normality in their distribution.

The first look at the data from the military sample shows that most of the recruits came from the center and bajío (center/north) regions (see Table 3). Most of the recruits were born during the turn-of-the-century decades. And most of the recruits in our sample joined the military during the 1910s and 1920s during the revolutionary and Cristero War periods (Figure 4). Most males were recruited between the ages of eighteen and thirty, but we do see that there were males recruited who were not within this age range (see Figure 5). Figure 5 suggests that recruitment in the military during this period did not enforce the minimum age requirement but was rather done according to the needs of the Department of Defense.

Figure 6 will support the notion that most of the recruitment was done in the regions where there was social and political instability. The recruitment centers changed over time according to the needs of the military. Unfortunately, there is no information on the recruitment centers or how and why they changed over time. However, from Figure 6 we can observe the

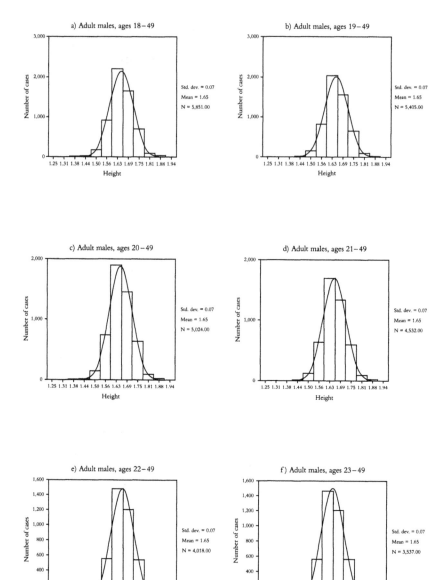

Figure 3 Height distribution profiles of males

SOURCE: Data from SDN archives.

TABLE 3

Military samples by decade of birth

	1840s	1850s	1860s	1870s	1880s	1890s	1900s	1910s	1920s	1930s	1940s	Total
Rurales soldiers total	345	1,232	2,097	1,432	1,194	520						6,820
Rurales (>159 cm)	319	1,169	1,994	1,358	1,155	463						6,458
Rurales (>160 cm)	313	1,147	1,965	1,338	1,137	453						6,353
Rurales (23 years and older)	341	1,159	1,631	1,022	888	7						5,048
Federal soldiers total				146	525	1,687	2,350	574	468	287	199	6,236
Federal (>159 cm)				131	445	1,371	1,957	510	364	223	175	5,176
Federal (>160 cm)				131	430	1,311	1,902	492	334	213	163	4,976
Federal (23 years and older)				118	436	1,271	1,330	287	290	79	54	3,865

SOURCES: Data from SDN and AGN archives.
NOTE: All soldiers are eighteen years and older.

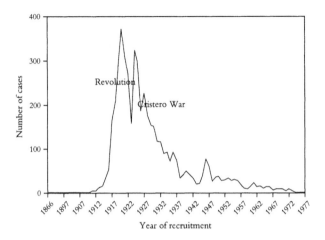

Figure 4   Federal soldiers' recruitment: Sample distribution
SOURCE: Data from SDN archives.

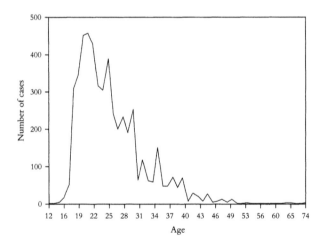

Figure 5   Federal soldiers: Age of recruitment
SOURCE: Data from SDN archives

trends in the regional composition of the recruits. The percentage of soldiers from the center remained constant. The number of recruits from the
bajío increased throughout the period of study. This coincides with the fact
that most of the Cristero movement took place in the bajío and the center
regions. The number of recruits from the south is low and stable, whereas

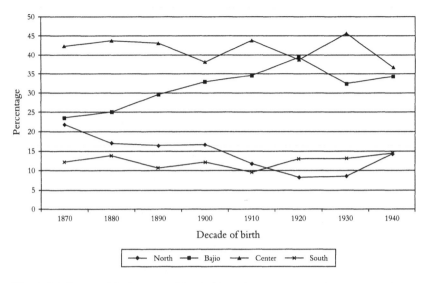

Figure 6 Geographical composition of recruits

SOURCE: Data from SDN archives.

the number of northern recruits declined over time. This decline suggests that after the revolution there was less need for a big garrison in the north. Still, the north of Mexico had a lower density of population than the rest of the country.

Most of the draftees were working-class males. Table 4 shows that most soldiers were day laborers and, to a lesser extent, skilled manual workers. The proportions do not change significantly over time. There is a slight decline in the percentage of unskilled workers compensated by an increase in the percentage of skilled manual workers. It is hard to infer what percentage of the unskilled workers was rural and what percentage was urban. The most common occupation that we find is day laborer (*jornalero*), which does not specify if this was in the countryside or in the city. The army was another job alternative for the lower classes, mainly peasants who did not have much to lose by joining the army and getting a chance to get to see different places.[72] In case they did not like it, they could always leave when they wanted without risking too much; the high number of desertions and the low number of soldiers arrested for intent to desert support this assertion.[73] Table 4 shows that the number of recruits with a white-collar occupational background was very small.

Figure 7 shows the percentage of soldiers who were recorded as literate or illiterate.[74] We observe that the percentage of literate recruits increases

TABLE 4
Military samples by socio-occupational status

	1840s	1850s	1860s	1870s	1880s	1890s	1900s	1910s	1920s	1930s	1940s	1950s
RURALES												
Unskilled	74	385	754	731	698	504						
Skilled manual	88	498	1,037	790	521	346						
White-collar	6	18	48	49	62	16						
Mean heights												
Unskilled	167.9	167.9	167.0	165.5	164.7	162.6						
Skilled manual	167.7	167.9	166.3	165.7	164.1	164.1						
White-collar	169.0	168.5	169.7	168.2	164.9	159.0						
FEDERALES												
Unskilled				97	339	1,129	1,429	352	265	147	97	14
Skilled manual				26	109	304	345	125	83	50	28	6
White-collar				n.a.	6	9	14	n.a.	n.a.	5	n.a.	n.a.
Mean heights												
Unskilled				165.0	164.0	163.0	163.0	165.0	164.0	164.0	165.0	164.0
Skilled manual				164.0	166.0	164.0	164.0	165.0	164.0	166.0	167.0	169.0
White-collar				n.a.	164.0	163.0	162.0	n.a.	n.a.	5	n.a.	n.a.

SOURCES: Data from AGN and SDN archives.

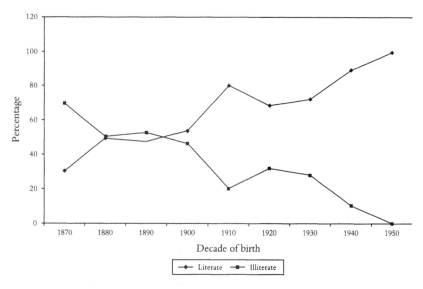

Figure 7 Literacy levels among federal soldiers

SOURCE: Data from SDN archives.

over time. This trend is consistent with the official information on timing of literacy improvement for Mexico as a result of the education campaigns launched since the 1920s. The official figures argue that literacy levels began to rise starting with the cohorts born during the decades of the revolution.[75] On the other hand, the literacy percentages are higher than for the working class as a whole during this period. This figure thus suggests that the recruits in our sample were unusual in this regard. This fact negates the possibility that the sample overrepresents the indigent portion of the working class. That is, we are not measuring the poorest of the poor.

Figure 8 suggests that most of the recruits came from rural communities and that the number of urban recruits tended to decline over time. The rate of urbanization in Mexico was high. Thus, the trend of the recruits is opposite to that of the rest of the population. Hence, for the last four decades of the study, the military sample overrepresents the rural population.

From Table 5 we can make some inferences on the degree of mobility of the recruits. Draftees were surprisingly mobile: on average 40 to 60 percent were recruited in a region other than that of their birth. This finding is consistent with the data on literacy and with the argument that the introduction of means of transportation fostered population mobility. Usually there is a positive correlation between migration and literacy. This finding

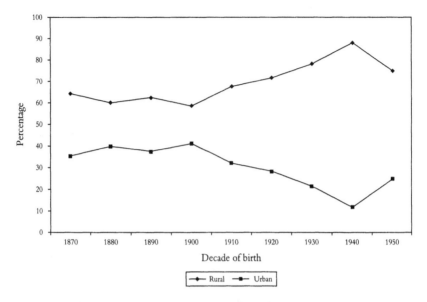

Figure 8   Urban/rural composition among federal soldiers
SOURCE: Data from SDN archives.

TABLE 5
Regional mobility among federal soldiers

	PLACE OF RECRUITMENT			
Place of birth	North (%)	Bajío (%)	Center (%)	South (%)
North	**39**	6	12	5
Bajío	33	**67**	24	21
Center	24	22	**55**	33
South	5	5	10	**41**
Total	99	100	99	100

SOURCE: Data from SDN archives.

also supports the argument that the sample is not biased toward the indigent portion of the lower strata of the population but rather toward the better-off portion of the lower classes. This indicates that the data set is biased against the hypotheses we are testing.

WHO WERE THE PASSPORT HOLDERS?

There were people of all ages applying for passports (see Table 6). All of these adults were literate and the birth certificates stated that they were all urban dwellers. The great majority of them belonged to the middle and

TABLE 6
Age distribution of passport applicants, 18 and older

	18	19	20	21	22	23 and up	Total
Total	354	421	421	616	670	14,131	16,613
% of total	2.13	2.53	2.53	3.71	4.03	85.06	
Male	226	291	308	408	465	9,700	11,398
% males	1.98	2.55	2.70	3.58	4.08	85.10	
Female	127	130	113	208	205	4,430	5,213
% females	2.44	2.49	2.17	3.99	3.93	84.98	

SOURCE: Data from SRE archives.

TABLE 7
Passport sample: Distribution by occupation

	Unskilled	Skilled	White-collar	Elite	Total
Total	1,116	7,510	3,976	3,995	16,597
Males	376	5,290	2,577	3,147	11,390
Females	740	2,220	1,399	848	5,207

SOURCE: Data from SRE archives.

upper strata of the population (see Table 7). There was a significant number of skilled workers. At first glance it seems well-to-do artisans and managers were likely to travel as much as the elite classes. However, the percentage of the elite is underrepresented. The reason for this underrepresentation is that the passports were issued to families as well as to individuals. Most of the nonelite passports were individual passports of people who visited relatives in the United States, or were men in the *bracero* program, or were men sent by their employers on business trips. In contrast, the majority of the people in the elite category traveled with family passports, where only the head of the household's height was listed. Very commonly the elite families traveled as groups of five or six members, usually to Europe. It was often the case that they traveled with a maid or a nanny. The maids' passports were issued separately. Thus, most of the working-class females from the passport sample fall in this category. It should also be stressed that there were numerous cases of students for which the occupation of the father was not available. In these cases I listed them as "skilled white-collar." The assumption for this classification was that, unless it was listed otherwise, someone who could travel abroad as a student was in a better economic position than the majority of the population.

The geographical composition of the passport sample favors the notion that there is a bias against frontier states. Table 8 confirms this notion as we observe that most of the passport applicants came from the center and bajío

TABLE 8
Passport sample: Regional composition

	North	Bajío	Center	South	Total
Total	2,059	3,378	9,797	1,363	16,597
% of total	12.41	20.35	59.03	8.21	
Males	1,398	2,309	6,694	989	11,390
% males	12.27	20.27	58.77	8.68	
Females	661	1,069	3,103	374	5,207
% females	12.69	20.53	59.59	7.18	

SOURCE: Data from SRE archives.

regions. As explained earlier in this chapter, the frontier states had the right to grant passports. Therefore, the nature of the sources forces us to undercount people from the north in this sample. The category "unknown" refers to those applications for which I could not read the place of birth on the birth certificate because of the poor quality of the microfilms. The category "foreigner" refers to all the passport applicants who were foreign-born residents of Mexico. It is not surprising to find that a considerable percentage of the people who traveled abroad were foreign born. However, this percentage overestimates the percentage of foreign-born Mexican residents with respect to the total population. Because the foreign-born population made up a very small proportion of the population, we will not include them in the analysis of heights. In addition, foreign people cannot be included in the Mexican population sample because the existing information in records does not clarify if applicants lived in Mexico during their growing years.

THE SAMPLE OF WOMEN

The sample of women contains the data gathered from both the military and the passport records. Table 9 shows that most of the women in the sample were born during the period 1880–1920. Let us remember that the data from the military sample covers women recruited since the 1930s, and the passport sample covers the applications of the period 1918–1942. Most of the women in the sample were from the center and the bajío, but we also see that there is an unknown category. This unknown corresponds to those cases in which the place of birth was not legible on the birth certificate. For the military sample, it corresponds to those cases where the information was not recorded on the recruitment forms. We should also stress that all women from both samples for whom we have complete information were literate and urban. All the women from the military sample were recruited

TABLE 9
Female sample: Distribution by decade of birth

	1860s	1870s	1880s	1890s	1900s	1910s	1920s	Total
Passport	51	215	500	857	1,656	1,717	217	5,213
Military	0	0	0	10	29	61	205	305

SOURCES: Data from SDN and SRE archives.

in Mexico City. The sample covers all the strata of the population. However, the number of elite women is undercounted because the passport sample does not cover all women who traveled with a male companion (husband or father) or with an older relative (mother, aunt). In these cases, only the height of the head of the family, usually a male, is recorded. The unknown category for the socio-occupational composition corresponds to the cases in the passport records for which women were described as having no occupation and the microfilm of the birth certificate was not legible, so we could not infer the social class by the occupation of the father. We should stress that although the number of elite women is underrepresented in the number of women who traveled abroad, it does not undercount the number of elite women as a percentage of the total population. Moreover, by not including the rural and the illiterate, the sample of women is then biased toward the better-off portion of the female population.

Conclusions

Well-being encompasses a wide array of spiritual, psychological, and material considerations. In this book I concentrate on the study of material well-being. In this chapter, I explained that material living standards can be estimated from different sources such as GDP per capita, price and wage series, demographic variables, and height and body mass. The representativeness of this measure of a population's general condition depends on its income distribution—namely, the levels of inequality—that can be calculated with Gini coefficients.

When presenting the sources I worked with I also described the intricacies of working with files containing information on heights: what can and cannot be used, as well as how to organize the information to build height data series. This presentation is followed by a statistical portrait of the people in our data series. In brief, this portrait depicts them as a mainly rural population, mainly concentrated in the center and bajío regions—these regions were the most populated parts of the country at the time. The vast majority of the people were unskilled or skilled manual workers. High illiteracy rates prevailed. These features correspond to the typical preindustrial life: poverty, slow growth, poor health, widespread literacy, and rural habitation.[76] The descriptive statistics of the data series I constructed provide a depiction of the main spatial, social, political, and economic features of the population samples I work with. Such a description allows the reader to get a sense of how the information we are working with is representative of the population at large over a one-hundred-year period and how it evolved over time.[77] Having information on different social classes will facilitate the use of trends in heights to estimate the evolution of biological standards of living of Mexico's population as well as to ascertain the trends in inequality across regions and across these classes. The data studied thus far affirm the importance of regional and social-class differences in Mexico. These trends and related issues will be covered in the next chapter.

After presenting and discussing in length the pros and cons of the different measures of material well-being at both the general level and for the specific case of Mexico, I argue that adult statures are the best proxy for assessing the evolution of biological standards of living of Mexico's population in the period 1850–1950. This argument is supported by an explanation of the advantages and shortcomings of the information available on variables other than adult heights from Mexican sources.

Chapter 2

The Tall or Short of It

Tracking Heights and Living Standards

I have always been tall by Mexican standards. With 167 centimeters of height, I am tall almost anywhere I go in Mexico. I go on the Mexico City metro and I can see over the heads of most of the people who ride it, except for the few, yet very distinctive, European or American tourists that take it. Growing up, I was the tallest girl in my class. When I was a four-year-old, Zoila, the Tzotzil woman from Chiapas who helped my mother at home, would hold me up and my feet would hang very close to the floor because Zoila was very short, like most indigenous women from Chiapas. However, when I first arrived at the Stanford University campus to start graduate school, I was amazed at how tall undergraduate women were; not one or two, but all of them. From then on I stopped thinking of myself as tall and wondered what parents fed these women as children.

As a graduate student in history, I learned that Europeans of the preindustrial era were much shorter than modern-day Europeans. Americans have followed a similar path and were even taller than the English at the time of the War of Independence in 1776.[1] The population of Japan, too, has experienced a significant increase in average heights since the post–World War II era, and the population of Spain has reported a spectacular increase in height since the end of the Franco dictatorship and the economic takeoff that followed.[2] I began to wonder about the height of Mexicans in the past and present. In Bernal Díaz del Castillo's chronicle of the Conquest of Tenochtitlán, he describes Mexican emperor Moctezuma as a man of "good size" (*buena talla*); no other comment is made with regard to the stature of the Aztec population.[3] The analysis of skeletal remains from samples of burial sites of indigenous settlements in the Central Valley of Mexico of parish burials from the early colonial period yields the same conclusion: inhabitants of precolonial and early colonial Mexico were not shorter than their Spanish counterparts.[4] Nonetheless, three centuries later, during her visit to Mexico in the late 1830s, English traveler Fanny Calderón de la Barca remarked that the people from the lower strata of the population of the central valley of Mexico were small "as two little bundles of ammunition."[5] It is interesting to note early twentieth-century pictures of Venustiano Carranza, a northerner, with revolutionaries from the south in which Carranza is consistently and significantly taller than his southern counterparts. The remark on the conquest and burial sites from the colonial period would lead us to conclude that Spaniards were not taller than the indigenous of Mesoamerica at the time of the discovery of the New World, which is consistent with the medical research findings that conclude that race per se does not make some populations taller than others.[6] These depictions, however, suggest that by the nineteenth century foreigners saw common country people from central Mexico as short, and that by the early twentieth century there was a substantial north–south disparity in heights. The anecdotes of Calderón de la Barca's travel account and Carranza's picture are consistent with the assertion made by traditional historiography that income was poorly distributed and that there were regional disparities in development and growth during the period covering the second half of the nineteenth century and until at least the first half of the twentieth century.

From the anthropometric history perspective, these anecdotes point to the hypothesis that disparities exist in the evolution of living standards of the Mexican population across regions and across social classes. These kinds of disparities are commonplace in the history of the world. Height disparity across social classes was common in many preindustrial societies. Eighteenth-century England is perhaps the best-known case of this kind of disparity; the classic example is that of boys from the slums enrolled in the Marine Society being approximately 13 centimeters shorter than boys who attended Sandhurst Academy.[7] With time, as English society became less unequal, the heights of different strata of the population began to converge. Regional disparities are also found in the case of several populations. The case of north–south disparity is well documented for different countries of Western Europe. People in the same social class but in different regions had different average heights, but their diets and environmental conditions

Photograph 8 F. Escudero—Gen. F. Angeles—Gen. V. Carranza. Photograph by Bain News Services. Courtesy Library of Congress.

were also different.[8] From the mid-nineteenth century and throughout the twentieth century, with the development and expansion of means of transportation, advances in public health and health-care provision, and the rising quality of nutrition, material living conditions have become more homogeneous, and consequently regional differences have been minimized.

Unlike most industrialized nations, Mexico followed a path in which events took place at a different tempo and intensity. Although in most industrialized countries the early phase of industrialization was hazardous to the quality of life, the negative trend was eventually reversed as societies reduced inequality and cities became healthier places to live.[9] But then, timing was different, too. In countries such as England, Germany, France, and the United States, the first wave of the Industrial Revolution had already taken place by the time great public works were undertaken in cities. So the causality of events occurred by steps. First there was the initial wave of industrialization; societies gradually became less unequal, and then cities became healthier places to live. Finally, biological standards of living improved continuously to the point where they currently are. In Mexico, the first wave of industrialization took place almost at the same time as big public works in the cities were undertaken. Shortly after the onset of industrialization, policy makers of the time recognized the germ theory of disease and public health principles. Urbanization remained limited up until the second decade of the twentieth century. Hence, the urban penalty of preindustrial and industrializing cities did not affect a large portion of the population. Thus, one might think that the decline in the quality of life commonly found in the early phases of industrialization would be offset by cities becoming healthier places to live. Industrialization was incipient in its first stages and was less labor intensive than it was in Western Europe or the United States. Therefore, the number of industrial workers was small compared to the entire working population, another reason to think that industrial work was not so damaging to the biological standards of living of the whole working class. Subsequently, advances in medical services and the introduction of a labor law protected the rights of workers in the early twentieth century. At first glance the combination of these circumstances would lead one to think that industrialization would not generate a decline in biological standards of living the way it did in the case of industrialized countries. Nonetheless, the evidence presented in this chapter will show the opposite, at least for a great majority of the population.

Differences in height have been noticeable to scholars and policy makers at different points in history, and many different explanations have been given for this phenomenon. During the late nineteenth century, it was suggested that Mexicans were short because it was one of the defining features of race. It was the time when the *Científicos* embraced the ideas of the positivist school; one of them was eugenics. This school of thought asserted that some people were prone to be underdeveloped and delinquent due to their racial origins, and they went on to examine which of these presumed racial characteristics were present in the Mexican race. Some went so far as advancing the argument that the Mexican race was one of the sources of Mexico's social problem and part of the solution resided in "whitening up" the population. Eugenics was considered a serious theory until the 1920s.[10]

Advances in the medical research undertaken throughout the twentieth century have proved the postulates of eugenics wrong.[11] These medical research findings have successfully proven that adult height is the result of net nutrition during growing years.[12] Therefore, adult statures mirror the material quality of life (health, food, shelter, and clothing) that any individual had during the first twenty years of his/her life. It is important to point out that there are two important growth spurts during these two periods of growth: infancy (i.e., the first three years of life) and adolescence. During these two periods growth accelerates. Hence, any potential environmental insult suffered during these periods could prevent individuals from attaining maximum potential stature.[13] Another relevant finding is that, at the individual level, the genetic endowment plays an important role in determining adult height; yet genetics are not inherited uniformly. This is why, in the same family, siblings raised under the same circumstances do not necessarily have the same final height. As a result, adult statures of any human population will have a bell curve distribution; this means that there will always be people who are short and others who are tall, and most of the people will be in the middle. The medical explanation of this phenomenon is that, at the aggregate level, the genetic endowment of individuals loses relevance. This implies that when we are studying the increase in heights of a certain population over time, we are interested in observing the trends in the average height of the population under study.

In the previous chapter, I explained how adult stature was one measure of well-being and the best measure at hand to study the Mexican population at large over the one-hundred-year period from 1850 to 1950. In those pages, I also described the sources I worked with as well as the methods I used to build the data sets, and I included the main statistical features of the samples. In this chapter, I will elaborate in more detail how we should analyze anthropometric measures to understand biological standards of living. For this, I will examine the trends in heights of the different samples and the compositional changes that influenced them. A special emphasis

will be given to the evolution of differences across regions and across social classes. Robert McCaa, the leading demographic historian of Mexico,
studied long-term trends in demography. Based on his research findings,
he asserts that Mexico's population history has been influenced by political
events; he also points out that demographic pressure has been altered by
environmental and cultural changes.[14] In the previous chapter we presented
demographic variables as measures of well-being. As they also concern the
evolution of statures, it is worth exploring the effects of certain variables—
political events and environmental and cultural changes. Research findings
in developmental biology, mainly on the nature of deoxyribonucleic acid
(DNA), show that there is a recurring interaction between human biology
and the sociocultural environment.[15]

   This chapter examines the evolution of living standards in Mexico from
1850 to 1950 by tracking the trends in heights of the population samples
presented in Chapter 1. This study focuses on the macrotrends in the long-
term perspective. Acknowledging that disparities across regions and across
social classes are ubiquitous in Mexican history, it remains important to
trace their evolution within this context as well. We will analyze the evolution of heights over time and make inferences concerning the evolution
of biological standards of living. As we examine our data, we will indicate
which of the independent variables that we are working with are the most
important determinants of height. We will run the tests of the main sample
of heights as well as of the subsamples (geographical, socioeconomic, liter-
ate/illiterate, urban/rural) to evaluate the differences among them in long-
term trends. In this way, we can get an idea of the compositional changes
of the population and their relationship with the average heights and the
biological standards of living.[16]

   We will test the relevance of political events on the population's well-
being. This means that we will ascertain if there was a structural break in
the trends in heights for people who were born after the liberal reforms
(Reform Laws) were passed and after the 1910 Revolution. In examining
the evolution of living standards of people born and growing up during the
second half of the nineteenth century, we will be able to tell if the disentailment of communal property or if the changes brought by the Porfirio Díaz
administration had any repercussion on the standards of living of the different segments of the population. We will also be able to figure out if people
growing up during the last decades of Porfirio Díaz's dictatorship experienced a decline in living standards severe enough to trigger a revolt against
the status quo. We will also test the effects on the material well-being of
cohorts born and growing up during the two decades of political instability

and armed uprisings that followed the famous revolution of November 20, 1910. Lastly, it will be possible to find out if the evolution of biological standards of living corresponds to the claims of welfare improvement made by postrevolutionary governments. Environmental and cultural transformations (or the lack thereof) will also be taken into consideration.

Applying a regression analysis to the data that I gathered on the heights of the Mexican military, rural police, and passport records, I will be able to infer if there was a secular increase in the average height of the Mexican population for the cohorts born between 1850 and 1950; this will give us an idea of the evolution of the biological living standards of the entire population.[17] I can also ascertain if there were different trends in height, or not, across regions and across social classes. This will answer more refined questions derived from geographical and socioeconomic differences. For example, it will be possible to know whether being from the north or the central region of the Mexican Republic mattered or not for the biological quality of life. Moreover, it will offer us an idea of the difference in adult heights and living standards among the different income strata of the population. It will be possible to determine if people who were literate had any advantage over those who were illiterate, and also if there was any difference between people who grew up in the cities and those who grew up in the countryside. Third, I can have an idea of the trend concerning heights of women; this will give us a basis for determining if we can safely extend our inferences to the population as a whole. Lastly, through an international comparison and a comparison with modern-day standards, I will be able to ascertain where the case of Mexico stands in a global context both in time and space. Having these results, I can then study their relationship to changes in nutritional status and disease environment with the information on health and diet available for this period.

The results of this study will tell us a story that can be considered a more accurate depiction of the history of well-being in Mexico during the period 1850–1950, as distinct from studies based on anecdotal evidence or price and wage series, for three basic reasons. First, the sources provide a more thorough representation of the Mexican population because they cover all regions of the country and all social classes, including information on both men and women. Second, given that adult height is the result of net nutrition during growing years, we can consider adult height as an output of living standards. Hence, it is a reflection of the income that entered a household by way of money or species and of how the income was allocated within the family. Height thus enables me to overcome the potential biases that could result from measuring living standards with more traditional

indicators in a period of Mexican history when a significant portion of the
population operated partially or completely outside of the monetized economy. Concerning those households in which the breadwinner did earn a
wage in money, it was a period in which low educational levels could not
guarantee that the income would be spent on food or health care for family
members instead of alcohol for the head of the household. In other words,
an alcoholic man earning wages did not necessarily provide food and health
care for his family.[18] Third, the use of adult height as a measure of material well-being to conduct this study allows me to write a history of poverty and inequality, as differences in height across regions and across social
classes are an accurate representation of regional disparities and income distribution. Height analysis will also allow me to test the hypothesis advanced
in Chapter 2 of Section 1 that the inadequate development of welfare institutions contributed to the perpetuation of high levels of inequality among
the Mexican population during the period 1850–1950. Later in the book,
the sections on health and nutrition will explain the biological, social, and
cultural causes that underlie such inequalities.

The rest of this chapter is organized around the analysis of each of the
samples gathered for this study, namely, the *rurales*, the military, and passport records. After tracking the trends of each of these samples along with
the composition effects, the analysis will focus on comparisons across regions and across social classes vis-à-vis the evolution of economic growth,
and will then show how results can be extended for the population in general. Comparisons of trends in heights with other countries as well as with
modern populations will follow.

The Trends Analysis

Let us briefly sum up the basic data classification and relevant information. The geographical classification of the sample was done by dividing
the country into four regions: north, bajío, center, and south.[19] The different occupations were collapsed into four categories: unskilled workers,
skilled manual workers, skilled white-collar workers, and elite. Following
the UNESCO convention, everyone who could sign their name in the
recruitment record or passport request was listed as literate. People who
reported being born in a settlement having fifteen thousand inhabitants or
more according to the 1878 and 1900 figures in the historical statistics are
considered urban.

I did not include race within the descriptive categories of any of the
samples. There are two reasons for this: one is legal and the other scien-

tific. First, with the abolition of slavery and *castas* at the onset of the period of independence, this category lost legal relevance. Therefore, since the early 1820s, official documents no longer required the description of racial background. It then becomes prohibitively difficult to determine the racial composition of the people in our samples. Moreover, it should be added that, as some social history studies argue, interracial mixing was so common throughout the colonial period that by the end of the eighteenth century racial differentiation in Mexico had come to mean little.[20] Second, auxology and medical research have found that race is not a determinant of stature; it is rather the interaction between gene pools and environment that influence adult size and shape.[21]

Adult statures are the reflection of nutrition and health during the growing years. In graphs, adult heights are correlated with the decade of birth. This means that the adult stature of someone born in 1880 would reflect his/her quality of life during the first two decades of life; adult height would be reached approximately in 1900. Adult height is determined by qualitative variables such as regions of birth (north, bajío, center, or south), decade of birth (e.g., 1850s, 1860, etc.), and social background (unskilled workers, skilled manual workers, white-collar workers, and elite). To analyze the trends in heights and how these differences in qualitative characteristics influenced their evolution, a regression will be carried out for all samples. Last but not least, human populations' statures have a normal distribution.

THE MILITARY SAMPLES

In the previous chapter I explained that one of the most common problems in military samples is shortfall, an erosion of height distribution caused by an HR that could vary over time. It is possible to ascertain HR-related deficiencies through a three-step analysis proposed by John Komlos. The steps are visual inspection of sample histograms; estimation of the direction of the trends of the means through the Komlos-Kim test (K&K); and a regression analysis with a truncated ordinary least square method (TOLS) or truncated regression (TR) "that [is] able to explore the effect of covariates [such as age, time, birthplace, socioeconomic environment, mortality rate, and population density] on heights, provided such data are available."[22] The previous chapter includes the first two steps. Mexican military armies were made of voluntary (and sometimes not so voluntary) recruits. The need for soldiers was driven by periods of peace and periods of political instability; the ability to keep them on the payroll depended on the health of public finances. It is therefore plausible to argue that the degree to which recruiters adhered to the standards changed at the same speed as political circumstances moved. Not having a professional army of the dimensions of those of Western European countries also explains the fact that Mexican recruiters were not as systematic and methodical in the measurement and enforcement of HR.

Given that the shortfall created by HR can bias the results, it is hard to calculate the intensity of the bias since we do not know how lax the enforcement of HR was or how it changed over time. Hence, to overcome this problem, I excluded recruits below 160 centimeters when conducting the height analysis both for the K&K test and the regression analysis. To make sure that there are no discrepancies due to rounding off practices when measuring recruits, I repeated the exercise excluding only recruits below 159 centimeters. The calculated trends will be upwardly biased but in a consistent way. Figure 9 shows a summary of the K&K tests performed on both the federal and the rural samples. We note that the direction of the trend does not change between raw samples and the truncated ones.

There is a downward trend in the height sample for the period 1850–1890 (see Figures 9 and 10). The forty-year period during which this downward trend lasted corresponds to people growing up during the second half of the nineteenth century and the first decade of the twentieth century; this suggests deterioration in the standards of living of the working classes during the last half of the nineteenth century. We should, however, keep in mind that the *rurales* sample, in which we observe the decline, is drawn from a particular portion of the popular classes: farmhands and craftsmen, but not miners or factory workers. It was men who worked in trades that were being displaced by the modernization of the economy, such as muleteers displaced by the introduction of the railroad or artisans driven out of business by machines and manufactures.[23] For the most part, these were men in their midthirties, temporarily unemployed, who enlisted in the *rurales* until something better came along. Over time, the height of men in this sample declined and this suggests that the biological standard of living of this portion of the popular classes was deteriorating, a reflection of what was happening in the sectors of the economy where they had worked prior to joining the *rurales* militia. The cause of this decline in heights sheds light on how the end of the preindustrial era in Mexico affected certain portions of the population. The transformation of the economy fostered growth but, in the process, it also left some sectors of the population out of work; hence, their standards of living deteriorated.[24] It is also interesting to note that heights of the *rurales* are not much lower than other populations in the Western world, as we will see later in this chapter. In light of this comparison it is also worth

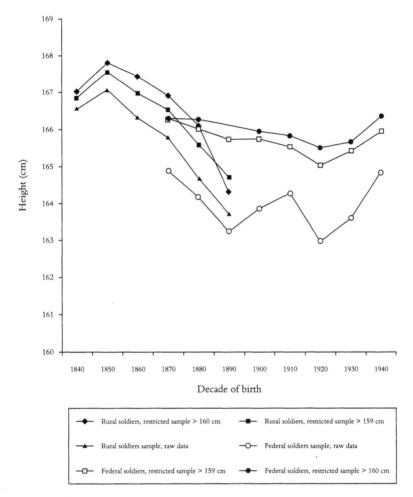

Figure 9 Military samples: Estimated trends in heights, Komlos-Kim method used for the restricted sample

SOURCES: Data from SDN and AGN archives.

emphasizing that this sample does not include the poorest strata of the population. Although truncated samples are upwardly biased, the height in the raw sample is not much lower (see Figure 9).

There is a difference in trends between *rurales* and *federales* for cohorts born in the 1880s and 1890s for the regression results (see Figure 10); this difference is driven by the number of observations for those decades in each sample. For the 1890s the number of *rurales* born in that decade age

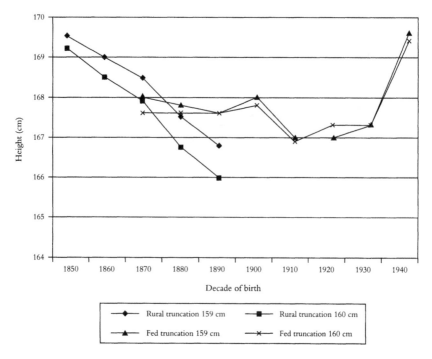

Figure 10 Military samples: Trends in heights, regression results
SOURCE: Data from SDN and AGN archives.

twenty-three or more is particularly small; most of the observations for that decade correspond to young men who had not attained their final height. Let us remember that the rural police dissolved in 1913 after Francisco I. Madero's assassination. The federal soldiers sample has a higher number of men twenty-three and older for those decades than the *rurales* sample. Moreover, the recruits in the *federales* sample come from a wider variety of trades than their *rurales* counterparts, some that pertained to a higher income level. The federal army even enlisted men from white-collar occupations, albeit in smaller numbers than manual workers.

Traditional historiography asserts that the Díaz administration was detrimental to the living standards of the popular classes because of the capitalist development model with which economic growth was set in motion. This model was based on the exploitation of the laboring classes, and in the case of peasants, it also meant the seizure of their lands.[25] Nonetheless, the evidence presented here suggests that the decline in standards of living began a little over two decades before the Díaz dictatorship was actually inaugurated; thus, the Porfirian administration's policies could not have been the only reason for this decline. Political instability, the transformation of modes of production that marked the end of the preindustrial era and displaced people from their traditional occupations, dire circumstances in the public finances, and the disentailment of communal peasant properties were all causes of this decline.

Recent studies of rural Mexico show that during the mid-nineteenth century there was a proliferation of ranches in the central and bajío regions. Peasant villages were able to flourish and exert their economic independence. These ranchos and villages produced basic staples for internal consumption and for local markets.[26] This form of production increased food supply for the average rural dweller. In the first years of its creation, the *rurales* militia drew half of its men from the bajío region.[27] Most *rurales* were drawn from regions that enjoyed a certain prosperity; thus, their stature being higher is compatible with the economic circumstances in which these soldiers grew up. Interestingly, in his study on the national income during the first half of the nineteenth century, Richard Salvucci asserts that food production increased toward the mid-nineteenth century with respect to the first decades of independence.[28] Still, it is important to keep in perspective that the *rurales* sample represents a portion of the popular classes that went from being relatively well-off during the mid-nineteenth century (1840s, 1850s, 1860s) to a gradual deterioration in their standards of living in the decades that followed. The *rurales* sample does not include the poorest strata of the population.

John Tutino explains, in his classic work *From Insurrection to Revolution in Mexico*, that although the disentailment of communal properties was decreed in 1856, it was not enforced immediately or homogeneously. The communities closer to large cities were the first to enter the privatization scheme, and it soon proved detrimental to the socioeconomic and political life of rural communities.[29] Those regions that were farther from the large cities were reluctant to enter the private property scheme mandated by liberal reforms, especially because it eliminated the possibility of having access to communal lands of wood and pasture and having a village fund to pay for festivities or to defend themselves.[30] For the most part, disentailment of communal property was harmful to the living standards of peasants and ranchero communities. The enforcement of disentailment and privatization laws was done slowly in the face of the opposition of rural dwellers. This gradual decline in living standards of people in the countryside explains the decline in heights of *rurales* who had worked in agricultural activities prior to their engagement in this militia.

The *federales* military sample covers a period that includes generations growing up during the Porfiriato, the revolution, and the first decades of the postrevolutionary period. Changes are not as steep as one would expect in a period marked by so many changes and instability. The first three decades covered in this sample show stagnation that would correspond to cohorts born during the dictatorship. This is followed by a slight improvement during the decade that followed; this includes people born during the last decade of the dictatorship and the revolution, with a decline in average statures for those born and growing up in the 1910s and 1920s. The last three decades of the period display a recovery trend that accelerates during the 1940s.

In terms of the evolution of biological standards of living there does not appear to be any significant deterioration due to the dictatorship that allegedly induced pauperization of the lower classes; the improvement observed for cohorts born toward the end of the Díaz period is modest compared to its economic performance. Policy makers were aware of the social improvement, and to them it did not seem modest. In 1902 Justo Sierra declared, "There exists . . . such a thing as Mexican social evolution. . . . This evolution no doubt is just beginning. When we look back at our conditions previous to the final third of the past century, we see what a long way we have come. . . . It is not insignificant."[31] Industrialization processes taking place and economic growth did not produce an improvement in the quality of life of populations from which the army was getting its recruits. This evolution in the average height of soldiers is understandable given that industrialization at its early stages does not necessarily translate into an improvement in the biological standards of living of a population.[32] In addition, as we mentioned earlier, changes in land tenure were not conducive to improving the livelihood of the average peasant.

The average stature of recruits born in the 1910s decade decreased; these are people growing up during the revolution and the first decades of the postrevolutionary period. It is not surprising to observe a decline. It might, however, be surprising that the decline is not steeper given the chaos created by the years of armed rebellion. After all, this was a violent war that took a heavy toll on human life. One explanation for this could be formulated under the Malthusian postulate that anything that raises the death schedule, for example, war, disorder, disease, poor sanitary conditions, will increase material living standards. A fixed amount of resources is distributed among fewer people. Although this postulate applies to preindustrial societies, given that industrialization was only taking place in a small number of regions compared to the extent of the Mexican territory, I would argue that in this case the Malthusian argument holds.

The high death rate increasing material living conditions hypothesis is compatible with the meager recovery in stature observed for cohorts born during the following two decades. Still, this seems too meager a recovery for a revolution based on the granting of workers' rights and the undertaking of an agrarian reform. The improvement observed in living standards is rather deceptive, but is congruous with arguments made in Section 1 concerning the extent of people who actually benefited from the new labor legislation and the land redistribution initiative. Institutional reforms mandated by the 1917 Constitution were meant to favor the popular classes but were only enforced to ameliorate the lives of a reduced portion of the working classes. The revolution did not do justice to all population strata on an equal basis. Politicians of the early postrevolutionary period expressed a commitment to social welfare, but failed to define what this commitment meant in concrete action. This explains the modest improvement in average height of recruits who were born and grew up during this period. For instance, Venustiano Carranza declared, prior to assuming power circa 1913, "The country has been living in illusion, starved and luckless, with a handful of laws that are of no help to it; we have to plough it all up, drain it and then truly construct."[33] Carranza's agricultural metaphor said a lot about the nature of his rhetoric and little about his plan of action. In contrast, the substantial increase in average stature for cohorts born during the late 1930s and 1940s coincides with the launching of a welfare state and with the government's commitment and recognition of its responsibility to assist the poor during the Lázaro Cárdenas administration, especially with the introduction of universal public health initiatives, such as national vaccination campaigns for children. The social development that stemmed from this commitment appears to have yielded positive results in the standards of living of the population from which the military were enlisting their recruits in the mid-twentieth century.

With regard to regional disparities and differences across social classes in these samples, we can say that regression results for both samples are consistent. Recruits born in the north and bajío are taller than their counterparts in other regions. Enlisted soldiers who were originally from the central and southern regions were shorter. With the exception of Mexico City and Veracruz, which were industrial development enclaves, disparities in regional average statures mirror economic performance; taller soldiers came from the north and bajío, which were more economically dynamic regions than many parts of the center and south at the time. The Appendix contains graphs of trends in regional and class disparities as well as regression results tables.

Environmental differences play a relevant role, too. The north and bajío had lower densities of population and were big cattle-raising regions. Lower densities of population meant a lower exposure to diseases and epidemics. Throughout history, it has been observed that hunter-gatherers, seminomadic groups, and communities living in small settlements were less likely to be exposed to infectious diseases and epidemics; hence, their health tended to be better in general than that of sedentary communities. This will be explained in further detail in the following section. Regions that have significant cattle production normally will have a higher meat intake in their diet and will sell meat at relatively lower prices than regions that do not raise cattle. Meat consumption during the growing years is an important determinant of final height. Children who have more meat in their diets usually grow taller and are more likely to reach their maximum potential stature. The dynamics of how meat intake among children and adolescents fosters growth will be explained at length in the following section. For the moment, suffice it to say that the traditional diet in the northern and bajío regions was richer in animal protein, and this had a positive impact on final adult statures.

Regression results also show that in both samples unskilled workers are slightly shorter than skilled workers (see Table A.1 in the Appendix). Such a height difference suggests that men who had a trade were taller than those who did not. Being trained in a trade is a form of human capital that correlates positively with a better biological standard of living. This kind of difference will become more evident when we analyze the passport sample.

PASSPORT SAMPLE

The stature of passport applicants increased throughout the period covered in this sample. The heights of applicants were also comparable to average heights of samples of males from the Western world. Such improvement suggests that men in this sample were not affected by the urban penalty of growing cities or the disentailment and privatization of communal property in the countryside. In contrast, it makes one think that the men in this sample benefited from all the positive transformations that were taking place, such as economic growth, investments in sanitary infrastructure, professionalization of medical services that allowed for more accurate diagnoses and prevention of most common infectious diseases, and last but not least, better nutrition due to the increased availability of a wider array of foodstuffs.

There is a regional disparity in this sample of the same nature as the military sample. This means that, among passport applicants, males from the

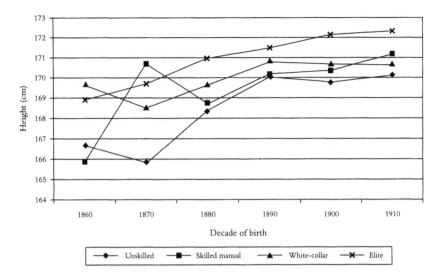

Figure 11 Passport sample: Evolution of male heights by occupation
SOURCE: Data from SRE archives.

south and center were shorter than their bajío and northern counterparts.[34] Nonetheless, as we can observe in Table A.2 and Figure 11, all subsamples show increases in heights; this suggests that all applicants were getting taller. There are disparities across social classes, but the gap tends to narrow over time: the elite and white-collar workers are taller than their unskilled and skilled manual counterparts, but there is a pattern of convergence (see Figure 11). What may raise some sort of conundrum is that the heights of all subsamples are increasing. Why are unskilled and skilled manual workers in this sample getting taller while their counterparts from the military sample are following a trend in the opposite direction?

In Section 1, I advanced the argument that within the working classes there were differences in opportunities for advancement. There were groups who benefited from institutional changes and others that did not. This applies to all groups, namely, skilled manual workers, unskilled workers, peasants, day laborers, and domestic servants. Once this assertion is taken into consideration, the differences in trends in height between the military and the passport samples no longer confound us. Passport applicants were individuals who could travel abroad legally, but for Mexicans going to the United States, this was far from being the norm. While crossing the U.S. border for work during the first half of the twentieth century was not a life-threatening venture the way it is today, many of the working-class

people who went to work in the United States did not go to the trouble of
obtaining official documents to leave the country.

To request a passport, applicants were required to present a birth certificate. This was a time when average working-class people were still not in
the habit of having that kind of document. Moreover, passport applicants
were all literate. This was a period in which literacy campaigns were being launched and the great majority of the working classes were illiterate.
Unskilled and skilled manual workers who applied for passports during the
first half of the twentieth century can be categorized as the aristocracy of
the laboring classes. Most likely, these applicants were workers who did
benefit from institutional transformations that granted them more rights
and higher incomes, and these workers were not affected by the absence
of a properly defined state welfare system. On the other hand, men from
military samples were representative of a portion of the lower strata of the
population different from passport applicants; recruits belonged to a segment living with a greater scarcity of resources. Except for recruits born in
the 1940s, soldiers in our sample did not have to present a birth certificate
upon recruitment, and a substantial number were illiterate. The average
stature of passport applicants improved. Although they remained shorter
than the better-off strata of society, there is a convergence in heights across
social classes. This suggests that at least for the better-off portion of the
working classes, the evolution of biological standards of living looked more
promising, and access to a sanitary infrastructure and a higher income, as
well as the possibility of a better diet, did become a reality for them. In brief,
we can say that passport applicants from a working-class background were
the small proportion who did benefit from economic prosperity generated
by Porfirio Díaz's policies and to whom the revolution did do justice.

WOMEN'S STATURES

In analyzing the trends in statures of the female sample there are several
points that need to be considered regarding sexual dimorphism, literacy, and
urbanization. Sexual dimorphism concerns the differences between males and
females. One difference is adult height. In a given population living under
normal circumstances, women are on average 12 to 13 centimeters shorter
than adult men. This is a consequence of the different timing in growth
spurts, which leaves boys an additional two years of growth before the onset of the spurt.[35] Another difference pertains to resilience to environmental insults such as food shortages and diseases that could be caused by war,
famines, or exposure to a new pathogen. Women's growth tends to be more
resistant to deprivation than men's; therefore, gender difference in stature is

relatively larger in good times and shrinks under bad conditions.[36] In addition, females tend to recover more quickly from environmental insults than males: "similarly girls recover from growth arrest more quickly than boys. The physiological reason for this greater stability is not known."[37] We should then expect to find less variation in stature for female height samples.

Literacy and urbanization are two other features that must be considered. All women in the samples examined are both literate and urban. Both of these features are representative of a somewhat privileged minority of the female population on both accounts, and I will explain why. Until the first decade of the postrevolutionary period, less than 30 percent of the Mexican population was literate.[38] Literacy campaigns launched by Vasconcelos in the early 1920s did not yield positive and compelling results until the 1930s, and it was not until the 1970s that Mexico became 70 percent literate. Women's education lagged behind due to the traditional view that it was less important to give formal schooling to women than it was to men. This means that at that time in Mexico, illiteracy rates in general were high and women's were higher than the average. At the outbreak of the revolution, Mexico was a predominantly rural nation in its population distribution and much of its GDP came from rural-related activities. Although both these features eventually transformed at great speed, this transformation did not occur until the 1930s and 1940s.[39] The fact that both of the female samples pertain to urban women makes them less representative of the general female population.

Being literate in an urban environment gave women in our samples a potential advantage in standards of living and in stature vis-à-vis their illiterate rural counterparts for at least three reasons. First, they had access to the limited sanitary infrastructure that made certain parts of the cities healthier places to live. Second, they had the skills and access to make the most of the information on best hygienic practices in the household. Third, they had the resources to implement their hygienic measures, thus preventing exposure to most common infectious diseases, which also included maintaining better nutrition for their families.[40] Women working and living in these households, albeit not part of the family in the stricter sense, also benefited from the healthier environment.

As to the passport sample there appears to be no substantial difference in heights across regions. Differences across social classes are smaller than in the male sample and they also show a convergence pattern. Sexual dimorphism can explain why differences are smaller among women than among men. For biological reasons, stature variation among females is expected to be smaller, and basic material living conditions across social classes in this sample were not too strikingly different. This means that although women from the upper and upper-middle classes had a substantially higher standard of living, working-class women in this sample did have the means to cover the basic material conditions for good health and nutrition.

Women from the military sample are shorter in stature than female passport applicants. There is, however, an increase in heights for the cohort born during the 1920s. The size of the female military sample is much smaller than that of the passport sample (see Table 10). Due to the small size of this sample, it was not possible to do a regression analysis. It is hard to infer with precision the economic background of women in the military sample beyond the fact that they were urban and literate. They were surely the first generation of women getting some type of formal schooling beyond grade school, but it is hard to tell if they grew up under less favorable conditions than women from the passport sample. The important fact here is that height does increase for those born in the 1920s.

Examination of the trends of different samples suggests that there is not one single trajectory in the evolution of biological standards of living. The trajectory of the military samples (*federales* and *rurales*) declines, stagnates, has a slight recovery, a slight decline, and then a substantial recovery that leaves cohorts born in the 1950s with a similar height to their counterparts born a century before. In contrast, the trajectory of the passport sample is one of constant increase. The military samples are built with working-class recruits from diverse backgrounds (agricultural workers, artisans, factory workers, etc.), whereas the passport sample is built with people from different income levels.

Richard Steckel suggests that in analyzing stature and living standards one should take into account three equally important elements:

1. Timing of industrialization relative to the recognition of the germ theory of disease and public health
2. The extent of urbanization
3. Diet[41]

TABLE 10

Sample of percentiles compared to modern standards: Males

	10th	25th	50th	75th	90th	Number
U.S. modern	168.5	172.4	176.8	181.2	185.1	
Unskilled (federal military)	156.0	160.0	169.0	168.0	171.0	3,893
Skilled manual (federal military)	157.0	160.0	165.0	170.0	173.0	1,368
Skilled white-collar (passport)	160.0	165.0	170.0	175.0	179.3	2,577
Elite (passport)	162.0	166.75	170.0	176.0	180.0	3,147

SOURCES: Mexico data from SDN and SRE archives; U.S. data from Steckel, "Percentiles of Modern Height Standards," 157–65.

In light of these elements let us analyze the different trends described above. In Mexico, industrialization and the recognition of the germ theory of disease and public health took place at basically the same time. (In Section 3 there will be a detailed explanation of the germ theory of disease and public health.) Urbanization was rather incipient until the 1920s, and a traditional diet prevailed in most of the country for the whole period except in cities. (In the following section the history of nutrition will be presented.)

Industrialization being concomitant with the recognition of the germ theory at a time when urbanization was incipient in the country would lead us to conclude that the "urban penalty" and the negative effects on standards of living of the early phases of industrialization observed in some Western countries did not affect the Mexican population to the same extent. Although cities were for the most part unhealthy places to live during our period of study, they were improving their sanitary infrastructure at a time when industries were developing. Therefore, the potentially deleterious effects of industrialization were somewhat neutralized. Moreover, if we take into account the size of industry and the number of workers in it with respect to the economy in general, it becomes evident that it was a small portion of both the economy and the working population. One potential benefit for the urban population was access to a wider array of foodstuffs— hence, the possibility of a diet with more variety. As we will see in the next chapter, the poorest segments of the population did endure the urban penalty typical of preindustrial cities, but these were not the people who applied for passports or were recruited by the army; they were mainly people working in the informal economy sector.

People from the passport sample were all listed as urban and literate. In light of the fact that there was not an urban penalty for people who operated within the formal economy, and that the majority of the population were illiterate up until the first decades of the twentieth century, passport applicants constituted a privileged portion of the population. These people benefited from the economic takeoff of the last quarter of the nineteenth century as well as the public health initiatives launched at the time in the cities. The upper classes increased their average stature and were the tallest group on average. The working classes from this sample were shorter than the rich, but did experience a growth in stature; their average statures were converging with those of the wealthy, at least for the period covered by the passport sample. This portion of the population was what the policy makers of the late nineteenth century would have wanted the entire population to be. Regardless of the existing social differences, everyone's standard of living was improving as judged by the evolution of average height. If all institutional transformations that address social issues (*cuestiónes sociales*) had covered the entire population, convergence in height could have eventually been attainable, but the reality was different.

The evolution of statures of the military samples provide a reality check of the policies to promote economic development as well as the extent and success of social policies implemented during the period 1850–1950. Nonetheless, it is worth keeping in mind that Section 1 explained that there was no real government concern followed by concrete action to improve the living conditions of the masses until the late 1930s, and even then action was piecemeal. The declining stature of adult men from the military sample over the second half of the nineteenth century speaks to the issue of the standards of living of the vast majority of the rural population, that is, there was no improvement; instead, there was deterioration and stagnation. Living standards did not improve until the 1930s. Mexico's economic development was heterogeneous; in places where industry developed, some groups were able to benefit from the growth that stemmed from industrialization. In places where the revolution fought its key battles, the people who lined up with the winning side were able to enjoy the fruits of revolution. The rest of the population remained excluded from economic prosperity and opportunities for progress. It is worth adding that—given the way recruitment was conducted—the military sample does not include the poorest segments of the population, both urban and rural. Therefore, we would guess that because the poorest people endured even harsher living conditions, they would also be shorter in stature; they had worse health conditions and a lower life expectancy.

Comparing these trajectories in the evolution of standards of living with the economic performance during the same period would shed light on the degree of prevailing inequality at the time. One way to establish this comparison is to examine the evolution of GDP per capita (see Figure 12) in contrast with that of heights of the different groups presented earlier. Passport samples follow a similar trend as GDP per capita, whereas the trends of the military samples are different. There are times when military heights and GDP per capita follow opposite trends, such as for cohorts born and growing up during the second half of the nineteenth century. In contrast, there is a period when the average statures followed the same trend as GDP per capita, such as the cohorts born after the 1930s. These changes in correlation between GDP per capita and adult male average stature are plausible in light of the fact that economic growth does not necessarily improve the biological standards of living of a given population. As highlighted in basic economics courses: economic growth is not a guarantee of convergence toward social equality.

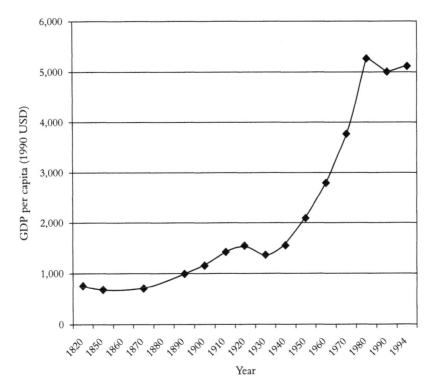

Figure 12   Geary-Khamis GDP per capita, 1990 USD

SOURCE: Coatsworth and Tortella Casares, "Instituciones y desempeño económico," 49.

In order to have an idea of the evolution of living standards in Mexico, it is important to determine the trend in average stature among the Mexican population and ascertain if there are differences among the various regional and social groups, and if these differences change over time. To attain a complete assessment of the evolution of biological standards of living, it is equally important to place Mexico in the international scene. To accomplish this, we examine the case of Mexico as it stood with respect to other countries and to what were then considered normal standards for populations born during the mid-twentieth century.

INTERNATIONAL AND MODERN

POPULATION COMPARISONS

The present history of the evolution of living standards emphasizes the importance of placing Mexico in a global context. Understanding Mexico's position with respect to other countries is helpful to assess the impact of industrialization and demographic transition on the biological standards of living. It is helpful to grasp the extent to which public policies failed to promote economic development among the entire population. It is also useful to clarify the extent to which existing social, political, developmental, and cultural conditions obliterated the possibility of enhancing the standards of living of the population at large.

As mentioned earlier in this chapter, in analyzing the evolution of living standards it is important to take into consideration the timing of industrialization, the recognition of germ theory in public health, and the extent of urbanization, because these events and phenomena did not all take place at the same time in all countries. Mexico industrialized later than most Western European countries and the United States; it remained a mainly rural country until the 1930s. Still, germ theory in public health was recognized and adopted shortly after its emergence in the Western world.

Figure 13 displays the evolution of heights for countries of the Western world and Mexico. We are drawing a comparison with the military sample because it is more representative of the average adult male than are the

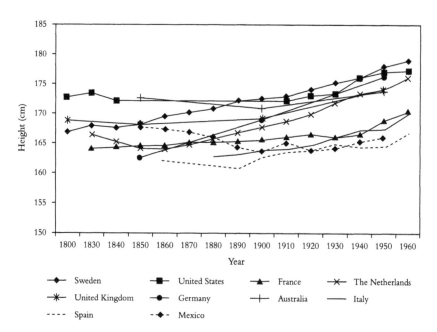

Figure 13 Adult male heights in cm: International comparison

SOURCE: Information in Table A.3.

working-class males from the passport sample. There are two points that draw one's attention in Figure 13. The first is that Mexicans do not start off as the shortest in the sample, suggesting that living conditions in preindustrial Mexico were comparable to countries in the Western world circa 1850. This is an interesting finding if we take into consideration that we are drawing a comparison with countries that had much higher per capita income and had higher literacy rates. The second point is that Mexico is the only country that does not have an overall increasing trend in height. Hence, by 1950 it falls to the last position in Figure 13, meaning that Mexicans were then on average as short as Spaniards.[42]

The evolution of living standards of the different countries in Figure 13 with respect to their time of industrialization, demographic transition, and degree of urbanization was heterogeneous; this fact serves to discredit the idea that in Mexico living standards improved slowly because of the delay with which economic transformations took place. In other words, contrary to what traditional historiography would lead us to believe, Mexico shares many common features with these countries in one way or another, and it is important to mention the most relevant ones. Like Mexico, some of these countries, such as Sweden, France, Australia, and the United States, had low rates of urbanization for most of the period 1850–1950. Hence, they were spared from the biological penalty of industrialization that is seen in England and in other countries with higher levels of urbanization.[43] Some countries industrialized while others, like the Netherlands and Australia, experienced more of what has been described as an economic "modernization," for they did not have the natural resource endowments to develop large manufacturing sectors and a heavy industry. The Netherlands developed its banking, shipping, and service sector; Australia focused on mining and agriculture.[44] Some countries had centralized authoritarian regimes that resembled the Porfirio Díaz régime, like Germany's Bismarck government. However, Germany developed a centralized welfare system during the era that improved the living standards of the working classes.[45]

Italy and Spain had trajectories similar to those of Mexico in the evolution of heights; these countries had a surplus of labor in the countryside as a result of demographic transformations that fostered several waves of emigration to the American continent during the period 1850–1950, and this worked as an escape valve for these nations. In Mexico the surplus of labor from the countryside was absorbed by migration into the cities and to the United States. Emigration from Mexico was a phenomenon of smaller proportions than for Spain and Italy, and was not the result of a demographic transition as was the case with the latter country. The labor surplus in the

Mexican countryside was caused more by a redefinition of property rights that resulted from institutional land reforms than from a lack of cultivable land due to growth in population. Land tenure reforms altered traditional landownership and forced peasants to look for better labor opportunities elsewhere; demographic transition did not take place until the 1930s.

Literacy is one welfare indicator in which Mexico systematically stayed behind throughout the whole period. The development of a public school system with national coverage did not take place until the 1920s with the postrevolutionary governments. Unfortunately, unlike countries such as Russia and Cuba in which the revolution accelerated the advancement of education, Mexico's efforts on the education front yielded meager results; it was not until the 1970s that a 70 percent literacy rate was attained.[46]

In order to have a notion of how close Mexicans of the period 1850–1950 were from reaching their maximum potential heights, it is important to know where these height values stand with respect to modern standards. As Steckel explains, "standards are essential for comparison involving ethnic differences in growth potential. . . . The yardstick of modern height standard gives a sense of perspective for any historical data and provides a way of assessing progress or deprivation against a level that we know is attainable under good environmental circumstances."[47] In the different samples that we have examined for Mexico, we see that there are divergent trends that suggest that only a portion of the population—namely, the passport applicants sample—experienced an improvement in standard of living. It is useful to have a standard to which we can compare the observed heights. It is possible to draw a comparison using the percentile of historical samples and those attained in modern height standards. Anthropometric historians have found the height data from the National Center for Health Statistics (NCHS) to be the most reliable source of information for drawing comparisons with modern standards of well-nourished populations.[48]

Tables 10 and 11 show that historical heights of the Mexican population are low with respect to modern standards of a well-nourished population. There are two basic points that are worth discussing from these tables. The first is that the heights of the better-off portion of the population show less difference with respect to modern standards. As we pointed out before, the trajectories of the biological standards of living measured by average heights are different across social groups. Passport applicants had heights that were closer to modern standards whereas the statures of the federal military remained at preindustrial levels. The second point is that the sample of males shows higher disparities than that of women; this substantiates the sexual dimorphism argument presented earlier. To assess the evolution of heights

TABLE 11

Sample of percentiles compared to modern standards: Females

	10th	25th	50th	75th	90th	Number
U.S. modern	156.2	159.8	163.7	167.6	171.2	
Unskilled and skilled manual (passport)	148.0	152.5	156.0	160.0	164.3	2,960
White-collar (passport)	151.0	155.0	159.0	163.0	165.0	1,399
Elite (passport)	150.0	155.2	160.0	165.0	170.0	848

SOURCES: Mexico data from SDN and SRE archives; U.S. data from Steckel, "Percentiles of Modern Height Standards," 157–65.

of Mexican women, it is useful to bring up the fact that, according to a survey conducted in Mexico on the quality of life in 2002, the average height of the women in the sample was 153 centimeters.[49] According to our regression results, this was the average height of women from the upper-middle class and elite born in the 1850s and under the tenth percentile of modern standards (see Table 10). This figure suggests that there was a very modest improvement in the biological standard of living of working-class Mexican women over the past century.

Conclusions

In this chapter, we have ascertained that the evolution of living standards has been heterogeneous across social classes during the period 1850–1950. The trend in heights of the military tells a different story than that of the passport applicants. Passport applicants get taller over time. The military, on the other hand, experience deterioration and stagnation and do not recover their 1850s height until 1950. There are regional disparities in both samples; the northerners and bajío dwellers are taller than their counterparts in the center and south. Regional differences are larger in the military sample. Nonetheless, regional differences are not as marked as those across social classes.

The comparison in results between passport and military samples sheds light on poverty and inequality issues. There are passport applicants from different social classes and, although the members of the upper strata are taller than applicants from the working classes, they all get taller and the gap between them decreases over time. This trajectory resembles the case of countries of the Western world, where heights converge over time. This trajectory mirrors the evolution of the economy when we draw a comparison with GDP per capita. These results should be taken into consideration without losing sight of the fact that passport applicants represent a minority of the population and are not representative of the population at large.

These were all urban, literate people who could afford to travel abroad legally. These three features are not common among average Mexicans born between 1850 and 1950; the passport sample is representative only of the wealthy and of the small portion of the working classes that were favored by Mexico's economic growth and development during this period. Industrial development, export-led growth, and the building of sanitary infrastructure contributed to the increase in stature of these passport samples. For the latter part of this period, it represents workers who did indeed benefit from the new labor legislation stemming from the 1917 Constitution. For those born and growing up during the decade of the revolution's worst warfare (1910–1920), we observe that there is no height penalty. This suggests that these people were not affected by biological stressors such as food shortages and disease, so ubiquitous in places experiencing warfare. The heights of working-class passport applicants can be used as a counterfactual hypothesis of what would have been the fate of the popular classes had the government's development policies also included efforts to integrate the population at large into the profound transformations that were taking place. The evolution of heights of the sample of women is similar to that of men. There is an increase over time.

The evolution of heights of the military samples reveals the impact of industrialization, the displacement of traditional sectors of the economy, periods of political instability, and the adoption of a development model that for the longest time gave little attention to human capital investments in the great majority of the population. The statures of the military recruits decreased for four decades (1850–1890); then they stagnated during the last decade of the nineteenth century. There is a modest improvement for the generation born around the turn of the century. This improvement is lost for the following generation; this reflects the penalty in living conditions for people who did endure the ravages of war during the Mexican Revolution. It should come as no surprise that the improvement in heights coincides with the launching of national-level public health campaigns as well as the launching of a welfare state in the late 1930s; before then, the majority of the population were excluded from positive changes and lacked opportunities for advancement. By the time the government launched welfare policies that aimed to include the population at large, the social lag had accumulated for basically all the time Mexico had been an independent nation. It would take time and effort to convince the popular classes to trust the new welfare institutions enough to modify their survival strategies.

In setting the case of Mexico within the international sphere, one must draw a comparison using the military samples. This is the realistic thing to do since these samples are representative of the population at large. Mexicans do not start as the shortest, but they do not show an improvement over time. We demonstrated that Mexico had circumstances similar to those of other countries in the Western world. Hence, the evidence suggests that Mexicans failed to grow taller during the period 1850–1950 for reasons related to the quality of institutions and the design of public policies rather than due to exogenous calamities or a lack of natural resource endowments. Although Mexico underwent modernization and industrialization that promoted economic growth and development, these societal advances were attained with persistent social inequality. The vast majority of the population continued to live under preindustrial conditions—poverty, slow growth, poor health, widespread illiteracy, and rural habitation—well into the twentieth century.[50] When we draw a comparison with modern well-nourished populations, it is clear that the better-off strata of the population, namely, the elite passport applicants, are closer to modern standards, whereas the military remain behind. The differences are similar for both men and women. These findings are conducive to the notion that Mexico is not a poor country. Rather, it is a country of inequalities. The contrast in the evolution of heights between both samples we analyzed constitutes a proxy of the income distribution.

We have noted earlier that the quality of health and diet are elements worth taking into consideration in analyzing the evolution of statures and the standard of living. In the following section, we will examine both of these elements to explain the biological, social, and cultural causes behind the different trajectories in standards of living.

The Synergies Between Health and Nutrition

Before the historian can judge wisely the political skills of human groups or the strength of their economies or the meaning of their literatures, he must first know how successful their member human beings were at staying alive and reproducing themselves.

—Alfred Crosby, *The Columbian Exchange*

In 2008, James C. Riley, a leading historian in the study of health, sickness, and mortality, published a comparative history study entitled *Income, Social Growth and Good Health: A History of Twelve Countries.* He argues that life expectancy is a better measure of well-being than GDP per capita. Under such a premise, Riley advances the hypothesis that countries do not have to be rich in income to improve the quality of life of their people.[1] High-income countries such as those of Western Europe, Australia, Canada, New Zealand, and the United States first became rich, and with the wealth they produced, they were able to invest in infrastructure and social programs that were conducive to increased life expectancy.[2] Riley argues that, in contrast, there were low-income countries that were able to increase life expectancy without first increasing their GDP per capita or laying the foundations to achieve sustained economic growth. He presents the case of twelve countries that, he asserts, between 1920 and 1960 were able to increase their life expectancy to levels comparable to those of high-income countries.[3] He explains that these countries, rather than investing in social capital the way high-income countries did, such as building schools, training teachers, and establishing health-care systems paid out of public revenues, invested in education and public health with some local and central government funds but mainly with the sustained collaboration of the community to build and use education and public health facilities.[4] These communities thus received a health education that turned out to enhance their living conditions by increasing life expectancy. Mexico is one of the countries in his study.[5]

This section will delve into the synergies between health and nutrition in the evolution of living standards in general and in the specific case of Mexico in the period 1850–1950. In doing so, this section will also show that Riley's postulates do not explain the case of Mexico prior to 1950. An overview of the history of health, demography, and nutrition in Mexico from 1850 to 1950 will show that life expectancy only showed a modest improvement and will shed light on the several factors that explain why the case of Mexico does not fit Riley's model. Although the examples he uses to assert that in Mexico there were investments in public health and education with the participation of the different communities are valid, this section will show they only took place during limited periods of time, such as the education campaigns launched by José Vasconcelos in the early 1920s, or in very localized areas, such as the public health campaigns sponsored by the Rockefeller Foundation in collaboration with the National Institute of Public Health.[6] These efforts yielded some results in very localized parts of the country; this is why, in 1950, life expectancy at birth at the national level was only 49.3 years.

During the first half of the twentieth century, setting high expectations for the improvement of the health of the population in a relatively short period of time became a possibility given the recent scientific discoveries in different areas that related to health. Advances in medical knowledge had expanded the scope of what the medical profession and public health administrators could do. In this section we will show that, although Mexican authorities had wanted to be at the forefront of modernization in public health since the 1880s, the major challenge for them was to provide the overwhelming majority of the population with the most basic health services. The different governments of the postrevolutionary era were centralizing and paternalistic. Consequently, in the political discourse, as well as in public opinion, there was the expectation that it was the state's duty to pay for education and public health infrastructure as well as to guide the people toward the improvement of public health. Contrary to Riley's assumption, proactive community efforts were not encouraged, especially if they challenged in any way the central government and its authorities. Also, contrary to Riley's postulate, the government in Mexico did try to emulate the path followed by high-income countries to attain a health transition. Since the Porfiriato (1876–1910), politicians and intellectuals were convinced that following the steps of the Western world would bring civilization, modernity, and economic growth to Mexico—as will be explained in the following chapter. These views were not challenged by the postrevolutionary (post-1910) governments. In the late 1940s, the government launched a health-care system that looked very much like French social security; it was managed by the state and financed with workers' contributions for the most part. It provided state-of-the-art health-care service to a narrow segment of the population, namely, those workers who had an affiliation with the political party in office, the aristocracy of the working classes. A substantial portion of the population thus continued to live without basic health services. Investments in education through literacy campaigns produced results that were far from being spectacular. Literacy rates improved at a moderate pace, a pace that would not have created the momentum to improve health education at a national level as Riley suggests for the case of Mexico.[7]

Concomitant to the health-for-all challenge were the persistently high fertility rates versus declining mortality rates. It was feasible to adopt Western patterns of medical and technological innovation, but the demographic behavior of the Mexican population was nothing like the models of the Western world. Riley does not comment on this issue in his analysis.

There was also the challenge of nutrition. At that time, there were dietary differences across regions and across social classes, and these differences contributed to marking the different trajectories in the evolution of living standards (as we observed in the previous section). People belonging to the more affluent segment of the population had adequate nutrition because they could afford a balanced diet, and this was conducive to cohorts growing taller over time. The laboring classes employed in the formal sector could also afford a diet nutritious enough to permit a gradual increase in average height. By way of contrast, the great majority of the population had a diet that supplied them with a caloric intake sufficient to subsist but insufficient to attain their maximum potential height.

In Section 1, I argued that institutions ruling Mexico's political and economic life were built in such a way that it would be easy to perpetuate inequality. Then in Section 2, I substantiated this argument by showing how sharp disparities prevailed in society for most of the period through the calculation of secular trends in heights and the analysis of the biological standards of living. Section 3 will show how health and nutrition influenced the trends in heights presented in Section 2; this will deepen our understanding of the evolution of living standards in Mexico in the period 1850–1950.

This section is divided into two chapters followed by a conclusion. The first chapter presents a narrative of the history of health and nutrition

during the years studied. Through the examination of the health and demographic history of Mexico as well as the evolution of dietary habits of
its population, this chapter will delve into the ways in which health and
nutrition influenced the evolution of the biological standards of living of
the population as presented in Section 2. I argue that the unequal provision of health services, dietary habits that perpetuated nutritional deficiencies among the popular classes, and unchanging fertility patterns all played a
crucial role in making the evolution of living standards among the Mexican
population as unequal as they were in the preindustrial era. Poor health
status contributed to the poor performance in the evolution of biological
standards of living of the working classes for cohorts born between 1850
and 1950. As exemplified by data on life expectancy, some figures on health
status showed modest improvements over time. However, there were others, such as average stature of the population, for which there was no sign
of improvement by the mid-twentieth century, even though the ongoing
economic, social, and political changes would appear to suggest otherwise.
Results from this analysis support the argument that innovations in medicine
along with government's investments in public hygiene and public works
were able to control the spread of infectious diseases to a certain extent, but
there was little improvement in nutrition for the population at large.

Government investments were a good start for improving public health,
but insufficient to service a population with very rapid demographic
growth. For the longest time, resources were unevenly distributed between
urban and rural dwellers. It was during the Porfirio Díaz administration
that the government increased the amount of resources devoted to improving public hygiene and to building a sanitary infrastructure. At first, like all
countries in the Western world, public health policy efforts and resources
were concentrated in the cities—in this case especially and disproportion-
ately in Mexico City. Unfortunately, it was not until the second half of the
twentieth century that rural areas began to benefit from public works. In
this regard, Mexico substantially lagged behind with respect to the developed countries, the countries that Mexico wished to emulate. Thus, by the
mid-twentieth century we observe a gap in the health status of population
in the countryside versus urban dwellers.

To assess the impact of disease prevention, public health policies, and
demographic transformations on the evolution of living standards of the
population, we first need to lay out the kind of health services that could be
provided in the Western world throughout the period 1850–1950. We will
overview how the quality and extent of health services available evolved
throughout this period. This overview will take into account scientific

discoveries made in the fields of biology and chemistry in combination with technological innovations in the field of engineering and explore how these advances provided more tools for diagnosis, prevention, and treatment available to medical professionals. On the issue of nutrition, I will argue two things. First, the dietary habits of the majority of the population barely changed during this time. Second, there were sharp contrasts in diet across social classes. These arguments will be examined through the analysis of literary works and official documents of the period.

The second chapter will continue to look into the synergies between health and nutrition by means of the analysis of the quantitative evidence available. This evidence comes from the military records and population and nutrition censuses. To assess the importance of nutrition in this chapter, I will clarify points that are relevant to a better understanding of the impact of nutrition on the evolution of biological standards of living and to better contextualize the information available within the time period in which scientific knowledge on nutrition evolved.

Chapter 1

Health and Nutrition: The History

In 1851, average ages of death for members of the parishes of San Sebastián and Santa Ana, located in poor quarters of the northern part of Mexico City, were sixteen and thirteen years, respectively.[1] This figure shows that the possibilities of reaching adulthood for children born in the poor areas of the Mexican capital were slim and that very few adults lived to be old, especially when an epidemic hit the city, as was the case with cholera in 1851. Under normal circumstances, the average age of death would have been twenty-two or twenty-three years, as compared with the average of a typical life expectancy at birth in a preindustrial society.[2] Dwellers in the better-off quarters of the city had a higher probability of living longer.[3] Higher life expectancy among well-to-do dwellers was due to better sanitary conditions in their neighborhood and better nutrition—such was their advantage over the poor. Rich people could afford to pay for doctor's visits, but at that time the best a doctor could do was establish a diagnosis of the illness, for little was known about prevention or cure of diseases.[4] Science and technology related to medicine and sanitary services evolved rapidly from 1850 to 1950, producing improvements that few would have imagined possible at the onset of the nineteenth century. Constitutional rights proclaimed equality before the law, entitling all citizens to the use of public utilities and health services. However, these rights did not go beyond a list of good intentions in politicians' discourse. Therefore, the poor had access to barely any of the few public works that were available in cities. The general quality of health in Mexico was not much different from that of other places in the world. The one difference was that poverty exacerbated the negative effects within the lower strata of the population. In countries of the Western world there were poor relief systems of the kind that failed to develop in Mexico.

In 1950, life expectancy at birth in Mexico at the national level was 49.3 years, and it was only then beginning to increase more rapidly. Starting in the 1930s, there was a full-blown demographic revolution. The government had launched health campaigns that had the objective of eliminating most common epidemic and endemic diseases both in urban and rural areas, but most of these programs only reached a reduced portion of the national territory.

Before examining and evaluating the evolution of public health, demographic behavior, and nutrition in Mexico, it is important to explain what was happening in the world at large in this matter. This is why the first part of the chapter will survey the most important changes in medical science throughout this period to acquaint readers with what was becoming available in the civilized world and the role of the state in its provision, as well as its effects on the populations where these advances were used. The second part of the chapter will provide a chronological overview of the health history of Mexico linked to its public health policies and demographic history. By briefly presenting the health, medical, and demographic history of the Western world as a point of departure and reference, it will be easier to contextualize Mexico's efforts on health policies. Hence, it will be easier to assess their performance in terms of the results on the evolution of biological standards of living. The third part of this chapter will present a brief history of Mexico's population to shed light on how and why demographic behavior greatly diverged from that of nations of the Western world. Since nutrition was not considered a field of scientific research until the mid-twentieth century, it is not possible to know in detail the nutritional content of people's diet for much of the period we are studying. I will thus circumvent this lack of quantitative information with qualitative sources that detail people's routines in daily life. This can be obtained from literary works and some official documents of that period. Most of the analysis on the nineteenth century is based on these kinds of sources.

Health, Medicine, and Demography in the Western World

Famous demographer Massimo Livi-Bacci refers to the period 1800–1914 as one of great transformations in the Western world.[5] During this time, the European population grew at a faster pace than in the previous centuries. This vital revolution was driven by different factors in each country; for instance, in England it was due to rising birthrates, whereas in Sweden it was declining death rates, and in France, the country with a lower rate of growth, the decline in deaths was largely offset by declining birthrates.[6] Social and economic historians specializing in the health history of Western Europe assert that such demographic transition was possible because of three main factors. First, more land became available for agricultural production. Second, new production technologies elevated the income levels and consequently living standards of the population. Third, there were changes in the epidemiological context. Technologies introduced as byproducts of the Industrial Revolution made it possible for individuals to have access to other forms of energy production that did not come from animal force or their own force. This change had an "effect on the potential for population growth similar to that of the Neolithic Revolution and the transition from hunting and gathering to one of settled agriculture."[7]

The Industrial Revolution in Western Europe increased food production and raised income levels of the average agricultural and industrial worker. By the nineteenth century, it was possible to avoid subsistence crises. Improvements in material living standards and a large food supply improved the well-being of working classes; this contributed to the increase in life expectancy. However, industrialization favored the spread of infectious diseases related to industrial occupations and to living conditions in urban industrial centers. The introduction of new crops and excessive reliance on these new staples resulted in the spread of certain nutrition-related diseases, such as pellagra among consumers of corn. Amelioration in living standards provoked rises in fertility in the countryside, therefore producing a surplus of labor that would swell the ranks of the urban industrial proletariat as well as immigrants overseas. Mortality rose especially in urban centers, and, more often than not, it ended up annulling the positive impact of larger food supplies. Scientific advances and economic growth in nineteenth-century Europe were a mixed blessing.[8]

At a time when development technologies that made the Industrial Revolution possible (steam power, wrought iron, textile machinery) were in full swing, scientific knowledge in microbiology was still in its infancy. Little was known about the causes of diseases; in the best of scenarios, doctors could diagnose a disease. There was not even a consensus on how diseases spread. In the mid-nineteenth century there was a bitter debate between *contagionists* and *anticontagionists*. *Contagionists* contended that infectious diseases were transmitted by living agents. *Anticontagionists* believed in the miasmatic theory, which postulated that epidemics spread because of peculiar changes in the state of the atmosphere. Each faction went on to develop their own research and actions according to their postulates.[9]

Contagionists developed the field of microbiology. During the second half of the nineteenth century, scientists throughout Europe like Pasteur, Koch, and Gram, among others, advanced the knowledge of bacteria: how these organisms reproduced and how they were at the origin of many epidemic diseases. These scientists were also able to develop vaccines to prevent diseases such as tuberculosis, typhoid fever, diphtheria, pneumococcus, meningococcus, and streptococcus. As a by-product of research on bacteria, the phenomenon of antibody production came to be better understood. Concomitant with research on microbiology was the adoption of antisepsis methods in surgery. Joseph Lister, a surgeon from Glasgow, was the pioneer in the use of this method. He used carbolic acid (phenol) in wounds at the time of surgery to prevent infections; eventually this method was replaced by sepsis, a method that entailed the sterilization of instruments that came in contact with wounds.[10] Research on the cause and cure of viral infections and chronic and degenerative diseases would gain momentum in the twentieth century (see Table 12).

In England, followers of miasmatic theory promoted the creation of infrastructure in public utilities. They were convinced that miasmas could be eliminated through the improvement of sanitation conditions. Civil engineering innovations rather than medicine were the key to the pursuit of these policies. The "sanitation movement" was active in England during the 1850s; Florence Nightingale and Edwin Chadwick were the main advocates of this initiative. The sanitation movement entailed the establishment in urban areas of effective sewage disposal, pure water supplies, paved streets, safer food supplies, and education in personal hygiene.[11] These public works were first made in London. Other cities in England and Europe would soon follow. Sanitary measures brought a great benefit to society in the prevention of waterborne diseases such as cholera and typhoid. Nonetheless, infectious diseases transmitted by the respiratory route, such as diphtheria, could not be prevented by the aforementioned sanitary measures.[12] Eventually, further microbiological research proved that the miasmatic theory was incorrect, but the policy conclusions were adequate and effective in the prevention of infectious diseases.

Although a number of significant advances in microbiology were made during the second half of the nineteenth century, their benefits in medicine did not go beyond diagnoses and, in some cases, the prevention of diseases.

TABLE 12

Discoveries in the control of major fatal infectious diseases, since 1800:
Mode of transmission and causal agent

MODE OF TRANSMISSION, 1847–1909			CAUSAL AGENT, 1880–1898		
Date	Disease	Investigator	Date	Disease	Investigator
1847	Measles	Panum	1880	Typhoid (ba-	Eberth
	Puerperal fever	Semmelweiss, Holmes		cillus found in tissues)	
				Leprosy	Hansen
				Malaria	Laveran
1854	Cholera	Snow	1882	Tuberculosis	Koch
				Glander	Loeffer and Schutz
1859	Typhoid fever	Budd	1883	Cholera	Koch
				Streptococcus (erysipelas)	Fehleisen
1867	Sepsis (surgical)	Lister	1884	Diphtheria	Klebs and Loeffler
				Typhoid (bacillus isolated)	Gaffky
				Staphylococcus Streptococcus	Rosenbach
				Tetanus	Nicolaier
1898	Malaria	Ross, Grassi	1885	Coli	Escherich
	Hookworm	Looss			
1900	Yellow fever	Reed	1886	Pneumococcus	Fraenkel
1906	Dengue	Bancroft	1887	Malta fever	Bruce
	Rocky Moun- tain spotted fever	Ricketts, King		Soft chancre	Ducrey
1909	Typhus	Nicolle	1892	Gas gangrene	Welch and Nuttall
			1894	Plague	Yersin, Kitasato
				Botulism	Van Ermengem
			1898	Dysentery bacillus	Shiga

SOURCE: Easterlin, *Reluctant Economist*, 105.

At the beginning of the twentieth century little could be done once an individual caught an infectious disease, especially if this developed into a severe illness. No remedies had been developed that could actually help cure infectious diseases. It was not until the 1930s with the introduction of sulfa drugs and with antibiotics like penicillin in the 1940s that medicine finally had the pharmaceutical means to cure infectious diseases (see Table 13).[13] The advances made during the twentieth century were rapid and spectacular. Once aseptic and anesthetic methods were mastered, modern surgery briskly evolved.

TABLE 13

Discoveries in the control of major fatal infectious diseases, since around 1800:
Vaccines and drugs

VACCINES			DRUGS		
Date	Disease	Investigator	Date	Drug	Investigator
1798	Smallpox	Jenner	1908	Salvarsan	Ehrlich
1881	Anthrax	Pasteur	1935	Sulfanomides	Domagk
1885	Rabies	Pasteur	1941	Penicillin	Fleming, Florey
1892	Diphtheria	Von Behring			Chain
1896	Cholera	Kolle	1944	Streptomycin	Waksman
1906	Pertussis	Bordet-Gengou	1947	Broad-spectrum	
1921	Tuberculosis	Calmette, Guerin		antibiotics	
1927	Tetanus	Ramon, Zoeller			
1930	Yellow fever	Theiler			
	Typhoid fever	Weigl			
1948	DTP	(Multiple)			
1950	Polio	Salk			
1954	Measles	Enders, Peebles			

SOURCE: Easterlin, *Reluctant Economist*, 106.

Up until 1900 scientific knowledge was developed in Europe. In spite of its staggering economic and industrial progress of the previous century, the United States was a follower in the adoption of pharmaceutical remedies, medical knowledge, and methods to control infectious diseases. Interestingly, during the Spanish-American war in 1898 the major killer of American soldiers was not the enemy but typhoid fever. This was because of the authorities' lack of knowledge about the prevention of this infectious disease.[14] However, things were to change rapidly during the decades that followed. At the onset of the twentieth century, the United States made substantial investments to improve public health and to develop scientific and medical research in hospitals and universities; funding came from both private and government sources. The catch-up proved to be so striking that as early as the 1920s the United States already had the economic and human capital resources to provide assistance on public health campaigns abroad. Latin American countries were among the main recipients of this form of assistance.[15]

Public health measures were a state initiative throughout the Western world. As scientific knowledge accumulated, it became evident that disease prevention could not be attained by mere individual action. Even if people knew how to prevent infectious diseases, they could not effectively take the necessary precautions on their own if they lived surrounded by "filth." The cleaning of cities was a problem that could not be left to be solved by market forces.[16] For instance, slum housing in working-class neighborhoods was both a typical source of infectious diseases and a profitable business for their landlords. Public works—so necessary to sanitize urban areas—were the kind of infrastructure that required state intervention for financing; in economics jargon: public utilities are a public good. Sanitation movements were thus state initiatives launched mainly in the cities because mortality rates were higher in cities than in the countryside, as higher population densities meant higher concentrations of filth in a specific place. Eventually the public utility infrastructure would also reach rural areas. Being a government initiative, the extent and efficiency of public health policies depended largely on the finances and politics of each polity. In this regard, the implementation and outcome of sanitation policies would be unique to each country.

The launching of public health measures improved the living standards of the populations that had access to such services insofar as they helped prevent epidemics and reduce the number of people contracting waterborne infectious diseases and the number of deaths due to such infectious diseases: morbidity and mortality were both reduced. The decline in infant mortality rates was perhaps the one thing that benefited society the most from this infrastructure because infants have not developed immunity to diseases. Thus, lower exposure to diseases increased their probability of survival and improved their living conditions. Better nutrition among the working classes is also mentioned as a significant cause for the reduction of morbidity and mortality. The larger supply of food resulting from higher agricultural output increased caloric intake of the popular classes; thus, people had more energy to fight diseases.[17]

Public health measures were one of the driving forces behind demographic transition in Europe during the second half of the nineteenth century and the first decades of the twentieth century, but not the only one. Demographic transition implied a rise in life expectancy and population growth. The causality of these phenomena is complex. Demographic historians point out that during the period 1800–1914, life expectancy in Western European countries rose at a pace of two or three months every calendar year.[18] They also note that population growth during this period was driven by higher fertility rather than by mortality decline.[19] More food available at more affordable prices made it feasible to feed more children. Nonetheless, well before the end of this period, fertility rates had begun to decline in some countries as a result of the conscious decision to limit the number of births on the part of individuals. Biological and medical factors had less relevance in this change in demographic behavior. During the first half of the twentieth century, fertility rates followed a downward trend; however, the world wars and the 1929 Depression would also influence fertility behavior.

Scholars across disciplines who have examined the causes of mortality decline in Europe in the period 1800–1950 recognize the difficulties of sorting out all of the determinants of mortality, the relevance of each, and the synergies among them. In spite of the complexities involved in understanding this phenomenon, they concur on the four main determinants: decline of subsistence crises, improved nutrition, changes in epidemiology, and the impact of medicine. Medicine was the determinant that played the least important role in this period, but it grew in importance thereafter. Lack of detail in statistics on mortality and morbidity up until the late nineteenth century is one of the factors that preclude the accurate identification of the causes of mortality decline and health status of the population in this period.[20] For instance, in England it was not until the last decades of the nineteenth century that it became compulsory to record cause of death in death certificates. Still, "deaths attributed to 'natural causes' in people regarded as elderly in the nineteenth century possibly masked industrial or degenerative diseases."[21]

After 1900, advances in biomedical knowledge, the widespread use of anesthetics, and antiseptic methods in surgery enlarged the scope and efficacy of hospital services. Hospitals ceased being perceived as the last stop before the grave. The medical profession gained prominence in society; doctors gradually became more able to diagnose and cure more diseases. Doctors could also perform more surgeries that were successful. Medical doctors asserted their social prestige over traditional healers, midwives, and apothecaries by lobbying to increase the requirements for being certified as a medical doctor. Biomedical innovations favored tightening the regulations of medical practice.[22]

Hospital care is one dimension of health care provision. Hospitals are one institution that underwent radical transformations during the twentieth century as a result of the increase in the number and quality of services they offered. Hospitals went from being charitable enterprises where patients could go to rest and recover from a disease and where married women could stay before and after birth to being efficiently organized institutions where people went more and more for specialized care (e.g., cures, surgery, etc.). Doctors' visits to homes were replaced by visits to doctors' offices, often located in hospitals or health clinics.

Hospitals were usually funded by religious orders (in France a hospital was known as a "hôtel de Dieu"); municipal, state, or central governments; philanthropic donations; and contributions from members of the community. The coverage and quality of service depended on the amount of resources available to the institution. The emergence of more sophisticated treatments increased the costs of treatment, and, over time, running a hospital became more costly. More and more hospitals were forced to decide if they could or could not receive patients who could not afford to pay for the services. Unlike the infrastructure in public utilities, which was a state enterprise for the most part, hospitals could be public or private institutions. Hence, from the wide array of health-related services available, some could be charged to individuals, such as a doctor's appointment, a surgery, or prescription medicine, whereas other services, such as paved streets or sewer systems, could not.

In Section 1, I mentioned that toward the end of the nineteenth century welfare institutions in different Western European countries underwent substantial transformations. These transformations were motivated by scientific advances that had bearing upon medical science: the construction of public works that revolutionized the possibilities of medical care. Transformations were also propelled by changes in labor relations that were by-products of the Industrial Revolution and the rise of an urban proletariat. The nature of industrial employment evolved in such a way that its workers became increasingly dependent on wages as their only source of income for survival. Moreover, industrial processes gave rise to new forms of disease and accidents. Having their income as their only means for survival, workers had to find a way to support themselves once they were too old to work or when they lost their jobs. Workers thus needed insurance mechanisms in case of sickness, invalidity, old age, or unemployment. Workers created associations of mutual aid to meet these needs. In some cases, employers and the government participated in some way in the provision of these services; the extent of their participation was different in each country. For instance, in Germany, state intervention in creating workers' insurance was substantial.[23] In contrast, in England workers tried to be as independent as possible of their masters and the state.[24] One thing was common among workers across countries—the awareness that their contributions gave them a right to the services they received; workers were not charity recipients.

Health services diversified at the end of the nineteenth century and the beginning of the twentieth century. Diversification made financing of these services more complex. Public health services had expanded beyond the mere provision of sanitary infrastructure. Sanitary infrastructure, being a public good, had traditionally been financed by local taxation although eventually central governments had to complement the costs. The new services included medical care for the popular classes. In Western European countries, hospitals and medical care were financed in part or entirely by government funds; the resources came from municipal, state, or central governments. The boundaries between poor relief and insurance services became blurred, especially in those countries in which the government intervened more actively in insurance provision. Workers complained that they did not want to receive medical care in the same place as the poor because they were not receiving charity.[25] It became necessary to draw a distinction between poor relief services and insurance services, and this is when a distinction between social assistance and social security became clear within the formation of a welfare state. Still, we can trace modern welfare systems back to poor laws and poor law mechanisms in this part of the world. It is also worth pointing out that, in the case of the United States, the distinction we just discussed was less of a problem, as medical care was left to market forces. Hospital services were financed by maintenance and physician's fees, which precluded those without insurance or without the means having to pay for this service. There was a minimal amount of federal resources going to hospital services for the poorest of the poor, namely, mothers, infants, and the mentally ill.[26]

During the first half of the twentieth century, state intervention in the organization of workers' insurance arrangements increased in Western Europe. State participation was motivated by the goal of meeting workers' needs at a time when socialist ideas were being actively discussed within workers' circles, especially after the Russian Revolution. Moreover, world wars and the 1929 Depression took a toll of such magnitude on the living standards of the working classes that state intervention became more necessary to help alleviate the cost of these calamities to the people. The mid-twentieth century was a golden era of the big welfare state.[27] The history of health and medicine, demographic evolution, and the emergence of the welfare state in the Western world that I have just presented is oversimplified given the amount of information available on the subject; the extant literature on the topics addressed is amazingly vast and complex (especially to the eyes of a Latin American historian posing the same questions). However, the purpose of this overview is to provide the reader with a context in which to better place and understand the experience of Mexico in the evolution of health, demography, medical care, and public health in the period 1850–1950.

More recent studies have contested the optimistic perspective on the evolution of the health of the world's population and demographic evolution from the late eighteenth century onward by conducting research beyond the case of nations of the Western world. These contesting views are worth examining in this chapter as they offer a perspective that facilitates the understanding of the evolution of health, disease, and demographic transition in developing and less developed countries. This is particularly relevant in presenting the Mexican experience on this subject.[28]

In 1989, a seminal work by anthropologist Mark Nathan Cohen argued that the extent of the so-called great transformation of the period 1800 to the present is overestimated. By looking at the living standards of contemporary hunter-gatherers and analyzing the living conditions of prehistoric societies from skeletal remains, Cohen asserts that these groups enjoyed health, nutrition, and living standards comparable to modern Western societies and better than impoverished contemporary urban populations.[29] According to his research findings, the transition from hunter-gatherer societies to farming and sedentism did not necessarily translate into better health and nutrition. Today more people survive and live longer lives, but not necessarily under better conditions.[30] His work invites us to reassess "scholarly and popular images of human progress and cultural evolution," and questions whether the adoption of new modes of production and technological innovation have, in fact, been as positive for certain Third World nations as they have for the Western world.[31]

Cohen argues that improvement in life expectancy during the nineteenth and twentieth centuries is more fragile than traditional views suggest, and that this misconception stems from the fact that research works tend to compare this period (1800 to present) with European urban populations from the fourteenth to the eighteenth centuries and then extrapolate trends back in history instead of drawing a comparison with prehistoric societies. Archaeological and historical research findings do show that European urban populations of the fourteenth and eighteenth centuries were "among the nutritionally most impoverished, the most disease-ridden, and the shortest-lived populations in human history."[32] The problem of comparisons between the achievements of the great transformation and previous periods is that they tend to be done with the most affluent sectors of today's population.[33]

A recent compilation of economist Richard Easterlin's research contests the alleged links between the Industrial Revolution and demographic transition. He calls the demographic transition of this time period a mortality revolution. He advances the hypothesis that these are two independent events: the Industrial Revolution and the mortality revolution.[34] Whereas both revolutions were the by-product of a cumulative process of empirically tested knowledge dating from the seventeenth century onward, the mortality revolution occurred later because biomedical knowledge, resulting from research in chemistry and biology, developed after the advances in physical knowledge related to the Industrial Revolution.[35]

The mortality revolution started in northwestern Europe, then its colonies (or former colonies), then Eastern and Southern Europe and Japan, then Latin America, followed by the Middle East and Asia and finally sub-Saharan Africa. It began after the onset of modern economic growth, but it did not occur at the same phase of development in all regions of the world. For instance, in countries such as England, economic growth resulting from the Industrial Revolution contributed to the improvement of life expectancy. However, in other countries such as those of sub-Saharan Africa, the mortality revolution started in the absence of modern economic growth.[36] Mexico's experience between 1850 and 1950 with regard to the mortality revolution, demographic behavior, implementation of integral public health policies, and adoption of innovation in biomedicine is an interesting case that falls between developed and less developed countries.

Public Health and Disease in Mexico

Concern for public health in Mexico goes back to the colonial period and has its roots in the biological encounter of the New and Old Worlds. The large number of human losses among indigenous populations due to epidemics in the early colonial period was an episode that Spaniards were willing to avoid at all cost. After all, an indigenous labor force was one of the main sources of wealth of the richest viceroyalty in Spanish America. Authorities of the viceroyalty had a legal obligation to supervise public health and sanitation.[37] At the time there were three basic services authorities had to make available and supervise: cleaning the streets, providing drinking water for the cities, and maintaining cemeteries. The state was the main authority in charge of providing these services. The Church, however, helped with the provision and care for the sick since both of these were among its traditional religious duties and charitable tasks.[38] Very frequently morbidity was followed by mortality, thus care for the sick came hand in hand with funeral services; therefore, it made sense that the Church would be in charge of both. Moreover, it was a common practice that people would be buried in churchyards. As early as 1541, the Spanish Crown issued an ordinance that required that both Spanish and Indian towns found hospitals to cure the sick who were poor. Indian towns tended to comply more with this initiative. Although managed by the Church, hospitales de indios were supported by indigenous contributions.[39] As we mentioned in Section 1, Hernán Cortés also founded a hospital as part of his efforts to give something back to the population that made his fortune. The Hospital de Jesús was founded in the mid-sixteenth century and it continued operating until

Photograph 9   Guanajuato, water carriers at the fountain. Photograph by Jackson William Henry, 1843–1942. Courtesy Library of Congress.

well into the nineteenth century. His was a lay initiative.[40] In 1582, Pedro López founded the Hospital de San Juan de Dios for mestizos and mulattos in Mexico City. It changed hands throughout the years, but it was in operation up until 1910 when it was repurposed to assist women with syphilis.[41]

Health and sanitation services were more readily available in urban and semiurban areas. Rural people generally relied on shamans, healers, and midwives for health care. Most of our knowledge about the history of health in Mexico during the colonial and nineteenth-century periods is about the cities. Little is known about the countryside. However, this dearth of studies on health history in rural populations is not unique to Mexico. Most studies on epidemics and diseases in general tend to focus on cities because in these urban locations the spread of infectious diseases and epidemics hit the hardest, and because these episodes were documented in cities.

Mexican colonial cities were unhygienic places to live, like any preindustrial city. There were no sewers. Most of the trash and human waste was dumped into the streets, then cleaned from the streets by municipal services, and then disposed of in the peripheries of the city, usually close to the poorer quarters of the city. Drinking water was brought from aqueducts and distributed in public fountains. It was often the case that this water was contaminated. In addition, contributing even more to the lack of hygiene, the Church condemned certain indigenous hygienic practices, such as frequent bathing.[42] Given that miasma theory was widely accepted as the explanation for contagions, baths were considered a source of contagion rather than a hygienic practice.

In the eighteenth century, an interest in public health and medicine from a scientific point of view began to develop. A number of reforms were undertaken upon the arrival of the Bourbons, filled with ideas of the Enlightenment, to the Spanish Crown. Bourbon bureaucrats issued an edict that legally elevated medicine to a professional status. As we mentioned earlier in this chapter, it would still be over a century before medical doctors would actually be accepted by the collective as capable of healing people. The Spanish Crown reformed and updated the Junta del Protomedicato, which was a board in charge of supervising the enforcement of sanitary measures. Most of the charitable activities that were traditionally carried out by the Church were by law transferred to the state. As we discussed in Section 1, in spite of this ordinance, the Church continued to be the main or de facto provider of charitable services, some of which provided public and private health services. Royal authorities published and distributed manuals aimed at giving advice on matters of public health. Given the growing awareness of the need to isolate the sick in times of epidemics, colonial authorities decided it was necessary to build more hospitals and centers of medical assistance.[43] A decision was made to construct cemeteries outside of cities. Had they been enforced, many of these measures would have indeed decreased the potential damage caused by epidemics. On the other hand, at this point in history, given the state of knowledge in the biological and medical sciences, the greatest benefit to the health of populations was likely to come from the construction of sanitary infrastructure. Nonetheless, the persistent lack of resources that characterized public finances of the time and the century that followed reduced new legislation to a list of good intentions. Perhaps one other important achievement from the point of view of policy makers was that, in the eyes of royal authorities, epidemics ceased being related to any sort of divine punishment and were recognized as the result of economic and social deficiencies. However, it would be longer before the Church and the common people abandoned the notion that famines, epidemics, and other calamities were a divine punishment.

Mexico's emergence as an independent nation did not change views on the issue of public health.[44] In essence, sanitary guidelines were the same as the ones established by the Bourbon reforms. For most of the nineteenth century welfare and public health were grouped together within the government's organization. Lack of resources remained a painful constant in Mexico's public finances; hence, the failure to enact sanitary guidelines. There were some new ordinances issued by the federal government in which obligations were established for municipalities to fight problems of public health and sanitation. In the political arena the main issue at stake was which level of government would bear this responsibility.[45] Following other countries' efforts to elevate the professional status of physicians as well as to preclude quacks from defrauding people, there were regulations in the mid-nineteenth century regarding the issuance of permits for doctors, surgeons, and midwives. This regulation applied only in those places where there were doctors; many places in the republic would not have access to a medical doctor for many decades to come.[46] Aside from emulating public health policies in other countries, these regulation initiatives also responded to the large number of complaints received about incompetent physicians obtaining permits to practice medicine.[47] Unfortunately, these ordinances were barely enforced, if at all. The most effective and tangible government attempts to improve public health during the period were the measures taken to face epidemic outbreaks. These requirements and measures were mainly designed for urban settlements.

Mexican public health officials recognized that streets had to be cleaned in order to prevent the spread of infectious diseases, just as many miasma theory advocates in other parts of the world did in the mid-nineteenth century. Government authorities were aware that indigence and malnutrition were also at the origin of disease and epidemics. Not only did poor people have higher rates of mortality, but, by living on the periphery of the cities, they represented a constant threat of contagion to the better-off people who lived in the center of the city.[48] It was of little use to improve hygiene in the center of cities, where the wealthy usually lived, if disease and contaminated waste continued to surround it. In theory, public infrastructure had to cover the entire city. However, public funds were seldom sufficient to reach the building of infrastructure in city quarters where the poor lived. Toward the end of the nineteenth century, the wealthy began to move from the center of the cities to the suburbs, where sanitary infrastructure and public utilities were readily available, while poorer strata of the population moved into the central part of the city. With them came a higher incidence of infectious diseases.[49]

Given the state of public finances and of scientific knowledge, little was achieved in public health matters from 1850 to 1876. As mentioned in Section 1, charity services and public health were still handled together and the government knew that the elevated number of destitute people in the cities was the origin of many of the public health problems. Nonetheless, other than legally taking away the Catholic Church's ability to provide any of the health services that they traditionally were in charge of, the government did not define a strategy of what it would do with regard to health issues directly related to the urban population living in destitution. Whether assistance to the poor was to be a governmental responsibility or not was still being debated.

There are some studies on the intellectual and cultural history of public health policies of the Porfirio Díaz era that depict an interesting picture of what was going on in the minds of policy makers of this time on this particular subject.[50] From this literature, we get a grasp of the intellectual origins of the introduction of public health initiatives by the Díaz administration in the 1880s. We also learn that Mexican scientists were in sharp synchronicity with scientific knowledge and technological innovations that were taking place in the developed world to an extent rarely matched at any other point in the history of Mexico.[51] This was possible due to the conjunction of two favorable facts. First, the country was regaining economic stability. Second, among the *Científicos*, there was a critical mass of professionals in the medical sciences who were keeping up with the scientific research and innovations that were being produced in Europe as well as with the debates on the need to make nations more hygienic. The influence of positivist ideas among prominent members of the Díaz cabinet, along with the desire to turn Mexico into a modern nation in the eyes of the international community, made policy makers of that time period aware of the need to clean the nation—the cities were the starting point. For this it was necessary to establish public institutions that would be in charge of designing and administering health policies as well as undertaking the construction of public works, including a sewage system and waterworks to bring potable water into the cities, especially Mexico City.

As early as 1879 a Public Health Council was created with a federal budget and a federal consultative group. On the agenda of policy makers, hygiene was considered "as part of the politico-cultural transformation called modernization. . . . Scientific hygiene emerged in Mexico as of major importance for the betterment of the sanitary conditions of the nation, and it was also indispensable for achieving a modern urban culture."[52] Social expenditure (*gasto social*) was first introduced in 1882 in the annual budget.[53] Scientists of that time had to convince policy makers of the importance of bringing their ideas on public hygiene into policy initiatives. The 1889 Sanitary Code was a result of these efforts. Likewise, there were construction projects undertaken to build drainage and sewer systems in Mexico City from late 1880 until 1905. At the same time in Mexico City, there were efforts to educate the population on these matters in what was labeled "hygienic education." The objective of this particular initiative was to clean the cities, prevent disease, and educate people to bring cleanliness into their homes.[54] Interestingly, all these policies were heavily oriented to improving Mexico's image abroad so as to attract foreign investments and European migration. Of these two objectives, only the first one was successfully achieved.

The positivist ideas of the *Científicos* produced the first scientifically based studies on demography. In fact, the 1895 population census was the first official census in Mexican history that we can refer to with a high level of confidence. The first statistics produced by the Porfirian government officials had a number of downsides for two main reasons. First, they lacked experience in running these studies. Second, the population was not used to being questioned so as to build a census. In spite of their downsides, the first statistics began to shed light on certain issues that led to a better understanding of the demographic profile of the Mexican population. For example, some traditional beliefs were dismissed, like the idea that coastal regions were the most unhealthy places of the country, and that the indigenous communities had the highest mortality rates due to their lack of hygiene and poor nutrition; both were a product of the people's ignorance. The first population figures told the opposite story. The coasts of Mexico along with the north were the regions with the lowest mortality rates in the country. Interestingly, the mortality numbers by region showed that the higher the altitude of the settlements, the higher the rates of mortality.[55] The indigenous communities were found to have lower mortality rates than the mestizos of the same income level, and did not show the signs of diseases of malnutrition that were common to the rest of the popular classes.[56]

Another feature of the comments of contemporaries on the first population census was the constant comparison of national figures with those of European countries. This was consistent with the objective of turning Mexico into a "modern" nation. From the work of the *higienistas* we learn that the intellectuals of the Porfiriato were concerned with the poor health, low life expectancy, and high mortality rates of the nation. Most of the comparative studies were focused on Mexico City. Mexico had the advantage of superb weather all year round, yet mortality rates were forty per one thousand inhabitants while Paris and London had only six to eight deaths per one thousand inhabitants. In the 1880s, life expectancy in Mexico City was 24.5 years; in Paris it was 46.6 years.[57] In 1904, infant mortality in Mexico City was 323 deaths per one thousand births. In St. Petersburg and London it was 256 and 114, respectively. Peasant women in Mexico gave

birth to approximately eight to twelve children of which only an average of three survived to adulthood. Epidemics, poor nutrition, and lack of
hygiene were pointed out as the origins of this problem. Nonetheless, this
was not a realistic or just comparison because Mexico at the time was at a
different stage of economic and technological development than its Western European counterparts. It would have been more accurate if the comparison had been made between Mexico City at the onset of the twentieth
century and European cities a century or two earlier.[58]

Policy makers recognized that mortality was high in Mexico. It was difficult, however, to have an accurate knowledge of the cause of death because, more often than not, the cause of death was not recorded. According
to the population census, in 1895 only 20 percent of the deaths had a medical diagnosis. By 1910, the number had only risen to 32 percent. In 1903,
government authorities decided to create a catalog of diseases in order to
have a better understanding of the pathologies that affected people the most.
The classification was the following: infectious, contagious, and virulent
diseases; respiratory- and digestive-related diseases (pneumonia, tuberculosis, diarrhea, enteritis); nutrition-related diseases (diabetes, kwashiorkor,
beriberi); and diseases of the nervous system.[59] To adequately contextualize
the case of Mexico within the international sphere, one should remember that in the late nineteenth century the possibility of establishing diagnoses for most common diseases was quite recent, even in countries that
were conducting the most advanced research. Moreover, the recording of
causes of death on a systematic basis was just beginning. For instance, in
England—a leading country in the collection of vital statistics—it was not
until 1872 that recording the cause of death became compulsory.[60] At the
turn of the twentieth century, the United States was also working on organizing vital statistics collections, and a consensus on how to carry out the
collections at the federal level had not yet been reached.[61]

The diseases were classified by degree of incidence. During the Porfiriato, epidemics like measles, typhus, and Asian cholera were still a serious
public threat. In addition, some diseases, both endemic and epidemic, were
more common in certain regions of the country. For example, *paludismo*,
which is a specific form of malaria, was very common in Veracruz and in
the coasts and places with nearby swamps. Measles and diarrhea, on the
other hand, were more common in the center of Mexico, and the high
plateaus observed the highest incidence of pneumonia and enteritis. For
the population in general (infants included), the most common causes of
death were diarrhea, enteritis, *paludismo*, pneumonia, measles, and whoop-

ing cough. Alcoholism was one disease that obsessed intellectuals at that time. It was a public health problem pointed out as the origin of most social problems suffered by the popular classes.[62]

In Mexico, most medical knowledge at the time came from Europe, especially from France, which was considered by the Porfirian government as the landmark for advances in medical knowledge.[63] The *Científicos* had a pool of doctors, urban planners, and specialists in public health, such as Francisco Altamirano, Eduardo Liceaga, Antonio Peñafiel, Leandro Fernández, José Ramírez, and José Ramos, among others.[64] On the agenda of policy makers, hygiene was considered "as part of the politico-cultural transformation called modernization. . . . Scientific hygiene that emerged in Mexico was of major importance for the betterment of the sanitary conditions of the nation, and it was also indispensable to achieving a modern urban culture."[65]

In some cases, the adoption of new techniques took decades to be accepted by Mexican doctors.[66] But in general the policy makers of the Porfiriato kept up with European advances in public health and sanitation, and as much as possible they tried to spread their knowledge so as to benefit the Mexican population.[67] It was during this period that bacteriology replaced miasma theories in the medical and public health communities. Efforts to improve sanitation and public health became clear through the construction of hospitals, support for the development of a school of medicine, the improvement of drainage, and the construction of new and modern infrastructure to bring clean water to the cities. It was also during this period that the first vaccination campaigns against the most common pathologies were begun (see Table 14). Nonetheless, these sanitary measures had little impact on the countryside given that the first vaccination campaigns were carried out only in the cities. Thus, the achievements of the Porfiriato reached only a reduced portion of the population since at the turn of the century Mexico was mainly a rural society (see Table 15). Neglected as usual, the people of rural Mexico continued to live under the same unhealthy conditions as they had on the eve of the Independence War.

TABLE 14

*Number of children vaccinated in
Mexico City, 1884–1886*

Boys	Girls	Total
16,783	16,783	33,566

SOURCE: *Estadística de la República Mexicana*, 1888.

TABLE 15
Urbanization index

Year	Total locations	Urban locations	Rural locations	Urbanization index
1910	70,830	530	70,300	8.2
1921	62,679	786	62,093	10.7
1930	64,448	603	83,845	13.7
1940	105,508	686	104,822	16.3
1950	98,325	908	97,417	23.7
1960	89,005	1,212	87,973	31.8
1970	97,580	2,170	95,410	40.4
1980	125,300	2,131	123,169	46.4
1990	156,602	2,586	154,016	51.1

SOURCE: *Estadísticas Históricas de México*, 2:1064.

The twentieth century brought two different forces in favor of public health: one internal and one external. The internal force included government plans and resources devoted to improving public health. The external force was the rapid advance in medical research that improved public health everywhere in the developed world. Among these external forces we find prophylactic measures to prevent and control infections, vaccines for diseases that used to be deadly, the development of better ways to preserve food, and advanced works in civil engineering to provide people with clean water and to dispose of wastes. All of these advances in public health also revolutionized the concept of personal hygiene. Things like daily showers, dental hygiene, and the daily change of clothes became part of everyday life. Achievements of the Porfirian government had been positive but insufficient. In order to be fully effective, public health services had to reach the entire population, not just the cities, and medical services had to be available for all social classes. This was laudable as a project but a titanic task in practice. Moreover, during the Porfiriato, it was never clear that the people in power had a commitment to improve the health conditions of the population at large.

During the first three decades of the postrevolutionary period, most government investments were spent on the improvement of public health; resources went to education and to the construction of public works. Awareness existed that, in order to improve the health status of the population, it was necessary to educate people on the importance of hygiene. Personal hygiene was included as one of the priority subjects in elementary education curricula, and this was a period when, for the first time, there were credible attempts to provide schooling at a national level. In terms of the construction of public works, the postrevolutionary government followed the project planned by the Porfirian government. There were monumental works to bring clean water to the cities, to pave streets, and build schools (see Table 16). As part of the institutional restructuring of the revolutionary government and the new 1917 Constitution, a Public Health Department (Departamento de Salud Pública, hereafter DSP) was created as stipulated by Article 73.[68] Still, it is worth keeping in mind that there was no welfare state apparatus in place yet; health services were not part of a welfare-state set of policies the way they are structured today. Therefore, the DSP's scope of action during its first years in operation was extremely limited with regard to both budget and health services coverage.

Another relevant feature in public health in "revolutionary" (post-1910) Mexico was the cooperation received from international health organizations to improve sanitary conditions in places that had traditionally been left in oblivion. International assistance came mainly from the Rockefeller Foundation International Health Division (RFIHD). An excellent study by Anne-Emmanuelle Birn looks at the history of this program in Mexico over a thirty-year period.[69] From 1921 to 1951 the RFIHD had assistance programs in Mexico in collaboration with the newly instituted DSP. Assistance was provided through a series of projects that aimed at eliminating certain diseases that were a constant burden on the well-being of communities and hindered development. It started with a yellow fever campaign along the Gulf Coast of Mexico down to the Yucatán peninsula. After the positive results of the first project, a hookworm campaign was launched in Veracruz, Oaxaca, and Chiapas years later. The establishment of cooperative health units in these states and Morelos followed. In the 1940s, malaria research projects were established in five states, and support health units were launched in northern states.[70]

Although the diseases that were being eradicated by the RFIHD campaign were not necessarily lethal, they debilitated those who contracted them. In the case of children, they hindered development to their full potential, and they diminished adults' productivity as laborers. For example, hookworm infection produces anemia, weakness, fatigue, and stunted growth. The populations affected by diseases lived, more often than not, in regions that were of some economic interest to foreign investors, such as ports, oil fields, and places devoted to the production of other valuable raw materials.[71] Therefore, the Rockefeller Foundation's assistance served a twofold purpose of fostering a public health international diplomacy and enhancing the health conditions of people who were potential workers for American businesses abroad.

TABLE 16

Federal social expenditure by sector (in millions of pesos)

Years	Total	Agriculture investment (%)	Industrial investment (%)	Transportation communication (%)	Social benefit (%)	National defense (%)	Trade/ tourism	Coordination agreement
1925–1930	581	13.8	—	77.5	8.8	—	—	—
1931–1935	484	14.5	—	73.8	11.8	—	—	—
1936–1940	1,081	17.2	8.3	64.5	64.5	0.5	—	—
1941–1945	2,874	16.7	10.3	60.0	11.2	1.8	—	—
1946–1950	8,476	20.6	22.0	43.9	12.0	1.4	—	—
1951–1955	17,783	16.5	30.2	37.7	37.7	3.2	—	—
1956–1960	31,297	11.6	35.7	33.1	17.7	1.9	—	—

SOURCE: *Estadísticas históricas México*, 2:623–24.

RFIHD assistance also entailed the training of doctors, sanitary engineers, nurses, and midwives. Doctors and nurses received fellowships to pursue graduate studies in the United States as well as to travel to see how public health programs worked in different parts of the United States. The objective was that, upon their return to Mexico, these public health workers would be leaders in public health policy making and would train more people who would work in the health units in different states where programs were launched. This way it would be easier to expand health services throughout the country. Modernization efforts in medical and public health practices came with some reluctance/rejection from the old guard of European-trained doctors. It had not been long since Europe was at the forefront of biomedical research. Hence, receiving help from the United States and dealing with young U.S.-trained doctors raised tensions. For some years, the medical profession would continue to be the fiefdom of French-trained doctors while public health would be directed by U.S.-trained doctors.

Notwithstanding the natural mistrust that Mexican government authorities professed toward any initiative that came from the United States, revolutionary governments were amenable to accepting the help offered by RFIHD. There were many voids to fill in health provision, and assistance was offered to regions that had historically remained untouched by the hand of any health initiative. In addition, this was a joint collaboration with DSP, so this initiative was not outside of the government's control. In the end, whatever positive outcome stemmed from these programs would reflect positively on government authorities. As Birn explains, the cooperation projects were not always undertaken in a congenial environment. There were tensions between RFIHD members and the Mexican DSP official on different points in the relationship. Nonetheless, this endeavor managed to last thirty years. By the early 1950s, nearly two thousand health professionals had been trained. Diseases had been eradicated in places once considered remote and many rural communities had received hygienic education.

During the Lázaro Cárdenas administration (1934–1940), a solid commitment to social justice was established. Cárdenas had the first six-year nonrenewable presidential term in Mexican history. His commitment to social justice was reflected in his six-year plan in which a clear program was laid out to fulfill revolutionary promises. Emulating the Soviet five-year plan, the six-year plan presented the social, economic, and political agenda of the administration. Improving public health was one pending assignment in the social development department. DSP's budget was increased significantly, and it established a nationwide public health program in coordination with state governments known as "coordinated health services in the states" (see Table 17). It was finally recognized that public resources had been allocated almost exclusively to cities and to Mexico City in particular. DSP had the main objective of creating sanitary services throughout the national territory. There were four basic problems to tackle: poor general health conditions; ignorance of medicine and personal hygiene among the population at large; lack of efficient health services (if they existed at all), especially in the countryside; and inadequate nutrition. The magnitude of these deficiencies was in part the result of the government's failure since independence to establish a welfare policy.

It was during the Cárdenas presidency that the distinction was made between social assistance to the poor and social benefits for the working classes. Health and social development would receive their share of the government's budget as two different items. In drawing this distinction, Cárdenas laid the foundations for the creation of a welfare state in the 1940s, and established a government position with regard to social assistance to the poor for the first time in the period of independence.[72] In 1939, Cárdenas acknowledged that it was the government's responsibility to assist the poor to improve their living conditions. In addition, an ambitious program to expand education services in the countryside enhanced the possibilities of improving public health at the national level as health education was included in the teaching curriculum.

Manuel Gamio, a prominent anthropologist of the first half of the twentieth century, worked at DSP during the Cárdenas administration. During his tenure at the public health department, he wrote reports on the health and nutritional status of the rural population in Mexico that clearly depict the theories and models that Mexican policy makers followed at the time with regard to welfare provision. It is important to highlight that Gamio was well known for his participation in the creation of a school of anthropology in Mexico and the discovery of important archaeological sites such as Teotihuacán. Moreover, his works contributed to the crafting of the official postrevolutionary indigenism discourse.[73] In documents he prepared while working at DSP in the late 1930s, he recognized that Mexicans living in the countryside, the majority of the population at the time, had poor health and nutrition. He explained that the issue of poor health was not evident at first glance because it was masked by very high infant mortality.[74] He also observed that the quality of diet was poor due to the almost universal lack of resources among the rural working classes. In

TABLE 17

Expenditure in health by the main health-care agencies and their percentage of the total sector

Year	Total in thousands of pesos	SSA		IMSS		ISSSTE	
		Thousands of pesos	Percentage of the sector	Thousands of pesos	Percentage of the sector	Thousands of pesos	Percentage of the sector
1910	2,260	n.d.	n.d.	—	—	—	—
1915	n.d.	n.d.	n.d.	—	—	—	—
1920	n.d.	n.d.	n.d.	—	—	—	—
1925	3,546	3,456	100.0	—	—	—	—
1930	8,715	8,715	100.0	—	—	—	—
1935	10,677	10,667	100.0	—	—	—	—
1940	38,670	38,670	100.0	—	—	—	—
1945	77,634	77,634	n.d.	n.d.	n.d.	—	—
1950	130,616	130,616	n.d.	n.d.	n.d.	—	—
1955	248,090	248,090	n.d.	n.d.	n.d.	—	—
1960	713,604	713,604	n.d.	n.d.	n.d.	—	—
1965	1,006,766	1,006,766	n.d.	n.d.	n.d.	n.d.	n.d.
1970	15,529,172	1,648,972	10.7	9,769,600	62.9	4,110,600	26.4

SOURCE: *Estadísticas históricas de México*, 1:156.

recognizing the ethnic and geographical diversity of the Mexican population, and therefore the difference in needs, he suggested improvements in three areas. First, he argued that fostering miscegenation (*mestizaje*) of Indians with Europeans would improve the health status of the population.[75] Second, he suggested that medical services be made available to all parts of the country; however, he stressed the need to insert medical services into the countryside only gradually. Otherwise, there would be a risk that traditional healers and the population in general would reject the services.[76] Third, he proposed that the diet be oriented toward more nutritious and inexpensive foodstuffs, such as soybeans.[77] We will elaborate more on this point later in this chapter.

Ávila Camacho's presidency (1940–1946) followed the guidelines established by Cárdenas on public health matters. First it upgraded DSP to a cabinet-level ministry, which meant that the head of the health department (SSA) would be part of the president's cabinet and the budget would be increased. SSA would provide health services to the population at large without making distinctions in income level or between employed and unemployed, informal and formal workers. Vaccination campaigns became more effective in covering the whole national territory. Infant mortality was reduced significantly. In 1942, a social welfare system through IMSS was created for workers affiliated with it. Health service was the first area to be developed by this institute, especially through the creation of clinics and hospitals. The quality of their health service was comparable to any hospital or clinic in the developed world. Not all workers were affiliated with IMSS. For instance, oil companies, the military, and railroad companies offered health services to their own employees.

The Cárdenas administration had an objective to expand health services in the countryside in response to the excessive attention given to health services in Mexico City by previous governments. This was an initiative of the federal government, and one initiative of limited success. IMSS began providing health services in Mexico City, then to other large cities in the country. They left the establishment of health clinics in the countryside to the end. This initiative only covered workers in formal sectors of the economy, who, as explained in Section 1, were far from being a majority of the labor force.[78] In 1947, only Mexico City had IMSS hospitals. This is not surprising in light of the fact that a significant number of industrial workers and other IMSS affiliate enterprises were based in Mexico City. By 1950, efforts to decentralize health services had not yielded visible results.

Demography in Mexico

It is hard to have an accurate depiction of Mexico's demographic history prior to the 1930s. Population data for nineteenth-century Mexico are incomplete as compared to data available for countries in northwestern Europe or the United States. It is not possible to prepare a demographic history of Mexico using parish records with the detail and accuracy with which it has been done in Europe.[79] There are two basic reasons for this. First, marriage patterns differed substantially across social classes and were very distinct from those of the United States or European countries; for instance, nonmarital fertility was common among the working classes. Hence, it is difficult to make strong assertions based on marriage patterns. Second, many parishes in the countryside were consistently understaffed; in addition, it was often the case that people did not have the money to pay for burial and baptism fees. Therefore, a good number of births and deaths went unrecorded.[80] The civil registrar was only established in 1857. Although the government made its certificates the legal proof of births and deaths as opposed to parish records, it was not until well into the twentieth century that people made a habit of getting birth and death certificates. The government carried out its first population census in 1895, and it took several decades before statistical methodologies and data gathering became fully reliable. Nevertheless, extant data sources do allow one to formulate certain assertions with regard to demographic history.

Lethal epidemics of the sixteenth century, a by-product of the biological encounter between Spaniards and indigenous populations, decimated locals to frightening levels. Eventually, Amerindian people became resistant to diseases brought from Europe and population growth in the New Spain recovered to its preconquest levels.[81] Demographic historians of Latin America refer to it as the second demographic transition, after the adoption of agrarian systems, as it was an intrusion of population and technologies from the Old World.[82] Throughout the colonial period, famines and epidemics were issues of constant concern among government authorities. Famines produced by cycles of crop failure were a constant threat until the early nineteenth century, when they seem to have stopped posing a problem.[83] Most famine episodes were followed by epidemic outbreaks; however, famines were not necessarily behind every epidemic disease. Certain epidemics became such because people had not been exposed to a certain pathogen, as was the case with cholera in the 1830s.[84] Although some diseases are not nutrition related, a certain level of malnutrition in the majority of the population made them more susceptible to contracting gastrointestinal and respiratory diseases, which were ubiquitous among the Mexican population for the whole period of study, as we will see later in this chapter.

Well throughout the nineteenth century, Mexico remained a high-fertility, high-mortality population. High mortality—especially driven by high infant mortality rates—prevented the population growing above 2 percent rates in spite of the prevalence of natural fertility. This demographic behavior was not unusual for a population of the Western Hemisphere.[85] To give us an idea of the growth of the population, Table 18 shows published official estimates of Mexican population; growth rates were rather modest.

Living conditions in cities were particularly dire during the second half of the nineteenth century, and mortality rates were comparable to European cities during the early Roman Empire or the medieval period.[86] Judging by

TABLE 18
Total Mexican population, 1793–1910

Year	Source	Population
1793	Virrey Conde de Revillagigedo	4,483,680
1795	Virrey Conde de Revillagigedo	5,200,000
1803	Barón de Humboldt	5,837,100
1808	Barón de Humboldt	6,500,000
1810	Don Fernando Navarro y Noriega	6,122,354
1815	Don José Salas	5,764,731
1824	Poinsett	6,500,000
1830	Burkardt	7,996,000
1831	A. J. Valdéz	6,382,284
1836	"Noticia de los Estados y Territorios"	7,843,132
1839	Sociedad de Geografía y Estadística	7,044,140
1852	Don Juan N. Almonte	7,661,919
1854	"Anales del Ministerio de Fomento"	7,853,395
1855	Don Miguel Lerdo de Tejada	7,661,520
1856	Don Miguel Lerdo de Tejada	7,859,564
1856	Don Antonio García Cubas	8,283,088
1856	Don Manuel Orozco y Berra	8,287,413
1862	J. M. Pérez Hernández	8,396,524
1869	Don Antonio García Cubas	8,743,614
1872	Secretaría de Gobernación	9,097,056
1873	A. Balcárcel	8,994,724
1874	Don Antonio García Cubas	9,343,470
1878	Secretaría de Gobernación	9,384,193
1880	Don Emiliano Busto	9,577,279
1882	Bodo von Glumer, Cuadro Estadístico	10,001,884
1886	Don Antonio García Cubas	10,791,685
1888	Dirección General de Estadística	11,490,830
1895	Dirección General de Estadística (first population census)	12,632,427
1900	Dirección General de Estadística (second population census)	13,607,259
1910	Dirección General de Estadística (third population census)	15,160,369

SOURCE: Dirección General de Estadística, *Tercer Censo de Población* (1910).

mortality rates in the statistics presented in Table 19, one would think that Mexico City "ate people up." The number of deaths substantially outnumbered the number of births during the second half of the nineteenth century, but the city continued to be populated thanks to the constant inflow of people from the countryside, a flow of substantial proportions since the late eighteenth century. We use Mexico City as an example for two basic reasons. First, given the centralism tradition inherited from the colonial period, the capital city was the center of economic, political, social, and cultural life in the country. Second, most of the funding allocated to building a sanitary infrastructure was spent in Mexico City.

In Figure 14 we observe how population growth did not take off until the Porfirian era (i.e., post-1876). There is no single compelling factor to explain this increase, but we can assert that it was not produced by a technological innovation in agriculture production as the Malthusian model explains for the case of England.[87] This is not to say that no technological innovations were adopted throughout the second half of the nineteenth century. During the Porfirio Díaz administration, the government facilitated the import of machinery in its quest to modernize the productive

TABLE 19
Population change in Mexico City, 1869–1886

Years	Births	Deaths	Births – deaths
1869	2,286	7,447	−5,161
1870	1,998	7,733	−5,735
Total	**4,284**	**15,180**	**−10,896**
1871	1,788	7,640	−5,852
1872	2,567	8,172	−5,602
1873	2,266	6,961	−4,695
1874	2,273	8,453	−6,180
1875	2,044	9,217	−7,173
Total	**10,938**	**40,443**	**−29,505**
1876	1,784	10,390	−8,606
1877	1,726	12,242	−10,516
1878	1,864	10,161	−8,297
1879	1,747	10,223	−8,476
1880	2,329	9,455	−7,126
Total	**9,450**	**52,471**	**−43,021**
1881	1,735	9,705	−7,970
1882	1,755	11,654	−9,899
1883	1,561	12,301	−10,740
1884	1,761	12,885	−11,124
1885	1,710	13,189	−11,479
Total	**8,477**	**59,734**	**−51,257**
1886	1,607	13,175	−11,568
Total, 1869–1886	**30,472**	**165,823**	**−135,351**

SOURCE: Estadística de la República Mexicana, 1888.

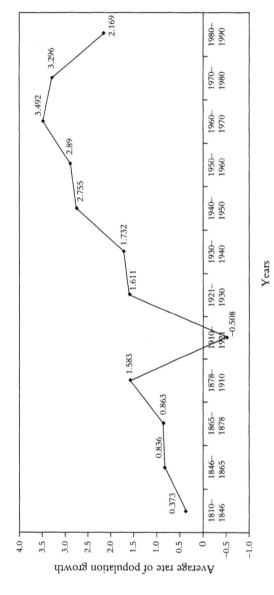

Figure 14 Mexico's average rate of population growth

SOURCE: INEGI, *Estadísticas históricas de México.*

sector.[88] New technologies were adopted in some regions, usually by wealthy *hacendados* involved in export agriculture, albeit not always with successful results.[89] Thus we cannot assert that growth in population during the Díaz administration was due to a technological innovation in agriculture that produced an increase in the amount of food available to the working classes. Basic staples continued to be produced with traditional cultivation methods in peasant communities, ranchos, or haciendas.[90] More land was opened up for cultivation during this time period, but this does not imply that the popular classes were eating more.[91]

Immigration did not cause an increase in population, either.[92] Mexico did not need to establish national programs to promote European immigration such as the ones launched by Brazil, Argentina, and Chile. The Porfirio Díaz government did extend invitations to Europeans to come settle in Mexico; the invitations were on a small scale compared to similar endeavors undertaken in South America. Moreover, they were not motivated by the need to populate frontier regions, but rather by the racist intention among politicians to whiten up the Mexican population.[93] This European immigration was not substantial in numbers, but the prosperity of the businesses they started upon their arrival in Mexico was of the utmost importance.[94] Government authorities led attempts to colonize certain regions that were successful, such as Italian groups in Veracruz and Michoacán, whereas others did not prosper, such as German settlements on the Tehuantepec Isthmus in Oaxaca.

The Mexican Revolution took a substantial toll on the population. Robert McCaa considers it a demographic disaster comparable to the Spanish Civil War.[95] It is estimated that "of a total demographic cost of 2.1 million[,] excess deaths accounted for two-thirds, lost births one-fourth, emigration considerably less than one-tenth of the total."[96] The population was able to recuperate naturally within a decade after the worst armed conflict in its history and continued to grow at an increasingly rapid pace until the 1970s, when government authorities finally decided to launch a birth control program that yielded results quite rapidly. Rapid demographic growth—observed since the late 1930s—unfortunately absorbed many of the benefits of the economic takeoff known as the Mexican Miracle.

Mexico's demographic evolution does not resemble those of Western countries. This fact raises two relevant questions to better understand Mexico's demographic dynamics: How is it that demography actually evolved, and how did fertility differ from the Western pattern? There was no substantial decline in fertility in this period in spite of the economic, scientific, and technological transformations taking place that in other countries created an incentive to limit fertility. On the other hand, mortality rates languished at a modest pace during the second half of the nineteenth century and at a more vigorous pace in the twentieth century. Three events should be taken into account in responding to these questions: the time when public health policies that stimulated the decline in mortality were introduced, the launching of welfare institutions, and the impact of cultural values on fertility behavior.

Mexico was not at the forefront of sanitary infrastructure building for most of the nineteenth century. Nonetheless, during the Porfiriato, the government made attempts to clean up its major cities, with a deep emphasis on the better-off sections of Mexico City. Public health infrastructure was unequally distributed. Vaccination campaigns and the improvement in health conditions in cities helped bring infant mortality rates down, leading to a rising life expectancy for the population at large. This was particularly evident in Mexico City at the end of the nineteenth century.[97] In most of the Mexican countryside, the traditional pattern prevailed until the first decades of the twentieth century, but the dynamics of demographic growth were not homogeneous throughout the country. In those places in the countryside where the land could not support all the offspring of peasant families, children would migrate to cities, to other regions that would offer better job prospects, or to the United States. Those communities that did not have an excess of population lived in the same archaic way they had been living for centuries. Increasing means of transportation fostered a rural exodus starting at the end of the nineteenth century; the process accelerated as the twentieth century unfolded. As the population began to grow, outlets to accommodate the excess in labor supply opened up, and so people in the working classes did not deem it necessary to limit fertility.

In Section 1, we learned that Mexico was not at the forefront of welfare provision, either; the exiguous development of welfare institutions had repercussions on fertility behavior, too. Although infant mortality declined—and this meant that a household would have more children to support—the general population continued to practice unrestricted fertility. People did not judge it necessary to have fewer children for a number of reasons: The 1910 Revolution had decimated the population and the government favored "the building up of the nation" (hacer patria) with more children. There was no confidence that in the future there would not be another war or epidemic that would kill youngsters and children. Salaries were not high or secure enough for the working classes, and there was no retirement pension system in place. Therefore, more children meant greater insurance for old age. Of the children who survived to adulthood, it was not clear that they would all be able or willing to care for elderly parents, so it made sense to diversify risk by having more children. In Mexico, the social security system was not created until 1942, and it only covered a small portion of the working population.[98] For nonaffluent Mexicans, children were (and still are) their parents' old age insurance, even for some of those who had a retirement pension. Lack of a reliable old age insurance system made children a part of the survival strategy among the Mexican working classes.

The pattern of unrestricted fertility and early marriage, with a high proportion of consensual unions also at an early age, did not mean that fertility among the Mexican working classes would be close to that of the Hutterites.[99] McCaa argues that, although there are few sources from which fertility patterns could be assessed, fertility declined somewhat starting in the late eighteenth century. Such a decline, however, was not the result of a conscious decision to limit births, but a result of institutional changes and political events that resulted in an increase in the age of marriage and a decrease in the number of women entering a union of any sort.[100] An imbalance in gender ratios due to frequent warfare and political instability restricted the number of males available to enter a union. At the end of the eighteenth century, a royal edict that recognized written pledges as the only legal promise of marriage had lasting consequences for mixed-race and Spanish groups. Throughout the colonial period, every time a woman lost her virginity to a man, he was forced to restore her honor by marrying her. The new edict changed this pattern, but it did not mean that couples stopped having premarital sex. It meant that fewer men married women they had sex with. Age of marriage rose and fewer women got married. Still, fertility rates were much higher and age of marriage much lower than those found in the Western world.

Given that consensual unions were less stable than marriages, women in consensual unions would have fewer children throughout their reproductive lives as they would not necessarily have a partner for the entirety of this period. Lower-class women in the cities would also interrupt pregnancies when they could not support another child, especially those in consensual unions or single mothers, even if this was prohibited by the state and the Church. Anecdotal evidence of abortion among lower-class women can be found in literature and in anthropological studies.[101] Widowhood restricted fertility for white and mixed-race groups. Except for indigenous peoples, women who were widowed normally did not remarry, whereas men did, and usually to younger women. Almost all women had children, but not all women

Photograph 10   Matilde Martínez and children. Photograph by Bain News Services. Courtesy Library of Congress.

Photograph 11   Making tortillas. Photograph by Jackson William Henry, 1843–1942. Courtesy Library of Congress.

Photograph 12 Mealtime. Photographer unknown. Courtesy IISUE/
UNAM/Fondo Octavio y Gildardo Magaña. Doc. 1014.

had stable unions throughout their reproductive lives; this translated into fewer pregnancies in spite of practicing unrestricted fertility. In Mexican society motherhood is what defines womanhood regardless of whether the children are born out of wedlock. In addition, Mexican society is a child-oriented society. Bastard children, as they were called, were integrated into extended households without it creating a social stigma. In this regard, there is no distinction between urban and rural dwellers. This is why marriage, be it civil or religious, is not a reliable factor for estimating fertility among Mexicans. English and French models of fertility do not serve to explain the size of the Mexican population. This is not to deny that in cities there were large numbers of orphaned and abandoned children, but rather that unchanged fertility behavior among the population throughout this period responded to cultural values that were decidedly distinct from what was observed in Western Europe.

A Narrative Overview of the Evolution of Dietary Habits in Mexico

Foreign travelers' accounts are a rich source of anecdotal information about the dietary habits of the Mexican population for the period for which there are no sources from which we could construct data series. During the nineteenth century, travelers from many European countries came to visit and explore Mexico. Like Brazil, India, and Egypt, Mexico represented the exotic. Travelers came from England, Germany, the United States, and Russia. Different trips produced different accounts, and various accounts reflect the different motivations for foreigners to come to Mexico. Some came for job-related reasons, such as government or diplomatic missions. Others came in search of the exotic. Some were interested in exploring new forms of fauna and flora; others were interested in studying the society. A good number of travelers came to explore business opportunities, especially during the second half of the nineteenth century. Some of the works produced from travel experiences have become reference points in the history of Mexico, such as the works of Alexander von Humboldt and Madame Calderón de la Barca. Mexican cuisine, its foodstuffs, and the dietary habits of the locals were among the most fascinating parts of Mexico; hence, they were often part of the accounts.

From these sources, we learn of the wide variation in the quality and quantity of food consumed by the population of nineteenth-century Mexico across social classes. For the upper strata of the population, there is little difference in quality across regions, for they had the means to acquire foodstuffs from any place. The diet of the upper classes was perhaps more exotic than that of the elite of the civilized countries in Europe due to the availability of fruits, vegetables, and indigenous spices of Mexico in addition to the foodstuffs brought from the Old World. All accounts devote a part of their description to the great variety and freshness of fruits in Mexico, especially in the markets.[102] A good example is provided by British traveler William Bullock's depiction of a Mexican fruit market: "Of vegetables and fruits there are few places that can boast such variety as Mexico, and one where the consumption is greater in proportion to the inhabitant. The great market is larger than Covent Garden, but yet unequal to contain the quantity daily exposed for sale; the ground is entirely covered with every European kind and, as I have already stated, with many the very names of which we have scarcely heard. I was never tired of examining these fruits and vegetables."[103] In terms of taste there were some travelers who were enchanted by the new flavors that Mexican cuisine had to offer, and there were others who could not find the taste in the spicy food, much as happens today with travelers who go to Mexico.

The description of menus of the upper class offered by Madame Calderón de la Barca—an English lady who lived in Mexico for two years in the mid-nineteenth century—supports the argument that the diet of the Mexican elite was refined. For example, the breakfast menu served to her and her husband (the Spanish consul) at Antonio López de Santa Anna's Veracruz ranch: "The breakfast was very handsome consisting of innumerable dishes, meat and vegetables, fish and fowl, fruits and sweetmeats, all served in white and gold French porcelain, with coffee, wines, etc."[104] The dinners offered by the clergy were no less rich and sophisticated than the ones served by the Mexican oligarchy. She describes being invited to the Convento de la Encarnación: "We came at length to a large hall, decorated with paintings and furnished with antique high-backed arm-chairs, where a very elegant supper, lighted up and ornamented, greeted our astonished eyes; cakes, chocolates, ices, creams, custards, tarts, jellies blancmangers, orange and lemonade."[105]

Mrs. Alec-Tweedie's comments on the diet of the upper classes later in the nineteenth century are consistent with those of Madame Calderón de la Barca. She notes, "The day begins with coffee taken early, in the bedroom—a custom that enables people to be in negligé attire for the greater part of the forenoon, as in France. This light repast is followed by an enormous mid-day meal usually served about one o'clock, when soup, fish, entrées, meats, puddings and numerous sweets always appear at the table in the better houses."[106]

These travelers also noted that the availability of foodstuffs outside of the big cities was of substantially lower quality. The meals served in little towns reflected the quality of food of the nonelite. While on the road to visit the nearby towns of Mexico City, they refer to the food in the inns: "After a tolerable breakfast, hunger mak[e] chile and garlic supportable"[107] or "at the posada they gave us rancid sheep's milk, cheese and biscuits."[108]

All travelers noted the contrasts in diet across social classes in both quantity and variety. Madame Calderón de la Barca makes a very interesting remark: "There is no country in the world where so much animal food is consumed and so little is required. . . . The consumers are not the Indians who cannot afford it, but the better class who generally eat meat three times a day."[109] Carl Sartorius, a German traveler passionate about the botanic, refers to these contrasts when he states, "The Mexican population presents the most striking contrasts, unlike that of any north-western Europe: On one side splendor and luxury, elegant carriages and Parisian toilette, on the other dirt and indigence, an exclusive life, with separate national type in its outward appearance, in language and manners."[110] Sartorius spent more time getting to know the lifestyle of the working classes and writes about the differences in diet between the mestizos and the Indians. "The food of the Indians . . . consists for the most part of vegetables such as maize in all its various methods of preparation, beans, squashes, and different kinds of roots and vegetables, which grow spontaneously in the fields, like portulaca, phytolaca, palm-cabbage, etc. They are very fond of fruits, and take great pains to cultivate them."[111] He writes about the diet of the elite as being very Spanish: "At 3 o'clock in the afternoon dinner is served, which has certain unvarying dishes. First a cup of clear broth, the 'sopa' of rice, pasta, or some kind of bread fruit, cooked in broth, till the fluid has completely evaporated, and highly season with tomatoes. The 'olla' is the third dish, and is met on every table. It consists of beef mouton, a little pork ham, fowl, small sausages, cabbage, French beans, parsnips, turnips, pear, bananas, onions, celery, a little coriander and parsley, all cooked together. The vegetables are placed on the tables apart from the meat, and each person helps himself according to his taste. The 'olla' is followed by some 'principios,' mostly ragouts with strong flavored broth of meat or fish; then comes a sweet dish, and finally some sweetmeats. Wine is rarely drunk at table; but the sweetmeats are succeeded by a large glass of water."[112]

There is also mention of the physical appearance of the working classes that suggests that they were malnourished. Some of the remarks were more metaphoric than others. For instance, Madame Calderón de la Barca refers to two guards from lower-class origins as "two little men, who with their arms and sarapes, looked like bundles of ammunition."[113] Sartorius, in a more scientific fashion, states, "The appearance of the men is sturdy, and they are seldom above the middle height; the women are short and fat."[114] According to his description, the children of the working classes suffered malnutrition. "The child is nursed long after he has been able to run alone. Meanwhile the mother enjoys every sort of prejudicial effect of it by allowing the child to share it with her. If she eats oranges she squeezes some of the juice into the child's mouth; if she drinks brandy the child received its portion also. Such a diet necessarily injures all the organs of digestion. After the child is weaned, its only food is maize-broth and bread or beans, and these it eats all day long without having any stated meal-times. The abdomen thus becomes affected by scrofulous swellings. Commonly they acquire the habit of eating earth and lime instinctively. . . . Can we wonder that under such a diet the greater part of the children die under four years of age?"[115] Sartorius's account was written before the germ theory was widely accepted in the Western world, and before the causes for a good number of pathologies were actually discovered. The symptoms he describes are very useful in ascertaining that the communities he visited had a high incidence of hookworm and other intestinal diseases. Lack of certain hygienic practices is at the source of these diseases; malnutrition only exacerbated the incidence and lethality of these pathologies. As we explained earlier in this chapter, these diseases were significantly reduced in many regions of Mexico starting in the 1920s.[116]

Decades later, Tserverkoi, a Russian traveler who visited Porfirian Mexico, made similar remarks to those of Sartorius regarding social inequality and the living standards of the lower classes. As he wrote, "working people were in bad physical condition in general, no matter what their age. They always had a hungry look, because indeed they did not have enough to eat or drink. In the city, their diet was composed primarily of corn, beans and peppers, and in the country these foods were all they ate, although never was there enough food of any sort to forestall hunger and malnutrition. They almost never consumed meat or other vegetables, and few dairy cows, pigs or chickens were to be seen. Finally, and to make their situation even worse, the poor and the working class had no understanding of hygiene, and they often fell ill."[117] Tseverkoi's remarks are consistent with health conditions in the cities in nineteenth-century Mexico discussed in earlier in this chapter.

Brantz Meyer, an American, noted in the second half of the nineteenth century that working-class Mexico City dwellers had the habit of eating outside the home. As a general rule, men left home very early and bought some fast food on their way to work. These fast foods consisted of some meat, beans, and salsa served in a tortilla.[118] During the twentieth century, the habit of eating in the streets became even more common among the urban population. Having described the diets of the popular classes, it is not surprising to find that the regular menu in the nineteenth-century Mexican army was similar to that of the working classes—both rural and urban. As explained in Section 2, the Mexican military did not have the degree of professionalization of European armies. When it came to feeding soldiers the same was true; the military did not have special personnel to cook for the troops. It was civilian women who cooked for soldiers. In wartime, women would follow their partners on campaign to cook for them. The typical menu for the military circa 1900 was white *atole*, coffee, chili, and bread for breakfast; broth with rice and vegetables, a small portion of meat, tortillas, beans, and chili for lunch; and beans and tortillas for dinner.[119]

Dietary habits of the Mexican population were also a subject of study for intellectuals of the time. Their motivation was to understand the causes of Mexico's social problems. Intellectuals in the second half of the nineteenth century were greatly influenced by social Darwinist ideas. Their observations on the diet of the working classes are rife with prejudices against the customs of the poor as well as with racist observations. These prejudices did not have a solid scientific foundation because nutrition as a science did not exist.

Francisco Bulnes's theories on diet are a great example of the influence of social Darwinist thought among Porfirian intellectuals. He divided cultures into corn eaters, rice eaters, and wheat eaters. According to Bulnes's classification, wheat eaters were the most civilized. He thus argued that in order to civilize the Mexican population, it was necessary to increase their wheat bread consumption and decrease their tortilla intake. Bulnes described the Mexican society in three classes according to the allocation of their wages: the lower, which "ate badly and drank considerably"; the middle, which "ate badly and dressed as good and fashionably as possible"; and the upper, which "ate badly and paid high prices for their *parvenu* luxuries."[120] Interestingly, these ideas persisted even after the revolution. Thus, it is not surprising that in the first population census one question on quality of diet was whether people ate wheat bread or tortillas.

Not all Mexican intellectuals wrote in the social Darwinist tradition. There were others who wrote about the dietary habits in nineteenth-century Mexico in the same style as foreign travelers did. They wrote about food in their memoirs. Antonio García Cubas provides a good example of this kind of literature. In his famous *El libro de mis recuerdos*, he speaks highly of the meals in Mexico City's restaurants and even small fondas,[121] and describes a late-night dinner of grilled chicken, salad, fresh fish from Chapala, beans, and tortillas combined with good wine.[122]

Postrevolutionary intellectuals were interested in seeing how the revolution affected the dietary habits of the population. Salvador Novo and Alfonso Reyes are the best examples of this group of postrevolutionary intellectuals. Novo, for instance, described the differences in diet of the population during the times of the revolution. For the poor, he described the diet as the traditional trilogy: corn, beans, and chili. The middle class added to this menu some soup, of rice or pasta or broth, along with some meat that had already been cooked with the broth.[123] In the late 1930s, Manuel Gamio recognized that people's diets in rural Mexico lacked variety and nutrients such as proteins, vitamins, fats, and minerals. He explained that this inadequacy could be rectified by adding meat, eggs, fruits, and vegetables to the everyday diet of the inhabitants of the countryside; at that time, however, it was not financially feasible for the government to invest resources to make this possible. Gamio suggested that this poor nutrition problem could be solved by making rural people eat soybeans as they did in other parts of the world. He proposed to increase the national production of soybeans and to teach people the different ways in which this food could be cooked.[124] This suggestion did not prove feasible either. Although soybeans were eventually produced in Mexico, it was not possible to change people's dietary habits based on the argument that soybeans were more nutritious. Gamio, as a policy maker, overlooked the importance of palatability and tradition in diet. The same error would be made by policy makers in the 1970s as they tried to find ways for the nation to regain self-sufficiency in food production.

Diet did not change much during the nineteenth century and the earlier decades of the twentieth century, especially regarding meat consumption, which reflects protein intake.[125] Some dietary habits did evolve. As the population became more urban, an increasing number of people were eating more or most of their meals in the streets than in the previous century. With the adoption and growth of the food-processing industry, fast food became more available to the population and fostered the tendency to eat nonhomemade meals. Finger foods deeply fried, commonly known as *antojitos*, and sweet beverages like canned soda became more common in the diet of the Mexican population as the twentieth century progressed. Researchers in nutrition have noted that this trend in dietary habits did have an effect on the quality of nutrition of the population and in their health status, as we will see in more detail in the following chapter. For our period of study, we observe that there is a gap in the quality of diet across social classes. It is our hypothesis that this gap does not narrow over time (1850–1950) because of persistent inequality, and that is why we observe a height differential across social classes and why the height of the popular classes barely improves over time. Whether this gap continued after 1950 is another story.

Chapter 2

Health and Nutrition: The Data Analysis

The previous chapter presented a narrative overview of the history of health, nutrition, and population in Mexico in the period 1850–1950 that provides a more integral view of the causes behind the unequal evolution of heights of the Mexican population. In this chapter, I will continue to look into the synergies between health and nutrition and their impact on living standards, but I will do so using the quantitative evidence available. I will first analyze the data on health and then those on nutrition.

Health

I will compare the health status of the Mexican population between the turn-of-the-century decades (1880–1910) and the mid-twentieth- and late twentieth-century decades to evaluate changes in the health status of the Mexican population over the period 1850–1950. Nineteenth-century data come from the military files of the Personal Extinto presented in Section 2. The post-1910 data are drawn from two different sources: the population censuses of 1940, 1950, 1960, and 1970, and medical reports published by INNSZ. Ideally, we would want to have longitudinal observations drawn from the same data source in order to do a follow-up of the health histories of the population. This information would help us understand the links to socioeconomic status. Unfortunately, this information is not available. The most we have is some information on health status and cause of death of

179

the federal military sample. We complement this information with data on health at the national level from the population sample.

Health Data Analysis

With information on health services drawn from the military archives and national statistics, we can ascertain the arguments made in the previous chapter. Mortality rates declined over the period 1850–1950, especially after 1930. There was a growth in population toward the end of the nineteenth century that was halted by the 1910–1920 years of armed rebellion linked to the revolution. Growth resumed afterward at a pace that accelerated toward the 1940s to levels leading to demographic explosion. Decreasing mortality rates coupled with unchanged fertility patterns during the first half of the twentieth century drove up population growth at an increasingly brisk pace. The most common pathologies were those related to respiratory and gastrointestinal infectious diseases. Rapid growth in population undermined government efforts to improve public health. Fertility rates remained high due to cultural norms that placed a high value on motherhood. Moreover, the absence of welfare institutions that could credibly substitute for children as insurance for old age and as a source of income through child labor contributed to this.

The first source of data is a sample constructed from the recruitment and services files of soldiers born in the period 1880–1910. This sample was drawn from the Personal Extinto sample I examined in Section 2. This means that soldiers in this subsample served in the military for at least six years and then retired or died while in service. The law required that the information contained in these records be thoroughly kept; based on these records, widows of deceased soldiers could claim their deceased husband's retirement pension. We thus have information on height, year and place of birth, occupation prior to recruitment, age, and cause of death. There are three basic limitations to these data sets. First, there is no information on the weight of the soldiers. Weight data is useful to determine the nutritional status of an individual after reaching final height.[1] Second, a soldier's height was measured only at the time of recruitment; this meant that in cases in which soldiers were measured at an age younger than the age when final height was achieved (eighteen to twenty-three years old), we could not make use of that observation because we cannot assume this to be the individual's final height. Third, aside from the cause of death, there is little information on diseases that soldiers suffered from while in service. This is understandable because during the last quarter of the nineteenth century medical diagnosis

and the recording of vital statistics were in their infancy even in the most scientifically and technologically advanced places in the world. The totality of
the data sample contains information for cohorts born from the 1860s to the
1950s. However, observations are insufficient for cohorts born before 1880
and after 1920 to do formal statistical tests.

The second source of data provides information on death as recorded
by INEGI in population censuses for different years; this information was
compiled by the government institutions that provided health services. Using this information makes it possible to evaluate the changes in most common pathologies among the population over time. What is expected from
this change is that as life expectancy has increased, infectious diseases have
been replaced by degenerative diseases. I assume that the population census
data do not count the entire population for two basic reasons: first, because
health services were still not provided universally even with the most recent
census taken into account (1990); second, because there were numerous
communities in the countryside where there were no doctors to certify the
cause of death, and so for all these communities there is no information
on the most common causes of death. An additional reason to be cautious
with the census data is that there is no explanation of how these data were
gathered by INEGI or how these series were constructed given that they
were gathered from different sources. In spite of these deficiencies, this
source of data provides the only information currently available on changes
in pathologies in Mexico with respect to earlier decades.

There is a general consensus on the relationships among nutrition, disease, and social conditions.[2] This consensus is that the nutritional status of a
population depends on the production, distribution, and quality—modified
by technology—of food as well as on the level of physical activity and the
effects of disease. This way, the level of nutrition combined with the effects
of disease establishes the health, capacity, and productivity of a population.
Although all infections influence nutrition, the reverse is not true. There are
some types of diseases that can appear regardless of the nutritional status of
the individual or where having had good nutrition has a minimal effect on
the outcome of the infection. These are detailed in Table 20. A part of the
military records sample contains information on the cause of death and/or
diseases contracted by soldiers.[3] This subsample was drawn from the Personal Extinto files.[4] It does not contain members from the upper strata of
the population or soldiers from the poorest backgrounds because the latter
were commonly found in the deserters sample. Hence, we can assert that
this sample is not biased toward the extremes of the social spectrum, and we
can take the main characteristics of these soldiers as a fair representation of

TABLE 20
Nutritional influence on morbidity or mortality of infections

Definite	Equivocal or variable	Minimal
Measles	Typhus	Smallpox
Diarrhea	Diphtheria	Malaria
Tuberculosis	Staphylococcus	Plague
Most respiratory infections	Streptococcus	Typhoid
Pertussis	Influenza	Tetanus
Most intestinal parasites	Syphilis	Yellow fever
Cholera infections	Systemic worm	Poliomyelitis
Leprosy	Encephalitis	
Herpes		

SOURCE: Bellagio Conference, "The Relationship of Nutrition, Disease, and
Social Conditions: A Graphical Presentation," *Journal of Interdisciplinary History* 14
(Autumn, 1983): 503–6.

TABLE 21
*Most common respiratory and gastrointestinal diseases
among soldiers*

	1878 (%)	1879 (%)	1880 (%)
RESPIRATORY			
Laryngitis	0	0	0
Bronchitis	0	0	0
Pleurisy	0	4.2	12.0
Pneumonia	22.0	24.3	24.2
GASTROINTESTINAL			
Enterocolitis	4.4	2.7	1.8
Dysentery	4.3	2.5	0
Hepatitis	20.5	2.7	7.0

SOURCE: SDN, *Memorias de guerra y marina*, 1881.
NOTE: Data expressed as percentages of the month that presented the
highest mortality.

the average Mexican at that time. The majority of the soldiers in this subsample were rural dwellers from the central and bajío (center-north) regions
of the country, which were also the most densely populated at the time.
These soldiers were, for the most part, unskilled manual laborers prior to
their recruitment. The average age of recruitment was twenty-six years and
their average stature was 165 centimeters (64 inches approximately).

There is information on the main diseases suffered by soldiers and their
death rates only for the first decades of the Porfirio Díaz administration
(see Tables 21, 22, and 23). This information was gathered and published
by the Ministry of Defense's memoirs (*Memorias*) in the 1880s. These statistics were not drawn directly from the Personal Extinto subsample. In the

TABLE 22

*Most common diseases among soldiers, numbers of
cases in 1879–1880*

Disease	1879	1880
Syphilis	994	1,196
Intermittent	272	152
Rheumatism	276	148
Alcoholism	115	127
Enterocolitis	117	117
Bronchitis	216	109
Pneumonia	111	103
Erysipelas	111	68
Tuberculosis	78	48
Typhus	18	28
Influenza	130	20
Scarlet fever	n.a.	8
Smallpox	12	7
Measles	20	6

SOURCE: SDN, *Memorias de guerra y marina*, 1881.

TABLE 23

Infectious, endemic, and epidemic diseases observed in military hospitals, 1878–1880

Disease	1878		1879		1880	
	Morbidity	Mortality	Morbidity	Mortality	Morbidity	Mortality
Erysipelas	95	3	62	4	68	2
Scarlet fever	0	0	0	0	8	0
Flu	0	0	130	2	20	0
Intermittent	381	1	78	0	152	2
Measles	0	0	20	0	6	0
Typhus	34	10	18	3	28	0
Smallpox	4	1	12	3	7	0

SOURCE: SDN, *Memorias de guerra y marina*, 1881.

Ministry of Defense's memoirs there is no distinction made between the division soldiers belonged to and if they were simple soldiers or officers. Also, in many cases the cause of death is not well specified because vital statistics recording was not done systematically, as was the case in almost every country at the time. This, of course, does not mean that a doctor did not issue the death certificate or that the deceased received no medical assistance. This is consistent with the information on public health during the Porfiriato that we described earlier. Except for syphilis, records show that the diseases for which people would go to get medical care are the same as the causes of death. At the time smallpox was mainly a children's disease. Those who had the disease as children and survived it were most likely to have permanent damage to their organs, and this would make an individual at higher risk of death early in adulthood. Very commonly in recruitment files, one finds soldiers listed as having scars from smallpox as particular features (*señas particulares*).

Unfortunately, for the Personal Extinto subsample, we do not have information at the individual level on the medical history of soldiers while they were in service or when they retired. There is also no information on the weight of the soldiers, which makes it impossible to calculate BMI.[5] However, we do have information on the causes of death of soldiers and can determine their nutritional influence. In Table 24 we observe that in the Personal Extinto subsample the most common causes of death were also related to the level of nutrition. This finding supports the argument that poor levels of nutrition influenced the high rates of mortality in the population in most preindustrial societies.[6]

TABLE 24

Number of deaths among the military, ranked by degree of nutritional influence, 1880–1910

| | NUTRITIONAL INFLUENCE | | |
Cause of death	Definite	Variable	Minimal
Tuberculosis	157		
Respiratory disease	75		
Intestinal disease	35		
Septicemia	6		
Malnutrition	1		
Liver and kidney disease		42	
Circulatory and rheumatism		33	
Consumption		9	
Cancer		4	
Syphilis		3	
Typhus		2	
Influenza		1	
Estreptococcemia		1	
Heart disease			30
Paludismo (malaria)			24
Others (madness, isolation)			23
Typhoid			8
Encephalitis			4
Smallpox			3
Meningitis			2
Poliomyelitis			1
Tetanus			1
Yellow fever			1
Total in number	274	95	97
Total in percentage	59%	20%	21%

SOURCE: Data from SDN archives. Personal Extinto de Caballería e Infantería sample.

Soldiers who died of disease did so at all ages, but there was higher mortality for soldiers in their midthirties, with an average age of death of thirty-five; one can verify this by looking at Figure 15.[7] Mortality among the military tends to be higher than that of the general population given that the military usually have a higher exposure to disease because of their close living arrangements while in service. Still, the mortality rate for the military obtained here is not much different from life expectancy at birth for Mexicans born during that time period drawn from population censuses.[8] This leads one to conclude two things: first, that there was no additional health penalty for soldiers at the time; second, mortality rates among the Mexican population were still at preindustrial levels at the end of the nineteenth century. By looking at the distribution of ages of death in Figure 15, one could infer that military authorities were not selective in terms of the health status of those they recruited. They frequently recruited soldiers who were already ill. In the sample it was not uncommon to find soldiers who died of chronic diseases, such as tuberculosis, within the first months of joining the military.

According to the disease classifications by nutritional influence presented in Table 20, the most common causes of death in Mexico at the

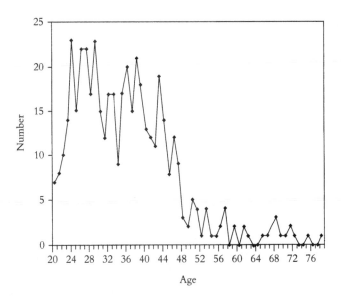

Figure 15 Distribution of the age of death of soldiers from the Personal Extinto sample

SOURCE: Data from SDN archives.

TABLE 25
Causes of death, percentages

Cause	1931 (%)	1940 (%)	1950 (%)	1960 (%)	1970 (%)	1980 (%)	1990 (%)
Infectious diseases and parasites	46	43	35	26	23	14	10
Malignant tumors	1	1	2	3	4	6	10
Nutrition and metabolic diseases	1	2	2	3	3	6	11
Circulatory diseases	3	4	6	9	11	16	20
Respiratory diseases	18	20	21	19	22	13	10
Digestive diseases	5	5	5	5	6	7	8
Malformation	3	2	0	1	1	1	2
Supplement, trauma, poisoning, etc.	4	5	6	7	7	16	14

SOURCE: Data from *Estadísticas históricas de México*, 1:160.

national level until 1950 are clearly affected by nutritional status (see Tables 25 and 26). Regarding the most common causes of death at the national level, there is a transformation over the course of the twentieth century, as was the case in countries of the Western world; epidemiological transition from infectious to degenerative disease went hand in hand with the rise in life expectancy. Additionally, after the 1950s, there is a substantial increase in the percentage of circulatory and endocrine gland diseases, namely, heart-related diseases and diabetes. Incidence of these two diseases is related to diet with high contents of fat and sugar combined with a sedentary life, which leads to obesity and malnutrition— two of the main health problems of Mexico at the onset of the twenty-first century.

How does the health status of soldiers compare to the health of people born in the last decades of this study? Reports on health from the INNSZ nutritional survey conducted in the mid-twentieth century show that anemia and intestinal parasites were the most common endemic diseases. The main causes of death in the communities studied in the survey were disease and respiratory diseases, with the exception of urban dwellers. In Mexico the epidemiological transition commonly observed in the Western world over the twentieth century was accompanied by an "epidemiological trap." This means that pathologies common in the preindustrial era diminished due to better health services in the form of sanitary infrastructure, disease prevention, and available cures for the most common diseases. Moreover, there was also an increase in the health problems related to a sedentary way of life combined with diets rich in sugar and fat so ubiquitous in postindustrial societies.

TABLE 26

Causes of death in 1990 ranked by nutritional influence

Cause	1990	NUTRITIONAL INFLUENCE			
		Definite (%)	Variable (%)	Minimal (%)	Not defined (%)
INFECTIOUS DISEASES AND PARASITES					
Diarrhea and enteritis	19,233	5			
Dysentery	n.a.				
Typhoid	602			0	
Paludismo (malaria)	39			0	
Measles	5,899	1			
Pertussis	458	0			
Tuberculosis	5,452	1			
Smallpox	n.a.				
Other infectious diseases	9,313	2			
Total	40,996				
MALIGNANT TUMORS					
Malignant tumors	41,168				10
Others	1,435				0
Total	42,603				
NUTRITION AND METABOLIC DISEASES					
Diabetes mellitus	25,782				6
Others	19,793				5
Total	45,575				
CIRCULATORY DISEASES					
Heart diseases	5,942				1
Brain−vascular	19,760				5
Other	4,331				1
Total	83,833				
RESPIRATORY DISEASES					
Bronchitis, asthma, emphysema	9,629	2			
Pneumonia and influenza	22,205	5			
Other	12,443	3			
Total	44,277				
DIGESTIVE DISEASES					
Liver diseases	24,170				6
Other	9,068				2
Total	33,238				
Malformation	8,969				2
Supplement, trauma, poisoning, etc.	58,904				14
Other	54,692				13
Sign, symptoms, and morbid states	9,716				2
Grand total	422,803				
Percentage		20.0	0.0	0.2	79.8

SOURCE: Data from *Estadísticas históricas de México*, 1:160.

Nutrition

Food is both a need and a pleasure. As a necessity, food is nutrition, essential for life. As a pleasure, food is gastronomy, the art of fine cuisine and good eating. Although the art of gastronomy is centuries old, nutrition as a field of scientific research is relatively young. In the Western world, a scientific approach to the study of diet and human food requirements for optimal nutrition did not evolve until the mid-twentieth century. The first studies on nutrition were soon followed by the hypothesis—formulated by Thomas McKeown in 1950—that a correlation existed between nutrition and the evolution of living standards.[9] In other words, changes in the quality and the quantity of what we eat have an effect on how long and how healthy we live. Mexican gastronomy has a worldwide reputation for its variety and palatability; tomatoes, avocados, chocolate, vanilla, and a wide variety of peppers are only some of its contributions to international cuisine. Still, despite its highly appreciated gastronomy, it is not possible to make the argument that the Mexican population has adequate nutrition.

Traditional diets rely heavily on foodstuffs indigenous to each locality, and these change across regions. The upper classes, however, tend to have a more homogeneous diet regardless of their location because their choice of meals depends more on taste than on price of foodstuffs. More constrained by their incomes, the lower strata of the population are more dependent on local foodstuffs, and these depend on the natural resource endowment of each region. One of the most relevant dietary differences concerns meat intake. Protein intake during the growing years is a key ingredient to reaching one's maximum potential height. There are historical examples in which populations were taller because of quality of diet along with lower exposure to diseases, such as Native American populations in the mid-nineteenth century.[10] In Mexico, northern and bajío populations had a higher meat intake because cattle production made meat more affordable than in the center and south. Since the pre-Columbian era, the center and south were oriented to agriculture production and the consumption of corn, beans, and squash. Consequently, within the popular classes, people from the north and the bajío were consistently taller than their counterparts in the center and south.

Before presenting the evidence to substantiate the argument of this section with regard to nutrition, I should clarify some points that are relevant to a better understanding of the impact of nutrition on the biological standards of living and to better contextualize the information available within the time period in which scientific knowledge on nutrition evolved.

Energy requirements during growing years will be roughly the same for all humans with slight variations depending on climatic conditions and differences in physical activity. For adults, on the other hand, nutritional requirements greatly depend on size and lifestyle. In general, taller people will need more calories to function than shorter people. Still, the greatest difference depends on lifestyle. An individual who performs a physically demanding activity, such as agriculture, will require a higher caloric intake than someone working in front of a computer.

Optimal nutritional requirements have changed over time for two basic reasons. First, as nutritional science has developed, we have acquired more refined knowledge of the composition of a balanced diet. Second, with the increase in the number of people living in urban settlements earning their living in sedentary activities, the nutritional requirements of a balanced diet have also changed. Usually a lower caloric intake is required. To this, we should add that the human species is extremely resilient to changes in diet. People can adapt to survive under the harshest nutritional conditions. That is why emaciated women from sub-Saharan Africa can give birth to children. As a survival adaptation, the human body is also efficient at storing fat when caloric intake exceeds energy requirements.

In examining the evolution of dietary habits in the Mexican population over the period 1850–1950, we should keep in mind that nutrition as a field of scientific research was nonexistent. Consequently, information available on nutrition for the period was not gathered for the purpose of scientific analysis. People's choices on nutrition as well as welfare policies that entailed food provision concentrated on giving more food instead of better food. Another relevant point is that during the one-hundred-year period covered by this study, there were no famines in Mexico. In years when crops failed due to adverse climatic conditions, the government imported grain from abroad, usually the United States. Although there were food shortages in some regions during the revolution, they were not severe to the point of provoking a famine.

Although malnutrition is often associated with extreme poverty, an increase in income would not necessarily improve the nutritional value of a lower-income household. Usually the decision of which foodstuffs to buy beyond the minimum caloric requirements depends on variety, palatability, and convenience rather than nutritional value. This is worth clarifying because in Mexico, as we will see later in this chapter, even people from the lower strata of the population had a caloric intake sufficient to live, but the nutritional value of their diet kept children in this strata in poor health and growing below their average maximum potential. This was the case for most peasants and low-income urban people. Urban dwellers had more sedentary lifestyles as compared to rural dwellers, even those whose work required physical activity. By 1950 in Mexico, despite having a lower energy requirement, urban people had a higher caloric intake than rural dwellers. In brief, with regard to nutrition, in Mexico the problem was not undernutrition but malnutrition.

In their famous *Essays in Population History*, Sherburne F. Cook and Woodrow Borah devote a chapter to Amerindian food production and consumption before and after the conquest in central Mexico.[11] Their interest in this essay is to explore changes in patterns of food production and consumption before the conquest and the 150 years that followed to find out how changes in these patterns were related to the epidemics and high mortality that decimated the Indian population after the coming of Europeans. Their work focuses on Central Mexico, which is the area for which there was more information available and the one part of Mesoamerica that had higher densities of population at the time. Cook and Borah are careful to warn the reader about the limitations of their findings given that the information available on the subject is incomplete; their findings are to be taken as a first approach to the subject. They mention that this particular topic had been of little interest to historians until the 1940s, when the issue of food production in the world became important and when more information became available.[12] Their analysis of the evidence leads them to argue that in central Mexico there was a wide variety of foodstuffs available that could "fully supply human requirements in protein, fat, vitamins and minerals. Although there were no large animals in the area, animal protein requirements were secured through fishing and hunting."[13] Still, the authors clarify that large regional variations in the quality of diet may have existed due to differences in climate and fertility of soil.[14] They assert that food resources were not distributed fairly across social classes. The Indian nobility and other elite people such as merchants, artisans, and the military had a rich and balanced diet. In contrast, peasants—who were the overwhelming majority of the population—had a leaner diet based on maize, beans, chili, and agave for the most part; to a lesser extent, they were able to supplement their diet with fruits, vegetables, fishing, and hunting. Cook and Borah have some information on the estimated height and weight of the average Mexican of that time, and they try to evaluate whether, based on their dimensions and caloric intake, they were eating enough to sustain endure their workloads. Based on their sources, they find that Mexicans were not shorter or leaner than the average Spaniard at the time; this was 160 centimeters height and 60 kilograms weight. Their findings suggest that, prior to the conquest, Indians had a lower caloric intake but they also worked fewer hours. The introduction of Old World animals increased the availability of meat to the population at large. Indians thus increased their protein intake after the conquest, but also the number of hours they had to work.[15] Interestingly, based on their analysis, Cook and Borah argue that sixteenth-century Mexicans were just as tall as the rural indigenous population of the mid-twentieth century.[16] Their findings are consistent with the assumption made in this study that the living conditions of the rural population of Mexico in 1950 were basically the same as in 1850, dietary habits included.

It is not possible to know in detail the nutritional content of people's diets prior to 1950 (after the INNSZ was founded) because the quantitative data necessary to study the quality of diet are only available for the post-1950 period. We can, however, ascertain what people ate across regions and across social classes during the one-hundred-year period we are studying. Indeed, we have qualitative information on people's daily life routines; this can be obtained from literary works and some official documents of that period. Most of the analysis on the nineteenth century is based on these kinds of sources. For the twentieth century, I use information on dietary habits from population censuses, the first nutritional census, and government documents on social assistance. It is worth pointing out that there is consistency among these different sources with regard to people's daily eating habits.

Research for the post-1950 period, including censuses undertaken in 1950, 1960, and 1970, mirror some similar and some different trends as compared to the period 1850–1950. The methodology in the population census and nutritional census provides insightful information that may be applicable to the period 1850–1950. The information available on the twentieth century comes from two different sources: the population censuses of 1940, 1950, 1960, and 1970, and the nutritional survey of the 1960s (*Encuestas nutricionales de México*). The population census data provide information on dietary habits. These are enumerated at the municipal level. Thus, it makes it feasible for us to study nutritional differences between rural and urban areas. However, the questions in the 1940 and 1950 censuses were rather vague; they asked if people ate wheat bread or not. This information does not give us a clue as to whether people were getting enough proteins and vitamins. The 1960 census asked if people usually ate meat, fish, milk, and eggs; and the 1970 census asked the frequency with which foodstuffs were consumed.[17] This source of data gives an idea of the quality of diet in terms of the protein intake of cohorts born during the latter years of this study. As we will see later, this is an important clue for determining how final height is correlated with quality and composition of diet.

The second source of data I use is the national survey done during the late 1950s and the early 1960s by the INNSZ, which provides information on height, weight, and health of children and adults. A useful feature of this survey is that it provides information on adults who grew up during the last years of the period that this book covers. Let us remember that these are the best years of the Mexican Miracle, which is supposed to have been a golden era of sustained economic growth and the least unequal period of Mexican history. Specialists in nutrition and related fields (doctors, nutritionists, and physical anthropologists) conducted the survey in different regions of Mexico. Although this study does not cover the entire national territory, it does have information representative of all regions and social classes. It also has extensive information on the height, wealth, and dietary habits of rural, semirural, and urban communities in Mexico, so it gives a reliable portrait of the nutrition and health of the Mexican population.

Anecdotal information presented in the previous chapter offers a glimpse of the quality of nutrition of the Mexican population. Two points become clear. First, there were sharp contrasts in diet across social classes. Second, the popular classes were malnourished. Their diet was high in carbohydrates and low in protein. One could argue against the assertion that there was a low protein intake because beans and meat both contain protein; however, the amount of meat consumed was small and beans are not a high-quality source of protein. Completeness and digestibility determine the quality of proteins. A complete dietary protein contains all the essential amino acids in relatively the same amounts as human beings require; it may or may not contain all nonessential amino acids. Generally, proteins derived from animals are complete. Proteins from plants have more diverse amino acid patterns, and some tend to be limited in one or more essential amino acids. Protein digestibility is a measure of the amount of amino acids absorbed from a given protein. Proteins are important, among other things, to restore bone tissue and to produce antibodies, essential for fighting diseases.[18]

The poor had a diet that had insufficient quantities of meat. This suggests that the majority of the Mexican population had an inadequate protein intake. Children also had a diet that did not contain adequate nutrients and so they grew stunted due to protein energy malnutrition (PEM).[19] One could argue against this assertion, claiming that Mexican children were weaned later than children in European countries and the United States, and that later weaning decreases infant mortality. However, Mexican children not only lived in conditions of poor hygiene, but they also had very

TABLE 27
Mortality and infant mortality rates

| Year | Mortality rate | DEATHS OF CHILDREN UNDER ONE | | | Infant mortality rate |
		Total	Men	Women	
1895	31.0	n.a.	n.a.	n.a.	n.a.
1900	32.7	n.a.	n.a.	n.a.	n.a.
1907	32.1	n.a.	n.a.	n.a.	n.a.
1922	25.3	n.a.	n.a.	n.a.	n.a.
1930	26.7	107,921	58,476	49,445	131.6
1940	22.8	110,037	59,868	50,169	125.7
1950	16.2	113,032	61,882	51,150	98.2
1960	11.5	119,316	65,708	53,608	74.2
1970	10.1	146,008	80,800	65,208	68.5
1980	6.3	94,227	52,713	41,514	38.8
1990	5.1	65,497	36,932	28,565	n.a.

SOURCE: *Estadísticas históricas de México*, 1:68.

poor nutrition once they were weaned. Poor nutrition after weaning and lack of hygiene were among the central causes of the high rates of infant mortality (see Table 27). The analysis of the diet of the population later in this chapter will shed light on the issue of protein intake.

In the mid-twentieth century, with the emergence of welfare and social assistance policies, the government saw the need to obtain more information on variables that would be helpful concerning the measurement of living standards. This meant gathering information on the basic material needs of the population, that is, food, shelter, and clothing. Therefore, since the 1940s, the population census has included information on diet. The 1940 and 1950 censuses asked if people ate wheat bread. This question has implications on the proportions of corn and wheat as main staples of the diet. It does not, however, say much about the quality of diet because eating bread as opposed to tortillas hardly changed the quantity of nutrients essential for a well-balanced diet.[20] The 1960 population census refined the questions on nutrition and included information on intake of meat and dairy products. The 1960 census asked if people ate meat, fish, eggs, and/or milk. The data is broken down by gender (men and women) and by location between urban and rural dwellers. This information provides a rough idea of the protein intake of the population to ascertain if the working classes did not usually consume or consumed insufficient amounts of proteins from animal sources. In addition, this is a good complement to the nutritional survey we will analyze later.

In Figure 16, we observe the results from the 1960 population census for men and women. We observe the proportion of people who did not include in their diet the following foods: milk, eggs, meat, and fish. In this census, we have information about the number of people and the percentage of children less than one year old. Children are not counted in the questions regarding bread, milk, eggs, and meat consumption. The implicit assumption is that they are not weaned during their first year of life. The questions were designed so that people would have the option to respond only "yes" or "no." Although most people responded "yes" to the question, the proportion of affirmative responses was higher among urban people, which indicates that the diet of urban dwellers had a higher content of proteins from animal sources.

According to the responses of the 1960 population census, there is no substantial difference between men and women in terms of protein intake, which suggests that there was no difference in their diets by gender (see Figure 16). We do find differences across regions and between rural and urban dwellers. In the north and bajío there was a higher percentage of people eating meat, fish, and milk. In urban populations, we have a higher percentage of people eating these animal sources of protein. The information on regions is consistent with the findings in height differentials presented in Section 2; thus, it substantiates the argument that those populations who have a higher protein intake in their daily diet are taller on average. The downside of this information is that we cannot be sure what proportion of the diet was made up of meat, fish, milk, and eggs. The expression "usually" (*por costumbre*) does not say much about the dietary habits of people. Consequently, we do not know if people only had one glass of milk some days of the week or if they had a diet that included all of these foods on a daily basis. In the nutritional census, the question was refined and allows one to get a more detailed notion of dietary habits.

During the late 1950s and early 1960s, the INNSZ ran a thorough survey on the quality of the diet of the population of Mexico. This survey is extremely useful to complement the information from the population census of 1960 that we are analyzing. The survey covered different communities across Mexico (see Figure 17). In each community, the specialists who ran the survey studied the menus, the number of meals, the quantities of food prepared, and the way food was allocated within the household. They also calculated the quantities of the basic nutrients in the diet and how well they satisfied the recommended daily allowances according to type of physical activity. In addition, to get an idea of the influence of beliefs and income level on diet, they incorporated questions in the survey on taboos about certain foodstuffs as well as on what families would consume if they

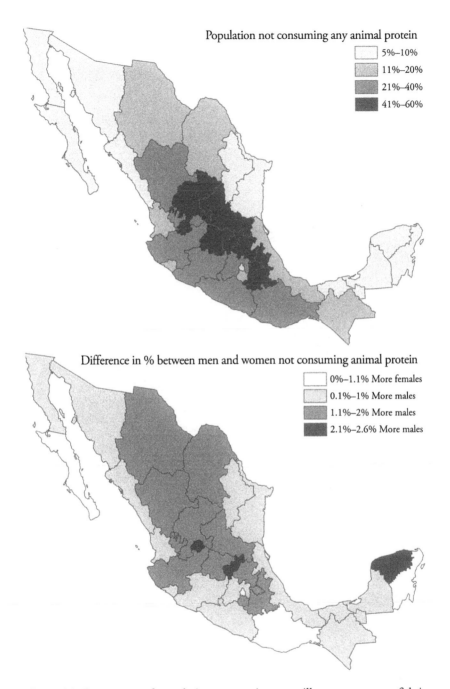

Figure 16 Percentage of population consuming no milk, eggs, meat, or fish in their diet / Difference between percentage of males and females consuming no milk, eggs, meat, or fish in their diets

SOURCE: Mexico, 1960 Population Census.

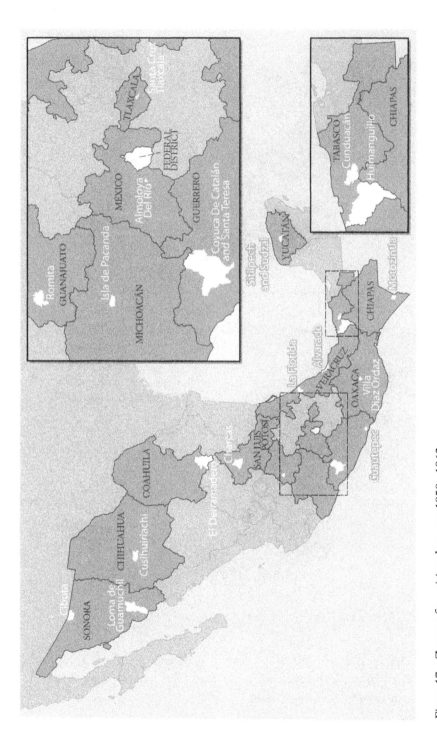

Figure 17 Zones of nutritional survey 1958–1962

SOURCE: *Encuestas nutricionales de México.*

had a higher income. Finally, they performed health exams of adults and children to detect nutrition and/or weight problems.

Table 28 shows the menus of some communities that illustrate the different rural and urban regions of the country. This sampling includes low-income to middle-class households. These menus show diets with a high proportion of carbohydrates and sugar and a low proportion of protein, vitamins, and minerals. Figure 18 presents a comparison of the intake of calories and proteins with respect to the recommended daily allowances. In them, we can observe clearly how the daily requirement for calories is normally met, but the intake of protein is rather low. These are figures for adult diets. The information for children shows that there are even more inadequacies. Unfortunately, this particular information was not gathered in all regions. In general, we observe a general deficiency in the intake of vitamins A and C, riboflavin, and the amino acid tryptophan. Most of the energy and protein intakes were from vegetables and not animal sources. As we explained earlier in the chapter, proteins obtained from vegetables are of lower quality. Although the degree of malnutrition is seldom due to famine—meaning that there is no caloric malnutrition—a considerable percentage of the population had some degree of malnutrition.

Why do people have such a poor diet? The levels of malnutrition and undernutrition reported in this survey depend on two basic factors: first, the natural resource endowment, which reflects mainly the quality of land for cultivation; second, a deficiency in dietary habits, which reflects the income and educational levels of the population.

In some localities, the quality of the land was so poor that agricultural production, although entirely destined for domestic consumption, did not suffice to feed the families throughout the year. The deficiency in dietary habits was more visible in places where, even though there were enough resources to provide a well-balanced diet, the dietary habits hindered this. Taboos about different foodstuffs had a negative impact on the nutritional levels of the population. The three most common taboos reported in the survey were: first, the belief that certain fruits, like citrus fruits, were bad for the health; second, the notion that children should not eat certain kinds of meats or should not eat meat at all during infancy; third, the belief that pregnant women should not eat fruit or meats. As a result, more often than not, the diets were classified as scarce and monotonous. The preparation of foods also had a negative impact. The most common example of this is the preparation of corn for tortillas and tamales, which involves washing away all the proteins and niacin that are in corn, making it a less nutritious meal.[21]

TABLE 28

Nutritional survey: Meal menus by region

Region	Type of breakfast	Type of lunch	Type of dinner
SOUTH			
Coyuca, Guerrero	Zucchini with milk, meat and chili, and tortillas	Meat with chili	Meat, beans, zucchini with milk, bread, and tortillas
Cuautepec, Guerrero	Coffee, sweet bread, and tortillas	Fish or beans, chili, and tortillas	Beans, tortillas, and chili
Díaz Ordaz, Oaxaca	Coffee or atole, bread, beans, and tortillas	Beans, tortillas, eggs, or meat	Coffee, tortillas, bread, beans
Motozintla, Chiapas	Coffee, tortillas, and beans	Meat, green leaf vegetables, tortillas, and coffee	Coffee, tortillas, and beans
Alvarado, Florida	Coffee, rice and beans, tortillas, and sometimes bananas	Rice, beans, fish, tortillas, and fruit	Coffee or atole, bread or tortillas
Cunduacán, Tabasco	Coffee with sugar	Meat, vegetables, rice, beans, and tortillas	Atole
Sudzal, Yucatán	Coffee and tortillas	Beans, chili, tortillas, and a little bit of meat	Coffee and tortillas
CENTER			
Almoloya, Edo. Mex.	Tea with sugar, beans, and tortillas	Meat with vegetables, beans, tortillas	Tea with sugar, tortillas
Santa Cruz, Tlaxcala	Coffee with milk (sometimes), sugar, beans, and tortillas	Rice or pasta, meat with vegetables, beans, salsa, tortillas	Tea, sometime beans with tortillas or bread
La Pacanda, Michoacán	Tea or atole, fish, tortillas	Fish, salsa, and tortillas	Coffee with tortillas
Romita Guanajuato	Atole or coffee, beans, chili, and tortillas	Beans, tortillas, and chili	Atole and tamales
NORTH			
Charcas, San Luis Potosí	Coffee or tea with milk, beans, tortillas or bread	Pasta or rice, vegetables, beans, tortillas (sometimes fruit)	Coffee or tea with bread or tortillas
Cusihriachic, Chihuahua	Oats with milk, coffee with milk, beans, and tortillas or bread	Beans, tortillas, cheese or eggs, and coffee	Rice or pasta, beans, tortillas, and coffee with milk
El Derramadero, Coahuila	Coffee, beans, potatoes, salsa, and tortillas	Beans, salsa, and tortillas	Coffee, beans, and tortillas
Cíbuta and Loma de Guamuchil, Sonora	Coffee, meat or eggs, beans, and tortillas	Sometimes rice or pasta, beans, tortillas, and coffee	Coffee, beans, and tortillas

CITY			
Semirural	Coffee, beans, and tortillas	Beans or meat or vegetables and tortillas	Coffee, beans, and tortillas No dinner
Suburban	Coffee, tortillas, and bread Coffee with milk and bread Coffee with milk, beans, and tortillas	Pasta, meat and vegetables, beans, and tortillas (sometimes rice)	Coffee or atole and bread Sometimes beans and tortillas
Barrios	Coffee with milk, beans, and bread (sometimes eggs)	Pasta, meat, vegetables, fruit or dessert, and tortillas	Coffee with milk and bread (sometimes beans)
Caseríos	Fruit, coffee with milk, eggs, beans, and bread Fruit, coffee with milk or atole, and bread	Pasta, meat, vegetables, fruits or dessert, and tortillas	Coffee with milk, meat, eggs, and bread Coffee with milk or chocolate, bread and butter

SOURCE: Data from *Encuestas nutricionales de México*.

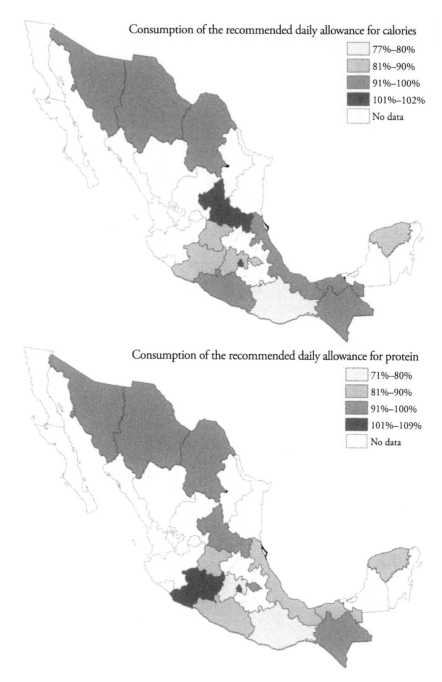

Figure 18 Percentage of daily recommended allowances: Calories and proteins
SOURCE: *Encuestas nutricionales de México.*

How can we know that this diet actually reflected the malnutrition and poor health of the population? Figure 19 presents some anthropometric indicators from the INNSZ nutritional survey. For each region for which we presented the diet, there are also measures of average height and weight. With these two measurements we can calculate the BMI to determine if on average the people in the survey were underweight or not, and we can determine how short these people were compared to modern height standards for a well-nourished population.[22] This figure is evidence that neither the men nor the women are underweight.

In the case of average heights, we find that they all rank in the lower percentiles of the modern height standards. People from rural zones are shorter than people from urban locations. The people from the north are taller than men and women from the center and the south. These results are consistent with the findings of Section 2. From these we can conclude that these people have a normal weight but are short. We should keep in mind, however, that having a weight that ranges within the normal limits does not necessarily mean that someone is well nourished. Thus, it is not surprising to find a high incidence of people with diseases linked to nutrient deficiency as we explained earlier. This survey also reported some information on diseases that will be discussed later in the chapter. The most important feature of these figures is that the intake of proteins is low. If we assume that this diet is better than that of people at the turn of the century, judging from the anecdotal evidence of the travelers' accounts, we cannot reject the notion that the diet of the Mexican population is high in carbohydrates and low in proteins.

Mexican intellectuals have stated that Mexican civilization ended where sauces and refined cooking ended and where grilled meat became the norm.[23] An expert gourmet would agree with this statement. Nonetheless, a nutritionist would not agree that a diet with a small meat intake would be appropriate for children, adolescents, and youths who had not completed their growing process. Palatability is not synonymous with optimal nutritional quality. From a gourmet perspective, the variety of dishes served from one end of Mexico to the other is so vast that numerous cookbooks on the market today present culinary delights originating in different regions. But this perspective did not and probably does not translate into a nutritional and balanced diet.

In Mexico during the period 1850–1950, people's dietary habits depended on income, foodstuffs available, and taste. Nutritional science has found that meat is an important input for those in growing stages to attain maximum height potential and be in good health. Mexicans liked meat,

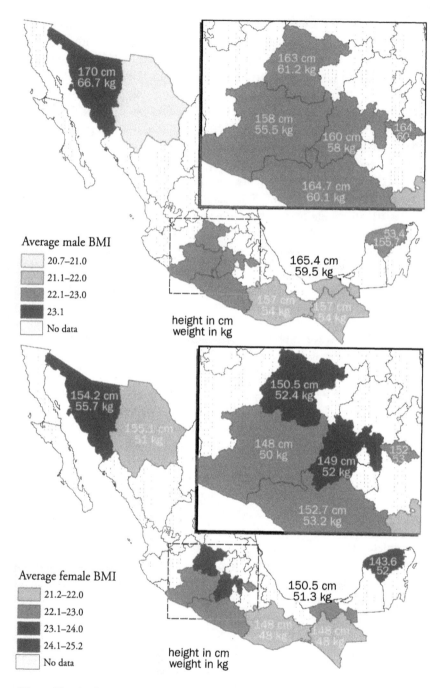

Average male BMI
- 20.7–21.0
- 21.1–22.0
- 22.1–23.0
- 23.1
- No data

height in cm
weight in kg

Average female BMI
- 21.2–22.0
- 22.1–23.0
- 23.1–24.0
- 24.1–25.2
- No data

height in cm
weight in kg

Figure 19 Anthropometric measures: Males and females

SOURCE: *Encuestas nutricionales de México.*

but only a few could afford to eat it on a regular basis. The upper strata of the population could eat meat as frequently as they desired. For the rest of the population, meat consumption depended on price and budget. Because of the natural resource endowment of each region, meat was more accessible in price for people in the bajío and the north; they thus had a higher meat intake and were on average taller than their counterparts in the center and south, where meat was a luxury reserved for festivities.

In this chapter, we looked at the basic characteristics of the traditional diet of the Mexican population over the period of study. By looking at the nineteenth-century sources, we can assert that there were quantitative and qualitative differences in diet across social classes. The evidence suggests that the diet of the Mexican elite was as good as the well-to-do classes in wealthier nations at the time, whereas the diet of the working classes—the majority of the population—was meager and had little meat in it. The description of nineteenth-century traditional diets of the popular classes is very similar to the information obtained in the twentieth-century nutritional survey and population census: they have a low content of proteins and they are based on corn, beans, and chilis.

Low protein intake has several effects on the standards of living of a population. The main repercussion is PEM; this kind of malnutrition is difficult to diagnose because, unlike people who have caloric malnutrition, individuals tend to have a normal weight. PEM presents two major negative influences: it hinders growth, so that children with PEM grow stunted; and it makes both children and adults more vulnerable to contracting certain diseases such as respiratory and gastrointestinal diseases. As we showed earlier in this chapter, these are the main pathologies among the Mexican population throughout this period of study. Children who frequently contract these diseases during their growing years will have an additional cause to grow stunted because the diseases will be constantly consuming the energy that is required for growing.

The contrast between the quality of diet in the nineteenth century and that of the twentieth century suggests that diet did not improve over time. Urbanization and the emergence of the processed-foods industry modified the traditional diet of the working classes. Unfortunately, such modifications were not beneficial. Medical reports show that in the second half of the twentieth century there was a substantial increase in fat and sugar intake. This modification does not add positively to the standards of living of the population but in fact creates new nutrition and health problems, such as diabetes and obesity, along with the already existing problem of PEM. By looking at the evolution of the quality of nutrition of the

Mexican population, we cannot expect the lower-income segment of the population to have grown taller. In addition, the lack of improvement in dietary quality can also be explained by the fact that Mexico maintained its high fertility levels parallel to the decline in mortality during this period; this forced the average laboring-class family to feed more children on the same wage. These effects were more negative for families in which the breadwinners were not working in the "formal" economy.

· · ·

In this section we analyzed the synergies among health, nutrition, and population growth in the evolution of living standards of the population in the period 1850–1950. We assessed if the information in this section was consistent with the analysis of the trend in heights presented in Section 2.

The evolution of Mexico's public health and history of disease just presented meant that up until the turn of the century, public health services could only be found in the more affluent sections of the main cities of the Mexican Republic, Mexico City in particular. These services included paved streets, clean water, and a sewer system. In addition, the pathologies found in the population were those common to preindustrial societies—namely, gastrointestinal and respiratory infectious diseases. During the second half of the nineteenth century, there were no famines because in years of bad crops, the government was able to obtain grain from abroad. Moreover, there were no big killer epidemic outbreaks. During the first half of the twentieth century, a series of institutional and technological changes that favored the improvement of public health services were put in place, and a substantial number of the most common infectious diseases were controlled. The government was able to spend more on building sanitary infrastructure, massive vaccination campaigns, and health education programs. International health organizations also helped bring health improvements to some remote localities through the introduction of sanitary services. Cities became less filthy and so did some regions in the countryside. By 1950, an epidemiological transition had gradually begun as well: incidence of infectious diseases declined and degenerative diseases became more common. Improvements in medicine made infectious diseases more tractable.

Government efforts to improve public health would have yielded staggering results had it not been for the path taken by population growth and the evolution of its welfare institutions. In the last decades of the nineteenth century, Mexico's economy was experiencing growth and industrialization. This was a time when scientific and technological research made it possible to live in healthier places and have access to effective medical care. Without having had to invest previously in research and development, Mexico could build state-of-the-art sanitary infrastructure and adopt the latest scientific advances in medical practice. Mexican authorities attempted to catch up in both areas, but efforts were limited when contrasted with the needs. Sanitary infrastructure did not cover all zones of the cities because government resources could not keep up with the rapid urban growth that took place during the first half of the twentieth century. Infrastructure usually covered older parts of the city and the better-off sections, which were not always necessarily the same. Resources to ameliorate public health in rural localities favored those regions that had some commercial potential, like ports or regions specializing in export agriculture. Regions lacking the export potential incentive were left in oblivion.

Whereas it was plausible to follow the Western model of scientific and technological advance by adopting their innovations, the pattern of demographic behavior shows different results. For one thing, fertility evolved under a different set of priorities and dynamics as age of marriage and the percentage of women entering a union were higher in the Western world. Fertility was still higher in Mexico. Although fertility declined over time, in some groups it remained unrestricted, including for indigenous and peasant communities. Mortality rates decreased as a result of improved sanitation, especially in times of political stability; however, the pace of decline was rather modest compared to Western standards. In 1950, life expectancy was only 49.3 years. This combination of mortality and fertility rates made it possible for the Mexican population to recuperate naturally from epidemic outbreaks and warfare without having to foster immigration. The Mexican population reproduced rapidly enough to generate a population surplus. Those who did not find jobs in their communities went seeking employment opportunities in the cities and the United States at increasing rates as early as the 1870s.[24]

This combination also led to demographic explosion, starting in the 1930s, when infant mortality rates were dramatically reduced. Although health services became available during the first half of the twentieth century, they had a limited coverage at first as they included mostly people who worked in the formal sector. Population growth added a challenge to the government's ability to enlarge its coverage. Demographic growth ate up the government's intention to expand public health services. By 1950, only a limited part of the population had access to some form of health care.

The diet of the majority of the population barely changed in caloric and nutritional value during the 1850–1950 period. In general, the traditional diet of the average Mexican was low in protein. Low protein intake affected the health of the population in two major ways. First, for children, it hindered growth; their traditional diet did not lead to attaining their maximum potential height. Second, low protein intake made both children and adults more vulnerable to respiratory and gastrointestinal diseases. There were differences in the quality of diet across regions and across social classes. The meat intake in the north and bajío was higher than in the rest of country, and people with higher incomes could afford to have more protein in their diets. These dietary differences mirror the different trajectories in the evolution of heights that I presented in Section 2.

We also tested the arguments on Mexico made by Riley in *Low Income, Social Growth, and Good Health*. The evidence presented in this section challenges Riley's assumptions with regard to the evolution of life expectancy and the role of health education and community participation in reducing mortality in Mexico from 1920 to 1960. Life expectancy did not show significant increases until after 1950. What did improve with respect to previous decades was the recording of the number of deaths and their causes, as well as the recording of most common pathologies among the population.

Education campaigns launched in the 1920s by José Vasconcelos did not have nationwide coverage or effectiveness to significantly improve literacy. It is not until the 1970s that Mexico reached the 70 percent literacy level. Although there were some attempts to bring hygienic education to the lower strata of the population, these programs had minimal outreach. For instance, in 1939 Manuel Gamio recognized that indigenous people in the countryside still had remarkably high mortality rates, and that it was necessary to consider designing public health programs tailored specifically for them.[25] Gamio believed Mexicans would be on the path to improving their health once they were able to learn the way of life of people with a European background; this policy recommendation did not place importance on community efforts to improve public health.

In 1948, decades after the postrevolutionary governments had presumably been making efforts on the health front, the results were not necessarily positive. Contemporaries like Jesús Silva Herzog were quick to point out the public health issues among the majority of the population. In his famous 1948 *Meditaciones sobre México*, Silva Herzog denounces the fact that most of the population lived without access to a sewer system or drinking water in their homes, and that this created terrible public health problems. The overarching challenge presented itself as a daunting task, a task that even with large efforts and resources invested to tackle the problem would take several years to overcome.[26] We cannot assert that Mexico was a good choice of example for Riley's *Low Income, Social Growth, and Good Health* group.

Overview and Final Conclusions

In the period 1850–1950 Mexico experienced profound social, political, and economic transformations that touched the different segments of society in diverse ways, altering their quality of life. Each is a different story in the evolution of living standards. The fate of each group was determined by their income level, participation in the process of economic modernization and growth, opportunities for advancement, and guarantee of respect for their property rights. *Measuring Up* identifies three different stories, each portraying people's place on the social ladder: the rich, the laboring classes who were integrated in the formal economy, and the remainder of the popular classes.

Using adult statures as a measure of the biological standard of living, I traced the history of each group. The group at the top of the social ladder got taller over the period covered in the passport sample. Despite political instability, economic stagnation, and the poor state of public finances suffered during the 1860s and 1870s, the better-off portion of the population saw their standards of living improve, and this continued up until the first decades of the twentieth century. The passport sample also included people belonging to the laboring classes. These were individuals who could afford to travel abroad on a passport and were therefore not at the bottom of the social ladder. This group, albeit shorter than the elite, also got taller over time, and their average statures tended to converge with the statures of the wealthier portion of the population. The trends in heights of these two groups are similar to the evolution of GDP per capita. Height differentials across social classes are steeper among men than among women. Nonetheless, as I explain in Section 2, the difference in trajectories between men and women are driven by sexual dimorphism, literacy rates, and urbanization.

In contrast, in the second half of the nineteenth century, the great majority of the population belonging to the working classes underwent a gradual deterioration in their biological standards of living. The average stature of Mexicans born between 1850 and 1890 declined, indicating that for those born during the last decade of the nineteenth century living standards stagnated. For cohorts born in the first decade of the 1900s conditions improved modestly, but then living standards deteriorated again for people born in the 1910s and 1920s. Living standards began to improve for cohorts born during the 1930s and onward, so by 1950 average statures were back to their 1850s levels. For most of the period studied, the living standards of the largest portion of the popular classes do not coincide with the evolution of GDP per capita. Neither do they coincide with the evolution of living standards of the middle and upper-middle classes. Drawing regional comparisons we find that, in general, people from the north and the bajío were taller than people from the center and south. Nonetheless, the gap is wider in the military samples than in the passport sample.

For the popular classes, biological standards of living do not accord with what the official history purports, that is, claims that their well-being improved. On the contrary, living conditions deteriorated for cohorts who were born and grew up after the launching of the liberal reforms. During the first two decades of the Porfirio Díaz dictatorship, standards of living stagnated. There was a mild recovery for cohorts born and raised during the third decade of the Díaz administration. Living conditions deteriorated again during the years of the revolution and the 1920s. Substantial recovery only started in the 1930s, coinciding with the launching of the welfare state.

The evolution of living standards with regard to poverty and inequality is the result of political decisions as much as economic performance, scientific advances, and technological innovations. Therefore, by examining the history of living standards through the lens of politics, social institutions, demography, health, and dietary habits, it is possible to understand how these factors interacted to create the different patterns in living conditions across social groups. We can delve more deeply into the underlying causes of endemic poverty and inequality in Mexico. In brief, such a multifaceted approach yields a more complete picture.

Political and institution-building factors are fundamental to an understanding of the history of welfare provision and social assistance, and reveal how this had an impact on the living standards of the population. For most of this one-hundred-year period, the different governments pushed welfare, charity, and assistance issues into the background and failed to establish an agenda for poverty relief until the late 1930s. For better or worse, political decisions did affect institutions and organizations related to welfare provision. However, this happened unintentionally, as the fate of the needy was not an issue of major concern for the government.

Anticlerical policies stemming from liberal reforms launched during the second half of the nineteenth century prevented the Church from assisting the poor the way it had done since the colonial period. The government's prime motive was to undermine the power of the Catholic Church by divesting its wealth and banning it from traditional activities, including educating children, caring for the sick, assisting the poor, and, last but not least, managing its holdings. Liberal politicians were too vested in debilitating the Church's power and in plundering their recently expropriated assets to consider the potential harm this reform could inflict on the people that the Church tended. Nor did they assume the responsibility of assisting the needy. Despite multiple anticlerical efforts, the Catholic Church's charitable enterprises did not disappear altogether. Toward the end of the nineteenth century, the Church channeled its charitable efforts to groups that held no interest for the government. The secularization of welfare institutions therefore exacerbated social polarization.

In the name of liberal reforms and while attempting to emulate development models from abroad, the government also decided that private property was the best form of land tenure. Consequently, the government proceeded to disentail communal property and tried to force everyone into a private ownership system. In one stroke, the government wanted to erase traditional organizations that had functioned effectively for centuries; in doing so, it jeopardized the ability of a large number of peasant communities to retain ownership of their land and their means of subsistence. Corporate organizations, so ubiquitous among the popular classes, were also viewed as backward and deemed undesirable if they had any link to the Catholic Church. As part of the liberal reform project launched in the 1850s, the government also banned religious corporations of lay members and ordered the disentailment of any property held by them. These corporations served as social safety nets for the popular classes. By rendering them illegal, the government was also delegitimizing a survival mechanism for people at the bottom of the social ladder. This reform was met with resistance, and these forms of corporate organization were not fully eliminated. These institutional transformations also exacerbated social polarization. This is not to deny that in some cases some individuals in the community were able to benefit from privatization, but in general no positive outcome came out of this initiative for the communities affected by it.

During the Porfirio Díaz administration some private welfare institutions emerged that were funded and founded by members of the oligarchy. In some cases, their creation was motivated by the desire of well-traveled elites to emulate the charitable initiatives of their European counterparts. In other cases, successful businesspeople wanted to do some good for the communities they lived in. Most of these efforts went to the urban needy.

The scope of these welfare institutions remained limited because the government failed to create legislation that would back them up. These institutions operated under feeble legal circumstances that made them vulnerable to government expropriation; more than anything, they operated in spite of the government. Assistance coming from these institutions helped the urban poor, yet the great majority of the needy were in the countryside.

New forms of production created new labor relationships. In addition, peasants who lost their land began to seek alternatives for earning their living. In general during the second half of the nineteenth century, more people began to work for wages. The 1857 Constitution did not contemplate the need to regulate labor. However, in 1865, Emperor Maximilian explicitly granted freedom of labor, although this freedom did not mean that other job opportunities existed. In addition, this freedom rendered workers more vulnerable to fluctuations in the price of foodstuffs and to hazards outside their control such as sickness, accidents, and unemployment. This vulnerability was common in societies that were inspired by liberal ideologies, and this was the case in Western European countries. Nonetheless, these countries had previously developed social mechanisms to assist workers who found themselves in a precarious condition. These assistance mechanisms operated through state or community-based organizations stemming from poverty-relief legislation. In Mexico nothing of this sort existed. Interestingly, it was fear of the spread of socialist and communist ideas coming from abroad that eventually motivated authorities of the Porfirio Díaz government to develop social legislation. In Mexico this type of social legislation was inspired by the need to regulate labor. One of the great gains of the 1910 Revolution was labor legislation emerging from the 1917 Constitution. Finally, in the late 1930s, the government enacted a social security law.

The postrevolutionary state decided to protect its laboring classes with a double incentive. First, in granting workers the benefits they demanded, the government kept its labor pool in good condition. After all, labor was an input in the productive process. Second, it guaranteed these groups would be political allies. The labor law was designed in such a way that the government became a mediator in the relationship between employers and workers. These groups were unionized for the most part. The laboring classes that benefited from the social legislation were able to improve their living conditions. This group, however, was a minority of the laboring classes because a good number of productive activities remained unregulated throughout this period.

In Mexico, the creation of a welfare state was a by-product of labor legislation but not of poor relief legislation, as in Western European countries. This is why it only covered a limited portion of the laboring classes. Why did the Mexican government defer the creation of a welfare law and its enforcement for so long? A brief overview of the economic history of Mexico of this time period can provide us with a clue: there was nothing in it for them. Business and political interests were closely intertwined to the extent that policy decisions were heavily based on the interest of the business class. Social assistance to the poor did not yield any profit to either businesspeople or politicians of the period. However, postponing the creation of a mechanism that would serve as a social safety net allowed social backwardness to reach proportions that would eventually become a heavy burden to society. It was not until the late 1930s that politicians came to recognize there were gains to be made from integrating people into the economy. Moreover, as elections to political office became more regular, the votes of the poor began to matter. Politicians seeking legitimacy through the popular vote realized that there were potential benefits from providing assistance to the needy. Yet, the amount of help given was insufficient to meet the needs of those at the bottom of the social ladder.

Global scientific advances and technological innovations of the mid-nineteenth and early twentieth centuries opened up opportunities for improving the living conditions of the world's population. Research in biology and chemistry made it possible to diagnose, prevent, and cure the most deadly infectious diseases of the preindustrial era. Developments in civil engineering permitted the construction of sanitary infrastructure that made cities healthier places to live. Such advances were developed and implemented in Europe, the United States, and wealthy European colonies like Canada, South Africa, and Australia. In Mexico, these improvements were adopted quite rapidly with the advantage of not having had to invest in research and development to make use of these scientific advances and technological innovations. Unfortunately, investments that were conducive to the improvement of public health only reached a small portion of the population. Sanitary infrastructure was built in the well-to-do areas of the main cities. Hospitals and clinics offering state-of-the-art medical treatments had very limited coverage.

In the first years of the postrevolutionary international era, health organizations provided assistance to eradicate diseases that were related to unhealthy sanitary conditions in rural areas. These programs were focused on building sanitary infrastructure and providing health education to the population. Not surprisingly, international aid focused on localities where there were business opportunities, such as ports and regions suitable for the development of agribusiness. The underlying motivation for groups sponsoring these programs was that healthier people made better workers. Although the health and living conditions of people in these areas improved, there were many others localities neglected by the government and international agencies. The period immediately preceding elections produced a flurry of government initiatives. For example, during this time period, the government launched massive vaccination campaigns. These campaigns did help reduce infant mortality rates. Still, by 1950 only a limited portion of the population had access to some form of health care.

Demographic behavior, on the other hand, posed a challenge to governmental efforts to improve public health. Since the colonial period traditional fertility patterns of the Mexican population had differed substantially from those of Western European countries. Age of marriage was systematically lower in Mexico. In addition, unrestricted fertility and unmarried fertility were common in the population. Higher rates of mortality kept population growth at preindustrial rates up until the late nineteenth century. In Mexico at the onset of the twentieth century, life expectancy at birth was circa twenty-five years when it was already circa fifty years in countries such as England. High fertility rates alone helped Mexico recover from the death toll of the 1910 Revolution. Even when mortality rates began to decline due to vaccination campaigns and better sanitation services, fertility rates remained the same among most of the population. Such behavior was also divergent from traditional European demographic patterns. Cultural values and the absence of social mechanisms that would serve as social safety nets help explain the persistence of high fertility rates. In the absence of a welfare state, children were considered an investment for old age. The high value attached to motherhood in Mexican society explains the fact that unmarried fertility, although frowned upon by the upper and middle classes, remained common among the lower strata of the population. As a result, by 1950 the Mexican population was on its way to a demographic explosion. Piecemeal efforts to provide social assistance and improve public health conditions were hardly ever enough to keep up with the needs of the rapidly growing population. Insufficient provision of health services could not improve the living standards of the population. Health improved for those sectors that had access to a sanitary infrastructure and to basic medical services; these were the well-to-do groups and workers protected by social legislation. In 1950, more people survived than a century earlier, but not in better health conditions.

The quality of diet can improve the living conditions of an individual or cause them to deteriorate. An examination of the evolution of dietary habits of the Mexican population allows one to determine the effects of diet on the biological standards of living of the population. With the development of transportation and the modernization of the economy it became easier to transport a wider variety of foodstuffs. Higher-income people were always able to gain access to the best foodstuffs available, so nutrition was not an issue for this group. Urban workers also had an increasingly wider variety of foodstuffs, and some could afford to have more meat in their diet. The diet of the popular classes, however, barely changed from 1850 to 1950. Nutritional censuses of the mid-twentieth century certify this. Evaluating the traditional diet of the majority of rural locations in Mexico alongside modern nutritional standards verifies that in general a great portion of the Mexican population had a low protein intake and insufficient intake of other important nutrients such as vitamins A and C. This insufficiency was conducive to stunted growth.

How different was the history of living standards in Mexico from the countries it tried to emulate? Placing Mexico in this international context is useful for at least two reasons. First, it allows us to ascertain Mexico's performance with respect to Western European countries and the United States. This comparison facilitates the understanding of the processes that shape the evolution of living standards, such as industrialization and demographic transition.[1] It is also helpful to grasp the extent to which public policies failed to promote an improvement in living conditions among the population at large. Mexico industrialized later than most Western European countries or the United States; it remained a mainly rural country until the late 1930s. Still, germ theory in public health was recognized and adopted shortly after its emergence in the Western world. Mexico's evolution of living standards was similar to Spain's and Italy's during the period 1850–1950. Nonetheless, their post-1950 paths would diverge dramatically.

Developing countries are at the frontier of the anthropometric history field.[2] This book hopes to inspire more studies of this kind in other Latin American and developing countries. In addition, it opens doors to further research on the anthropometric history of Mexico in at least three different directions.

First, the study of living standards in the period 1850–1950 offers a macrolevel, long-term approach and provides a point of departure for further, regional studies perhaps covering shorter periods of time. Although "every field of scholarship, not just human history, experiences tensions between narrowly focused case studies and broader syntheses or general-

214 Overview and Final Conclusions

izations . . . scholarly understanding requires both approaches."[3] Anthropometric history studies could offer a more detailed picture of the evolution of biological standards of living of various populations. Such studies could provide a more thorough perspective on the role that regional politics, natural resource endowment, opportunities for industrial development, and demography played in defining the living standards of each population. Anthropometric studies may shed light on the level of economic growth and modernization in the region.

Second, *Measuring Up* demonstrates that it is possible to undertake studies prior to 1850. This can be done using additional sources of data. There were censuses made during the last years of the colonial period that have information on heights, as well as military records of the early national period. To examine periods that go further back in time, there are samples of skeletal remains from which it is possible to estimate heights, as well as to portray "aspects of health over the life cycle, as opposed to the growing years."[4] Because modern Mexico was the core of Mesoamerica, there are a large number of skeletal remains to be studied to uncover the biological standards of living as far back as the precolonial era. Physical anthropologists have conducted extensive research on osteological evidence that has yet to be explained through the lens of anthropometric history and put to use in other disciplines.[5]

Third, as regards the post-1950 period, it is possible to work with more detailed data and with more accurate and sophisticated models. This is of the utmost importance in light of the fact that after 1950 Mexico transformed at an even faster pace while still carrying lags from the past. With extant information it is possible to build larger data sets with more detailed information; for example, information on weight is available for the post-1950 period. Examining the anthropometric history of this period will enable researchers to establish links between lags in social development and public health problems of the twenty-first century such as diabetes and obesity.

The purpose of this book has been to provide a national perspective on living standards using multidisciplinary tools. It was structured in such a way that it could be accessible to people in different disciplines. For historians of Mexico, I expect that this book can complement cultural history studies on the working classes. By offering an account of the material living conditions and their effects on the biological standards of living, it sheds light on another dimension of the life of the marginalized living in the period 1850–1950. *Measuring Up* shows that there are topics in which there can be a dialogue between cultural history and economic history. It also contributes to the field of Mexican economic history by studying a topic that has received little attention in recent scholarship.[6]

For social science historians interested in a macrolevel, long-term perspective, this book is a contribution designed to fill the void on studies concerning living standards prior to 1950. I contend that new methodologies available make it possible to examine the history of those who were not integrated into the formal economy. Anthropometric history is useful for assessing how the flaws in the process of economic modernization and growth coupled with piecemeal policies affected a large portion of the population. After all, the negative impact took its toll.

For economists and public policy makers, this book contributes to an understanding of the origins of poverty and inequality prior to the first measurement of income distribution in 1957 by demonstrating that history matters. The information it provides invites researchers to stop focusing exclusively on the examination of inputs—namely, the policies and the resources spent on allegedly improving living standards—and to begin to add balance to their analysis by examining the results of the implementation of such policies while assessing the efficiency with which resources were actually allocated.[7] In brief, this book seeks to convey a much-needed long-term perspective. *Measuring Up* shows that there *can* be a dialogue between historians and economists: historians can still write economic history books with findings that can be useful for economists and policy makers.[8]

This study in historical economics also aims to motivate researchers who design public policies intended to alleviate poverty. In addition to their skilled use of the basic postulates of modern economic theory, they can gain an appreciation that scholarly research in the social sciences can contribute to an understanding of the complex problem of poverty.[9] Indeed, the research and methods described in this book may have applications that go beyond the issue of poverty. Last, but not least, *Measuring Up* provides an explanation of how it was that Mexico got to the mid-twentieth century with such high levels of poverty and inequality. There is a need to raise awareness of how leaving social development at the bottom of the government's agenda created and can still create very critical lags. Over time, these lags accumulate and make problems of poverty grow larger, more complex, and more difficult to solve.

APPENDIX

TABLE A.1

Regression model for military samples: Dependent variable of height (cm)

Independent variables	FEDERAL TRUNCATION POINTS				RURAL TRUNCATION POINTS			
	159 cm (1a)	160 cm (1b)	159 cm (2a)	160 cm (2b)	159 cm (1a)	160 cm (1b)	159 cm (2a)	160 cm (2b)
Constant	167.6*	167.1*	168.0*	167.6*	170.5*	169.9*	168.4*	167.7*
OCCUPATION								
Unskilled					−1.21	−1.24	−1.21	−0.57
Skilled manual workers	0.7**	0.7**	0.4	0.5				
Skilled white-collar workers	1.1	0.9	1.1	0.8				
PROVENANCE								
North	—	—	—	—	—	—	—	—
Bajío	−1.2*	−1.2*	−1.4*	−1.4*	−0.46	−0.5	−0.43	−0.47
Center	−3.3*	−3.4*	−3.3*	−3.5*	−1.20	−1.42	−1.19	−1.40
South	−4.1*	−4.1*	−3.8*	−3.6	−2.43	−0.29	−0.24	−2.91
AGE								
18	−2.2*	−2.3*			−2.41	−2.47		
19	−2.1*	−2.4*			−1.21	−1.14		
20	−1.7*	−2.1*			−2.65	−2.74		
21	−0.9*	−0.8*			−2.12	−2.29		
22	−0.7**	−0.6			−1.67	−1.75		
BIRTH DECADE								
1850s					1.11	1.52	1.12	1.53
1860s					0.56	0.81	0.57	0.82
1870s					0.07	0.24	0.07	0.24
1880s	−0.1	0.2	−0.2	0.0	−0.93	−0.96	−0.89	−0.93
1890s	−0.2	0.2	−0.4	0.0	−1.60	−1.71	−1.62	−1.70
1900s	0.0	0.2	0.0	0.2				
1910s	−0.3	0.0	−1.0	−0.7				
1920s	−0.9	−0.2	−1.0	−0.3				
1930s	1.2	1.8**	−0.7	−0.3				
1940s	1.2	2.1**	1.6	1.8				
Deserters	−0.4**	−0.4	−0.6**	−0.5				
X^2					86.76	91.67	81.55	87.32
R^2	303.0	265.3	171.9	142.5				
N	5,176	4,976	3,309	3,194	6,129	6,027	4,495	4,412

* significant at the 1% level; ** significant at the 5% level

NOTES: The regressions were estimated with STATA's trunc reg routine (trun reg). Regressions 1 pertain to the whole population eighteen years and older, regressions 2 pertain to adults only. *Federales*: constants refer to adult illiterate, unskilled, nondeserter workers from Northern Mexico born between 1870 and 1879. *Rurales*: constants refer to adult skilled manual workers from Northern Mexico born between 1840 and 1849.

TABLE A.2
Regression model for passport samples

Independent variables	PASSPORT SAMPLES			
	Males (1a)	Females (1b)	Males (2a)	Females (2b)
OCCUPATION				
Unskilled	—	—	—	—
Skilled manual workers	0.93**	1.22*	0.84**	1.01*
Skilled white-collar workers	1.21**	0.62**	1.06**	0.41*
Elite	2.45*	1.32*	2.33	1.04*
PROVENANCE				
North	2.82*	2.53*	2.59*	2.32*
Bajío	2.11*	1.66*	2.04*	1.57
Center	1.37*	0.81**	1.18*	0.64
South	—	—	—	—
AGE				
18	—	—	—	—
19	−0.77	−0.51		
20	0.35	−0.67		
21	−0.15	−0.03		
22	0.47	0.10		
23 or more	0.54	−0.03		
BIRTH DECADE				
1870s	0.96	2.54**	0.95	2.59**
1880s	1.15	3.97*	1.14	4.01*
1890s	2.28**	4.85*	2.27*	4.89*
1900s	2.57**	5.16*	2.58*	5.23*
1910s	3.06*	5.13*	3.02*	5.15*
1920s	3.29*	5.62*	(dropped)	8.59
Constant	164.83*	153.50*	165.64*	153.76*
R^2	0.0235	0.0277	0.0229	0.0286
N	11390	5207	9693	4424

* significant at the 1% level: ** significant at the 5% level
NOTES: Method used is OLS. Constants refer to adult unskilled workers from Southern Mexico born between 1860 and 1869. Regressions 1 pertain to the whole population eighteen years and older, regressions 2 pertain to adults only.

TABLE A.3
Evolution of heights (cm): International comparison

Decade	Sweden	United States	France	The Netherlands	United Kingdom	Germany	Australia	Italy	Spain	Mexico
1800s	167.0	172.9			168.9					
1830s	167.9	173.5	164.1	166.5						
1840s	167.6	172.2	164.3	165.3						
1850s	168.2		164.5	164.2	168.2	162.6	172.7		162.1	167.8
1860s	169.5		164.6	164.0					161.7	167.4
1870s	170.2		165.1	164.8					161.1	166.9
1880s	170.9		165.2	165.7				162.7	160.8	166.1
1890s	172.3		165.3	166.8				163.1	162.6	164.3
1900s	172.5		165.5	167.8	169.3	169.0	170.9	163.8	163.5	163.6
1910s	172.9	172.9	166.0	168.7				164.1	163.8	165.1
1920s	174.1	173.5	166.5	169.9				164.7	164.7	163.8
1930s	175.2	172.2	166.0	171.9				166.0	164.4	164.2
1940s	176.1	172.9	166.5	173.4				167.2	164.4	165.3
1950s	177.9	173.5	168.8	174.1	174.1	176.3	173.8	167.4	166.7	166.0
1960s	179.1	172.2	170.3	176.0				170.0	162.1	

SOURCES: **Sweden:** Lars Sandberg and Richard Steckel, "Was Industrialization Hazardous to Your Health? Not in Sweden!" in Steckel and Floud (eds.), *Health and Welfare During Industrialization* (Chicago and London, 1997), 129 (recruitment years); **United States:** Dora L. Costa and Richard Steckel, "Long Term Trends in Health, Welfare and Economic Growth in the United States," in Steckel and Floud (eds.), *Health and Welfare*, 172 (birth cohorts); **France:** David R. Weir, "Economic Welfare and Physical Well-Being in France, 1750–1990" in Steckel and Floud (eds.), *Health and Welfare*, 191 (recruitment years); **The Netherlands:** "Paradoxes of Modernization and Material Well-Being in the Netherlands During the Nineteenth Century," J. W. Drukker and Vincent Tassenaar (1997, 357–59) (birth cohorts); **United Kingdom:** Steckel and Floud, *Health and Welfare*, chapter 11, 424; **Germany:** Steckel and Floud, *Health and Welfare*, chapter 11, 424; **Italy:** José Miguel Martínez-Carrión, "Estaturas, desigualdad regional y desarrollo económico en Italia y España durante el siglo XX," Mediterráneo e Historia Económica (Cajamar, 2005) (recruitment years); **Spain:** José Miguel Martínez-Carrión, "Estatura, salud y bienestar en las primeras etapas de crecimiento económico español: Una perspectiva comparada de los niveles de vida," Documento de Trabajo de la Asociación de Historia Económica, No. 0102 (Murcia, 2001) (recruitment years); **Mexico:** Data from 1850–1890 Rural Military Sample and 1900–1950 Federal Military Sample (birth cohorts).

Introduction

1. Diario Oficial de la Federación, Acuerdo de Creación de la Comisión del Programa Nacional de Solidaridad, 6/12/1988.

2. Asa Cristina Laurell, "Pronasol o la pobreza de los programas contra la pobreza," *Nueva Sociedad* 131 (May–June 1994): 162.

3. Alicia Hernández Chávez, *Mexico: A Brief History*, trans. Andy Klatt (Berkeley: University of California Press, 2006), 305.

4. Diario de Debates del Senado, 14 de diciembre 1937, in Moisés González Navarro, *La pobreza en México* (Mexico City: El Colegio de México, 1985), 193.

5. There is a debate with regard to when the Mexican Revolution ended; here I refer to the end of warfare and the drafting of the 1917 Constitution.

6. The origins of this traditional view can be traced back to the Bible.

7. Friedrich Katz, *The Secret War in Mexico: Europe, the United States and the Mexican Revolution* (Chicago: University of Chicago Press, 1981), chap. 1; Arturo Warman, *"We Come to Object": The Peasants of Morelos and the National State*, trans. Stephen K. Ault (Baltimore, MD: Johns Hopkins University Press, 1980), 106.

8. Friedrich Katz, "Labor Conditions on Haciendas in Porfirian Mexico: Some Trends and Tendencies," *Hispanic American Historical Review* 54, no. 1 (1974): 46.

9. Adolfo Gilly, *The Mexican Revolution* (New York: The New Press, 2005), 36.

10. Katz, *Secret War*, 8–9.

11. Jesús Silva Herzog, "Meditaciones sobre México: Ensayos y notas," *Cuadernos Americanos* 14 (1947): 25.

12. Luis González, "El liberalismo triunfante," in *Historia general de México*, ed. El Colegio de México (Mexico City: El Colegio de México, 2000), 683.

13. Gilly, *Mexican Revolution*, 19. "Land deprivations became particularly severe during the Porfiriato. Meanwhile, in the surrounding villages, the now landless peasants (turned wage laborers), and impoverished farmers eyed the hacendado's terrains in envy, anguish, and calculations" (David F. Ronfeldt,

"Atencingo and the Politics of Agrarian Structure" [PhD diss., Stanford University, 1971], 12). "From the villagers' point of view, work on the hacienda was always insecure. Sometimes there was work, and sometimes not; it could last six months or could end in a conflict" (Warman, *We Come to Object*, 74).

14. For an increase in prices of standard of foods of the working classes during the Porfiriato, see Marjorie Ruth Clark, *Organized Labor in Mexico* (Chapel Hill: University of North Carolina Press, 1934), 9–10.

15. Charles Cumberland, *Mexican Revolution, Genesis Under Madero* (Austin: University of Texas Press, 1952), 15.

16. Frank Tannenbaum, *The Mexican Agrarian Revolution* (1928; repr. Hamden, Archon Books, 1968), 144.

17. "According to good sources, during the colonial period and in years of good crops, a good crop of corn would sell for six *reales*, equivalent to 75 cents per hectoliter. The daily wage of an Indian then was twenty-five cents, his real wage in corn was thirty-three liters and thirty-three cents of a liter. In 1910 the mean price of corn was, in years of good crops in the production places, three pesos and fifty cents per hectoliter. The great majority of laborers earned thirty to thirty-seven and a half cents per working day, which made its real wage eight liters and fifty-seven cents of a liter" (Alfonso Teja Zabre, *Historia de México. Una moderna interpretación* [Mexico City: Imprenta de la Secretaría de Relaciones Exteriores, 1935], 357).

18. Friedrich Katz, "Liberal Republic and the Porfiriato," in *Mexico Since Independence*, ed. Leslie Bethell (Cambridge: Cambridge University Press, 1991), 111.

19. According to James Wilkie, "the Revolution's program of state directed integration of Mexican social and economic life has always been justified on the basis that it has given the poor classes a better standard of living" (*The Mexican Revolution: Federal Changes and Social Change Since 1910* [Berkeley: University of California Press, 1967], 20).

20. Alan Knight, *The Mexican Revolution*, vol. 2, *Counter-Revolution and Reconstruction* (Cambridge: Cambridge University Press, 1986), 518.

21. Alan Knight, "The Rise and Fall of Cardenismo, c. 1930–c. 1946," in *Mexico Since Independence*, ed. Leslie Bethell (Cambridge: Cambridge University Press, 1991), 264.

22. Wilkie's calculation of a poverty index in Mexico for 1910–1960 is an example of an ad hoc interpretation. The index uses such characteristics of poverty drawn from the population census as illiteracy, speak only an Indian language, live in a community with less than twenty-five hundred people, go barefoot, wear sandals, regularly eat tortillas instead of wheat bread, and absence of sewage disposal. They were given equal weight. Direct evidence on nutrition and health is absent from the index.

23. Daniel Cosío Villegas, "Mexico's Crisis." This essay was originally published in 1947, and it is included in translation in Gilbert Joseph and

Timothy Henderson, eds., *The Mexico Reader* (Durham, NC: Duke University Press, 2002), 470–81.

24. "For several reasons, some of which could not be considered as foreseeable and avoidable effects in the political economy, and others associated with trends and omissions of that policy, we have fallen into a notably unfavorable income distribution due to its trends and its current and potential implications on living standards and the country's economic development" (Fernando Rosenzweig, *El desarrollo económico de México, 1800–1910* [Mexico City: Colegio Mexiquense A.C.-ITAM, 1989], 132).

25. El Colegio de México, *Estadísticas históricas del Porfiriato: Fuerza de trabajo y actividades por sectores* (Mexico City: El Colegio de México, 1961).

26. John H. Coatsworth, *Los orígenes del atraso: Nueve ensayos de historia económica de México en los siglos XVIII y XIX* (Mexico City: Alianza Editorial, 1990), 177.

27. In the last footnote in his essay on food production, Coatsworth writes, "While it is true that *per capita* food production and beverages grew during the Porfiriato, it is important to note the possibility that there were changes in income distribution. . . . We cannot, however, exclude the possibility that part of the population earning lower incomes would have suffered a decline in its food consumption despite the increase in average production" (*Los orígenes del atraso*, 177).

28. Jeffrey L. Bortz, *Los salarios industriales en la ciudad de México, 1939–1975*, trans. Eduardo L. Suárez (Mexico City: Fondo de Cultura Económica, 1988), 270.

29. Jeffrey L. Bortz and Marco Aguila, "Earning a Living: A History of Real Wage Studies in Twentieth Century Mexico," *Latin American Research Review* 42, no. 2 (2006): 138.

30. Aurora Gómez-Galvarriato, "The Evolution of Prices and Real Wages in Mexico from the Porfiriato to the Revolution," in *Latin America and the World Economy Since 1800*, ed. John H. Coatsworth and Alan Taylor (Cambridge, MA: Harvard University Press, 1998), 351.

31. Mauricio Tenorio-Trillo and Aurora Gómez-Galvarriato, *El Porfiriato* (Mexico City: Centro de Investigación y Docencia Económicas/Fondo de Cultura Económica, 2006), 86.

32. Ibid.

33. John H. Coatsworth, "Structures, Endowments and Institutions in the Economic History of Latin America," *Latin American Research Review* 40, no. 3 (2005): 130.

34. As mentioned in note 5, for certain scholars, the revolution ended with the drafting of the 1917 Constitution; others claim it ended with the assassination of Álvaro Obregón in 1928 and Plutarco Elías Calles announcing the end of *caudillismo*; others argue that the revolution did not end until 1940.

35. Richard Easterlin, *The Reluctant Economist: Perspectives on Economics, Economic History, and Demography* (Cambridge: Cambridge University Press, 2004), 19.

36. This section draws heavily on material in Richard Steckel's "Stature and the Standard of Living," *Journal of Economic Literature* 33, no. 4 (December 1995): 1903.

37. Ibid., 1906.

38. Ibid., 1905.

39. Roderick Floud, "The Human Body in Britain," in *The Economic Future in Historical Perspective*, ed. Paul A. David and Mark Thomas (Oxford: Oxford University Press, 2006), 405.

40. Floud, "Human Body," 405.

41. Timothy Leunig and Hans-Joachim Voth, "Height and the High Life," in *The Economic Future in Historical Perspective*, ed. Paul A. David and Mark Thomas (Oxford: Oxford University Press, 2006), 431.

42. Ibid., 435.

43. Steckel, "Stature," 1909.

Section 1

1. González Navarro, *La pobreza*, 254.

Section 1, Chapter 1

1. "The hierarchy of human wants is well reflected in the employment structure and the allocation of hours of work in traditional societies. Food, clothing, shelter, and fuel were the basic necessities of life, the three last increasingly in relative importance with increasing distance from the equator" (E. A. Wrigley, *Poverty, Progress and Population* [Cambridge: Cambridge University Press, 2004], 213).

2. Adam Smith, *An Inquiry into the Nature and Causes of the Wealth of Nations* (Chicago: Cannan, 1976), I, 9, 10.

3. David Ricardo, *On the Principles of Political Economy and Taxation* (Cambridge: University Press of the Royal Economic Society, 1951), chap. 2.

4. "[I]t is only, then, because land is not unlimited in quantity and uniform in quality, and because in the progress of population, land of inferior quality, or less advantageously situated, is called into cultivation, that rent is ever paid for the use of it" (ibid).

5. T. R. Malthus, *An Essay on the Principle of Population; or, a View of Its Past and Present Effects on Human Happiness; with an Inquiry into Our Prospects Respecting the Future Removal or Mitigation of the Evils Which It Occasions*, selected and introduced by Donald Winch using the text of the 1803 edition as prepared by Patricia James for the Royal Economic Society, 1990, showing the

additions and corrections made in the 1806, 1807, 1817 and 1826 editions (Cambridge: Cambridge University Press, 1992).

6. Wrigley, *Poverty, Progress and Population*, chap. 1, 41.

7. Karl Marx, *Capital*, New World Edition, 10th ed. (New York: International Publishers Co., 1983), 1:239.

8. Unlike *poverty*, the term *marginalized* is of fairly recent mint, and it has been used to describe different social phenomena. For the purpose of this study, I will use the more economic definition, which describes the marginalized as those who have an unskilled manual job but lack social and economic security: more often than not these people are underemployed or unemployed.

9. E. P. Hennock, *The Origin of the Welfare State in England and Germany, 1850–1914: Social Policies Compared* (Cambridge: Cambridge University Press, 2007), 2.

10. "The general recognition that the community rather than the family ought to support its poorer members was not new in the sixteenth century" (Paul Slack, *The English Poor Law, 1531–1782,* New Studies in Economic and Social History [Cambridge: Cambridge University Press, 1991], 5–6).

11. Oscar Lewis, *Five Families: Mexican Case Studies in the Culture of Poverty* (New York: Basic Books, 1959), chap. 1; Lourdes Márquez Morfin, *La desigualdad ante la muerte en la ciudad de México: El tifo y el cólera (1813 y 1833)* (Mexico City: Editorial Siglo XXI, 1994), 89.

12. For a thorough description of the strategies of survival of Mexican extended families, see Larissa Adler de Lomnitz, *Cómo sobreviven los marginados.* 10th ed. (Mexico City: Editorial Siglo XXI, 1991), chap. 5.

13. "The data on the family are organized and presented under the headings of material culture, economic life, social relations, religious life, interpersonal relations, and so on. . . . Because decent housing is not available at reasonable rents, many people stay in their one-room apartments long after they are financially well off. Their little dwelling fills up with new furniture, china, TV sets, refrigerators, electric appliances, and even perhaps a washing machine, until there is hardly space for the family to move about" (Lewis, *Five Families*, 3–4, 11).

14. For the case of England, see Anthony Brundage, *The English Poor Laws, 1700–1939* (New York: Palgrave, 2002); Slack, *English Poor Law, 1531–1782*; for the case of the United States, see David Rosner, *A Once Charitable Enterprise: Hospitals and Health Care in Brooklyn and New York 1885–1915,* Interdisciplinary Perspectives in Modern History (Cambridge: Cambridge University Press, 1982), 22: "The importance of community support for small nineteenth-century hospitals cannot be stressed enough. In the absence of an organized set of public social services, and in a time before the notion of corporate responsibility for health care had developed, the community-supported charity hospitals were an indispensable resource for the community's dependent poor." For the case of Mexico, see Lewis, *Five Families.*

15. "Institutions exist to reduce the uncertainties involved in human inter-action. These uncertainties arise as a consequence of both the complexity of the problems to be solved and the problem-solving software (to use computer analogy) possessed by the individual. There is nothing in the above statement that implies that the institutions are efficient" (Douglass North, *Institutions, Institutional Change and Economic Performance* [Cambridge: Cambridge University Press, 1990], 25).

16. "Institutions provide the structure for exchange that (together with the technology employed) the cost of transacting and the cost of transforma-tion. How well institutions solve the problems of coordination and produc-tion is determined by the motivation of the players (their utility function), the complexity of the environment, and the ability of the players to decipher and order the environment (measurement of enforcement)" (ibid., 34).

17. This section is based on Brundage, *English Poor Laws, 1700–1939*; Slack, *English Poor Law, 1531–1782*.

18. "Up until the nineteenth century, the state and the market were two realities characterized by frequent confrontations in which the state attempted, successfully for the most part, to stop the market's moving impulses and to subdue it to its political and administrative ends" (Marcello Carmagnani, *Estado y mercado: La economía pública del liberalismo mexicano, 1850–1911* [Mexico City: Fondo de Cultura Económica, 1994], 355).

19. Title I, Section I, Article 4: "Being useful and honest, every man is free to embrace the profession, trade or job that suits him, and to appropriate its products. Either faculty cannot be impeded, except by a judicial sentence when it would attack the rights of a third party or by a gubernatorial sentence, dictated in terms marked by the law, when it offends the society"; see Felipe Tena Ramírez, *Leyes fundamentales de México, 1808–2005* (Mexico City: Editorial Porrúa, 2005), 607, 612.

20. See the following: Claudia Agostoni, *Monuments of Progress: Modernization and Public Health in Mexico City, 1876–1910* (Calgary: University of Calgary Press, 2003); Katherine Bliss, *Compromised Positions: Prostitution, Public Health and Gender Politics in Revolutionary Mexico City* (University Park: Pennsylvania State University Press, 2001); Ann S. Blum, *Domestic Economies: Families, Work, and Welfare in Mexico City, 1884–1943* (Lincoln: University of Nebraska Press, 2009); Pablo Piccato, *City of Suspects: Crime in Mexico City, 1900–1931* (Durham, NC: Duke University Press, 2001), Elisa Speckman Guerra, *Crimen y castigo: Legislación penal, interpretaciones de la criminalidad y administración de justicia (ciudad de México, 1872–1910)* (Mexico City: El Colegio de México/Universidad Nacional Autónoma de México, 2002).

21. González Navarro, *La pobreza*, 49–50.

22. "The appeal to public assistance or private welfare went against the ethical sense of the workers, who felt unjustly humiliated. . . . Workers were aware that they did not need to be forced to appeal to public or private

charity as if they were people who by their own volition or due to a physical impediment would never have worked" (Mario de la Cueva, *El nuevo derecho del trabajo mexicano* [Mexico City: Editorial Porrúa, 1983], I:16).

23. Jesús Silva Herzog, *El pensamiento económico, social y político de México, 1810–1964* (Mexico City: Instituto Mexicano de Investigaciones Económicas, 1967), 167, 214, 239, 259, 296.

24. Jean Meyer, *La Cristiada*, vol. 2, *El conflicto éntre la iglesia y el estado, 1926–1929*, 19th ed. (Mexico City: Editorial Siglo XXI, 2005), 49; Paul V. Murray, *The Catholic Church in Mexico: Historical Essays for the General Reader* (Mexico City: Editorial E. P. M., 1965), 1:337.

25. Meyer, *La Cristiada*, 52; Murray, *Catholic Church*, 345.

26. Meyer, *La Cristiada*, 49.

27. Ibid., 50.

28. "Trinidad Sánchez Santos . . . wrote that the Indian suffered the misery of rags for clothes, the troglodyte's home and the nourishment of a quasi stable, because the hacienda could not pay him more than twenty-five cents per working day" (González Navarro, *La pobreza*, 27); see also Trinidad Sánchez Santos, *Obras selectas* (Puebla: Linotipografía, 1945), 1:104.

29. Sánchez Santos, *Obras*, 92.

30. Ibid., 99.

31. William J. Suárez-Potts, "The Making of Labor Law in Mexico, 1875–1931" (PhD diss., Harvard University, 2005), 123.

32. Ibid., 125.

33. "Thus Antonio Ramos Pedrueza, a lawyer and deputy in the lower congressional house in 1901, criticized government notions of freedom of labor that tolerated the exploitation and abuse of workers" (ibid.).

34. Juan Carlos Moreno-Brid and Jaime Ros, *Development and Growth in the Mexican Economy: A Historical Perspective* (Oxford: Oxford University Press, 2009), 64; Donald B. Keesing, "Structural Change in Early Development: Mexico's Changing Industrial and Occupational Structures from 1895 to 1950," *Journal of Economic History* 29, no. 4 (1969): 723.

35. Alex Segura-Ubiergo, *The Political Economy of the Welfare State in Latin America: Globalization, Democracy and Development* (Cambridge: Cambridge University Press, 2007), 260–61.

Section 1, Chapter 2

1. "In defense of the property rights of the church, Munguía opposed the Lerdo Law because the church was the 'only mother of the poor,' in contrast to the 'hypocritical and hateful empty talk of philanthropists and progressives' because only the church has given alms a code and has turned the poor into natural born individuals beholden to the priests of that part of their rents left after they had paid for their subsistence" (González Navarro, *La pobreza*, 56).

2. "The best way to prove the influence of the Church in New Spain is by using proof of the opposite: the proof that the amazing stability of power, three times secular, of Spain in Mexico rested in good part on the Church. It is the antagonistic policy of the Bourbons that is one of the essential factors if one wants to understand the spreading of the war of independence. By alienating the support of the clergy and the people, and by uniting its cause to that of ecclesiastic immunity with Mexican independence, the power of the crown destroyed its foundations" (Meyer, *La Cristiada*, 2:10).

3. González Navarro, *La pobreza*, 57.

4. Tena Ramírez, *Leyes fundamentales de México*, 665.

5. Jan Bazant, *Los bienes de la Iglesia en México, 1856–1875: Aspectos económicos y sociales de la revolución liberal*, 2nd ed. (Mexico City: Colegio de México, 1995), 220.

6. "The weak point of the secularization of welfare institutions was that its assets now belonged to the government, which, in case of need, could make use of them. In fact that is what happened after May 5, 1862. . . . The national emergency forced the government to sell cheaper" (ibid., 227).

7. Arrom's work on the Mexico City Poor House provides a thorough review of welfare policies in Mexico in the period 1774–1871, and it documents the history of this unique institution in the history of Mexico; see Arrom, *Containing the Poor*.

8. "The utopianism of its founders soon gave way to the realization that it was far easier to provide lodging, food, and medical care than to reform adults" (ibid., 279).

9. Bazant, *Bienes de la Iglesia*, 230.

10. Ibid., 221.

11. The *Memorias* published in 1871 is a good example of the influence of religion in the services provided by this institution; see *Memoria de las obras de las conferencias de la Sociedad de San Vicente de Paul, dependientes del Consejo Superior de la República Mexicana durante el año de 1871* (Mexico City: Imprenta de la V. é Hijos de Murguía, 1871).

12. The Junta was created to issue guidelines for the material and moral improvement of the needy and to expand educational services as well as to determine how to make the best use of vacant lands to foster the colonization of the central part of the country; see *Decretos y reglamentos a que se refiere el estatuto provisional del Imperio Mexicano* (Mexico City: Imprenta de Andrade y Escalante, 1865), 103–4.

13. José María Andrade, *Informe sobre los establecimientos de beneficencias y corrección de esta capital*, escrito póstumo de Don Joaquín García Icazbalceta (Mexico City: Moderna Librería Religiosa, 1907). Interestingly, although written in the 1860s this report was not published until 1907.

14. Ibid., 215.

15. Ibid., 226–37.

16. "The 'Porfirian pax' was useful for the Church, that put in place at that time a true Reconquest. . . . Especially after 1860, the Mexican Church returned to the people, that had endured sixty years of revolutions and wars, and to the countryside, that had been neglected for the most part" (Meyer, *La Cristiada*, 2:45).

17. González Navarro, *Porfiriato: Vida social*. In *Historia moderna de México*, 2nd ed., edited by Daniel Cosío Villegas (Mexico City: Editorial Hermes, 1970), 4:499.

18. González Navarro, *La pobreza*, 101.

19. Ibid., 199.

20. In the mid-1940s, Miguel Alessio Robles published a historical overview of philanthropic institutions published in 1907. It suggests that there was continuity in the number and operation of private welfare institutions. In the mid-1980s Moisés González Navarro published a book on poverty in Mexico. In it he argues that private welfare institutions functioned during the end of the nineteenth century and well into the twentieth century unrelated to political events or the government's revolutionary goals. Interestingly, it is the same assertion Arrom makes with regard to the existence of the Mexico City Poor House a century earlier. Miguel Alessio Robles, *La filantropía en México* (Mexico City: Editorial Botas, 1944); González Navarro, *La pobreza*; Silvia Marina Arrom, *Containing the Poor: The Mexico City Poor House, 1774–1871* (Durham, NC: Duke University Press, 2000).

21. González Navarro, *La pobreza*, 254.

Section 1, Chapter 3

1. Sandra Kuntz Ficker, ed. *Historia económica general de México: De la colonia hasta nuestros días* (Mexico City: Colegio de México/Secretaría de Economía/Comisión Organizadora de las Celebraciones del Bicentenario, 2010), 314.

2. Article 3: "Education is free. The law will determine which professions will require a license to allow its practice and what the requirements are to obtain such a license" (Tena Ramírez, *Leyes fundamentales de México*, 607).

3. "Provisional Statute of the Mexican Empire. Title XV. Individual Guarantees. Article 69. No one can be obliged to render personal services, just temporarily and for a determined enterprise. Minors cannot do so without their parent's or guardian's intervention, and, if they have none, by intervention of political authority" (Tena Ramírez, *Leyes fundamentales de México*, 669).

4. González Navarro, *La pobreza*, 124–30.

5. For example, Carmen Romero Rubio, Porfirio Díaz's wife, sponsored the Fraternal de Costureras (Mutual Aid Society for Seamstresses) for women

who were mainly widows or orphans of the middle class. Her brother, Manuel Romero Rubio, was head of several *mutualistas*. Other *mutualistas* were organized by the Catholic Church as part of their social justice agenda (ibid., 128).

6. Ibid., 352.

7. Hennock, *Origin of the Welfare State*, 332.

8. González Navarro, *La pobreza*, 105.

9. González Navarro, *Porfiriato*, 511.

10. "Twenty years after Guillermo Prieto emphasized the importance of political economy for law and workers' rights, Emilio Pardo Jr. contended it was a monstrous error to legislate on behalf of workers social and labor regulations that countered natural laws of political economy" (Suárez-Potts, "Making of Labor Law," 109).

11. Keesing, "Structural Change in Early Development," 723.

12. Ibid., 737.

13. I will discuss this particular topic further in the chapter devoted to health.

14. "In 1912, several deputies supported M. Laison Banuet's initiative that any factory that employed more than 25 women would establish a nursery in the owner's charge, in which women could leave, as well as breastfeed, their children" (González Navarro, *La pobreza*, 155).

15. Ibid., 148–49.

16. Hernández Chávez, *Mexico: A Brief History*, 228.

17. "Hunger attacked the entire nation; some local authorities tried to solve the problem by distributing free cereals and other foodstuffs to the needy or by selling food at low prices: a liter of corn at 6 cents and 8 in Oaxaca" (González Navarro, *La pobreza*, 159).

18. Hernández Chávez, *Mexico: A Brief History*, 235; Robert McCaa, "The Peopling of Mexico from Origins to Revolution," in *The Population History of North America*, ed. Michael R. Haines and Richard H. Steckel (Cambridge: Cambridge University Press, 2000), 293.

19. Gilly, *Mexican Revolution*, 232.

20. Hernández Chávez, *Mexico*, 233.

21. Gilly, *Mexican Revolution*, 238–39.

22. Ibid., 238.

23. Ronald M. Schneider, *Latin American Political History: Patterns and Personalities* (Boulder, CO: Westview Press, 2006), 10–11.

24. Gilly, *Mexican Revolution*, 232.

25. Ibid., 238.

26. "There is a great variation among Latin American countries with respect to the timing and subsequent expansion of their welfare system. . . . A second group of countries followed suit in the late 1930s and 1940s (i.e., Colombia, Costa Rica, Mexico, Paraguay, Peru, Venezuela, and Panama)" (Segura-Ubiergo, *Political Economy of the Welfare State*, 27).

27. Segura-Ubiergo, *Political Economy of the Welfare State*, 33.

28. Hernández Chávez, *Mexico*, 240.

29. Other provisions included making employers responsible for work-related accidents and occupational illnesses; see Suárez-Potts, "Making of Labor Law," 172.

30. "The paper 'Eugenic Heritage and Mexico's Future' presented by Dr. Antonio F. Alonso of the Mexican Society of Biology, shows to what extent positivism persisted, at least in those circles. . . . As in previous years scientists had pontificated, Alonso—based on Darwin and Lamarck—argued that the world owed more to Whites than to others. Mexico should therefore favor the migration of Whites to promote 'miscegenation favorable to our race. . . . In contrast unions with people of yellow and black racial origins should be avoided'" (González Navarro, *La pobreza*, 188).

31. Ibid., 190.

32. Ibid., 193.

33. Ibid., 199.

34. The government had a Departamento de Pensiones (Pensions Department) since 1925; in 1955 it became the ISSSTE.

35. González Navarro, *La pobreza*, 378.

Section 2, Chapter 1

1. John H. Coatsworth, "Welfare," *American Historical Review* 101, no. 1 (1996): 3.

2. "Although economists recognize the magnificent achievements of the national accounts, research momentum has shifted to alternatives or supplements that address shortcomings in GNP as a welfare measure or that indicate living standards in time periods or among groups for which conventional measures cannot be calculated. Stature is an example now used extensively in the fields of economic history and economic development" (Steckel, "Stature and the Standard of Living," 1903).

3. See Joel Mokyr and Cormac O'Gráda, "Poor Getting Poorer? Living Standards in Ireland Before the Famine," *Economic History Review* 41, no. 2 (1988): 211; John Komlos, "Stature and Nutrition in the Habsburg Monarchy: The Standard of Living and Economic Development," *American Historical Review* 90, no. 5 (December 1985): 1153.

4. Mokyr and O'Gráda, "Poor Getting Poorer," 230; Stephen Nicholas and Richard H. Steckel, "Tall but Poor: Nutrition, Health and Living Standards in Pre-Famine Ireland" (NBER Historical Working Paper No. 39, [August 1992], 14).

5. For a good example of these kinds of data, see the *Encuesta de ingresos y gastos de los hogares*, published in 1994 by INEGI.

6. See Bortz, *Los salarios industriales*; Gómez Galvarriato, "Evolution of Prices"; Bortz and Aguila, "Earning a Living."

7. M. O. Lorenz (1905) invented the Lorenz curve. The Gini coefficient is named after its inventor, Corrado Gini (1936). The Lorenz curve examines the shares of the total income accruing to specific income groups. To construct a Lorenz curve we need to draw a square whose dimensions represent the total income of this society (100 percent of the families and the income in the economy). The horizontal line measures the sum of the percentages of all families starting from the poorest. The vertical line measures the sum of the shares of income received by these households. A point within the square represents each observation (e.g., each family). The line that connects every point gives the Lorenz curve. There are two basic features of the Lorenz curve. First, it begins at zero and ends up at the upper-right corner; this is following the logic that zero people have zero income and the total of the households receive all available income. Second, in a perfectly equal world, all the data points in the square would make a perfectly diagonal straight line. This means that the poorest 20 percent of the households receive 20 percent of the income, the poorest 40 percent of the households receive 40 percent of the income, and so on. The further the Lorenz curve deviates from a perfect diagonal straight line, the more unequal the distribution of income.

The Gini coefficient is the area between the Lorenz curve and the diagonal. In a perfectly equal society the Gini coefficient would be zero. This means that the more unequal the society, the larger the Gini coefficient. The Gini coefficient is thus a summary measure of inequality.

8. Rosenzweig Hernández, *El desarrollo económico de México*, 132.

9. Before the introduction of vaccines, infant mortality used to be very high everywhere. Nowadays, infant mortality is a feature that divides developed from developing and less developed countries.

10. "Since 1900, a revolution has occurred in human childbearing. Today throughout much of the world, parents deliberately limit their fertility, and the average number of births per women over the reproductive career is approaching two or less. Before then, and throughout most of human history, parents typically did nothing intentionally to restrict fertility, and women averaged six births or more" (Easterlin, *Reluctant Economist*, 166).

11. McCaa, "Peopling of Mexico," 241, 295.

12. Robert William Fogel, "Economic Growth, Population Theory and Physiology: The Bearing of Long-Term Processes on the Making of Economic Policy" (National Bureau of Economic Research, Working Paper No. 4638, February 1994), 25.

13. Timothy Cuff, *The Hidden Cost of Economic Development: The Biological Standard of Living in Antebellum Pennsylvania* (Burlington, VT: Ashgate Publishing Company, 2004), 10–11; Kenneth Sokoloff, "The Heights of Americans in Three Centuries: Some Economic and Demographic Implications," in *The Biological Standard of Living on Three Continents: Further Explo-*

rations in Anthropometric History, ed. John Komlos (Boulder, CO: Westview Press, 1995), 134.

14. Roderick Floud, Kenneth Watcher, and Annabel Gregory, *Height, Health and History: Nutritional Status in the United Kingdom, 1750–1980* (Cambridge: Cambridge University Press, 1990), 163.

15. Richard H. Steckel, "Height and Per Capita Income," *Historical Methods* 16, no. 1 (Winter 1983): 1; Steckel, "Stature and the Standard of Living," 1904.

16. Cuff, *Hidden Cost*, 29.

17. Kenneth Sokoloff and Georgia Villaflor, "The Early Achievement of Modern Stature in America," *Social Science History* 6, no. 4 (Autumn 1982): 461.

18. Cuff, *Hidden Cost*, 23.

19. See H. T. Waaler, "Height, Weight and Mortality: The Norwegian Experience," *Acta Medica Scandinavica* 679 (1984): S1–S56.

20. Komlos, "Stature and Nutrition," 1153.

21. See Coatsworth, *Los orígenes del atraso*, chaps. 4 and 5.

22. Komlos, "Stature and Nutrition," 1151; Komlos, "Shrinking in a Growing Economy? The Mystery of Physical Stature During the Industrial Revolution," *Journal of Economic History* 58, no. 3 (September 1998): 780.

23. El Colegio de México, *Estadísticas históricas del Porfiriato*.

24. See Bortz, *Los salarios industriales*, chap. 1.

25. See Peter H. Lindert and Jeffrey G. Williamson, "English Workers' Living Standards During the Industrial Revolution: A New Look," *Economic History Review* 36, no. 1 (February 1983): 1–25; Mokyr and O'Gráda, "Poor Getting Poorer," 211.

26. Komlos, "Shrinking," 794.

27. Bortz, *Los salarios industriales*; Gómez Galvarriato, "Evolution of Prices"; Hernández Chávez, *Mexico*, 260.

28. Aurora Gómez-Galvarriato and Aldo Mussachio, "Un nuevo índice de precios para México 1886–1929" (Working Paper CIDE, No. 113, 1998).

29. "Because the makings of good rates for Colonial Mexico, primarily denominators, much of its demographic history remains unknown and unknowable. Only where registration is relatively accurate, and reliable population censuses are available can series of baptisms and burials be converted into birth and death rates. Everywhere in Colonial Mexico many deaths went unrecorded" (McCaa, "Peopling of Mexico," 268–69).

30. The records of the officers are located in the Archivo Histórico with the same logic as the other divisions. I worked for several weeks in the Archivo Histórico, and I found that for each officer where records contained height information, I had to go through approximately fifty files that did not have it. I then decided this was not the best source for constructing a sample of the heights of the better-off strata of the population, for it could have taken me two years to construct a two-hundred-soldier sample. I left the search for

a sample of the height of the upper strata of the population to the passport records that I will discuss later in this chapter.

31. Secretaría de la Defensa Nacional, *Memoria de la Secretaría de Guerra y Marina, 1896–1899*, vol. 1.

32. From the records I reviewed, it is not clear how important the minimum HR was to the Mexican military. At least for the period of this study I did not find any record of soldiers rejected for not meeting the minimum height.

33. It was not until 1856 that the government created the General Directorate of Weights and Measurements (Dirección General de Pesos y Medidas), and until 1884 that a decree was issued on the exclusive use of the metric system. Patricia Galeana, *Los siglos de México* (Mexico City: Nueva Imagen, 1991), 245.

34. This phenomenon is very common even today.

35. "Illiteracy in 1921 was 72 percent; in 1934 it was still 62 percent" (Jean Meyer, "Mexico in the 1920s," in *Mexico Since Independence*, ed. Leslie Bethell [Cambridge: Cambridge University Press, 1990], 208).

36. Cancelados included soldiers recruited throughout the whole twentieth century.

37. Fluctuations in recruitment I found were consistent with those described by Paul Vanderwood in his study on the *rurales*; see Paul Vanderwood, *Disorder and Progress: Bandits, Police and Mexican Development* (Lincoln: University of Nebraska Press, 1981), 49.

38. I should point out that I reviewed 90 percent of the files in the Personal Extinto section; not all the files had information on heights of the twenty-five hundred mentioned.

39. Official documents in Mexico did not start recording weight until well into the twentieth century.

40. This is how we have a record of Valentina Abitia, one of the legendary *soldaderas* who did exist and was one of the first if not the first female nurse in Mexico.

41. Historically there was an incentive to not being classified as Indian. In the colonial period Indians had to pay tribute whereas mestizos did not. By the eighteenth century, still in the colonial period, it was already very hard to differentiate them, in part because people moved from their hometowns more frequently.

42. Between 1821 and 1857 there were forty-four changes of government and three foreign invasions.

43. "Kidnappings were not in any way limited to the countryside. The bandits also braved Mexico City" (Vanderwood, *Disorder and Progress*, 48).

44. "The plan called for the creation of four corps of rural policemen, each with its commander, paymaster, 18 officers and 255 enlisted men" (ibid., 49).

45. Ibid.

46. Ibid., 53.

47. "Díaz invested 55 percent of Mexico's revenue in military and police services, and another 30 percent to maintain a contented bureaucracy. . . .

Díaz made them loyal to him by setting very strict examples of political discipline" (ibid., 68).

48. Ibid., 176.

49. In order to build this sample, we reviewed all boxes that contained the recruitment files and muster rolls. There were recruitment files in approximately 60 percent of the boxes. Seventy percent of the recruitment files corresponded to soldiers twenty-three years and older. Most of the recruits were born between 1860 and 1890.

50. Vanderwood, *Disorder and Progress*, 121–23.

51. Ibid., 108.

52. Ibid., 109.

53. "Captured deserters ended up with an army battalion in the hellholes of Veracruz and Yucatán but most who deserted were never captured or even pursued" (ibid.).

54. "By 1880 he (the president) had expanded the force by 90 percent to 1,767 men" (ibid., 70).

55. Ibid., 118.

56. Ibid., 107.

57. Ibid., 125.

58. Ibid., 113.

59. The sample stops in 1942 because in November 2002 this archive was closed to the public under the new transparency law that protects the privacy of Mexican citizens. After this date the archives can only be consulted with a judicial order.

60. Adolfo Chávez et al., *La nutrición en México y la transición epidemiológica* (Mexico City: Instituto Nacional de Nutrición Salvador Zubirán, 1993).

61. Ethnic diversity in Mexico is well documented by research in the field of anthropology. Since the mid-twentieth century there has been a school of physical anthropologists that have studied the ethnic diversity of the Mexican population from pre-Columbian times to the present. These works are published by the INAH and the Escuela Nacional de Antropología e Historia (ENAH).

62. John H. Coatsworth, "Indispensable Railroads in a Backward Economy: The Case of Mexico," *Journal of Economic History* 39, no. 4 (December 1979): 954.

63. Edward Beatty, *Institutions and Investment: The Political Basis of Industrialization in Mexico Before 1911* (Stanford, CA: Stanford University Press, 2001), 43.

64. "Railroads favored the growth of certain regions and the extraction of minerals that without them would not have been income-producing; they also contributed to a certain extent to the internal circulation of cargo and the linkage to local productive processes" (Sandra Kuntz Ficker, *Empresa extranjera y mercado interno, El ferrocarril central mexicano, 1880–1907* [Mexico City: El Colegio de México, 1995], 356).

65. Barry Bogin, *Patterns in Human Growth* (Cambridge: Cambridge University Press, 1999), 30.

66. John Komlos, "How to (and How Not to) Analyze Deficient Height Samples: An Introduction," *Historical Methods* 37, no. 4 (Fall 2004): 161.

67. This is one of the most standard regional classifications of the country; others are north, center, and south. Due to the demographic distribution of the population and to balance the size of each subsample, I decided to use the division into four regions.

68. INEGI, *Estadísticas históricas de México.*

69. Following Tanner's findings that adult growth is not reached before age twenty-three. "In historical populations, those who were older than 23 had reached their final height and can therefore be considered adults. One should analyze the height distributions of younger soldiers separately, because the time during which their growth could be influenced by environmental circumstances is not perfectly coincident with those of adults" (Komlos, "How To," 163).

70. "The normality of adult heights is a commonplace of contemporary public health" (Kenneth Watcher and James Trussell, "Estimating Historical Heights," *Journal of the American Statistical Association* 77, no. 378 [June 1982]: 280); see also Floud, Watcher, and Gregory, *Height, Health and History*, 13.

71. Phyllis B. Eveleth and James M. Tanner, *Worldwide Variation in Human Growth*, 2nd ed. (Cambridge: Cambridge University Press, 1990), 1; Floud, Watcher, and Gregory, *Height, Health and History*, 13.

72. Some literature on the revolution gives anecdotal evidence of the allure of going with the crowd (*irse con la bola*).

73. The deserters section of the military archives is the largest one. While working in this section, I was able to note that deserters were rarely caught.

74. I constructed my sample from those files that had information on heights; sometimes these files did not have information on literacy. Graph 3.7 was constructed with those files for which there was information on literacy; thus, it does not cover the entire sample from the military.

75. Rosemary Thorp, *Progress, Poverty and Exclusion: An Economic History of Latin America in the 20th Century* (Washington, DC: Johns Hopkins University Press/Inter-American Development Bank, 1998), 37.

76. Steckel and Floud, *Health and Welfare*, 428.

77. As we explained earlier, there is an undercount of northerners in the passport sample due to the nature of the sources.

Section 2, Chapter 2

1. A. Theodore Steegman Jr. and P. A. Haseley, "Stature Variation in the British American Colonies: French and Indian War Records, 1755–1763," *American Journal of Physical Anthropology* 75, no. 3 (March 1988): 414.

2. "The fastest growth in stature among Spaniards during the second half of the twentieth century was due to environmental, economic, and social improvements, perhaps more intense starting in the 1960s, and due to the fact that they started out with very low standards of living caused by losses suffered by generations that lived during the Spanish Civil War and the postwar period" (Martínez Carrión, "Estaturas," 7).

3. "The Great Montezuma was about forty years old, of good height, well proportioned, spare and slight, and not very dark, though of the usual Indian complexion" (Bernal Díaz del Castillo, *The Conquest of New Spain*, trans. J. M. Cohen [London: Penguin Books, 1963], 224).

4. Robert McCaa et al., "Health and Nutrition in Prehispanic Mesoamerica," in *The Backbone f History: Health and Nutrition in the Western Hemisphere*, ed. Richard H. Steckel and Jerone C. Rose (Cambridge: Cambridge University Press, 2002), 321; Moramay López-Alonso, Lourdes Márquez Morfin, and Laura Gómez Santana, "Living Standards in Pre-Industrial Mexico" (paper presented at the "Biological Welfare and Inequality in Pre-Industrial Times: A Political Economy Workshop," Yale University, 2005).

5. Fanny Calderón de la Barca, *Life in Mexico* (Berkeley: University of California Press, 1982), 54.

6. "Growth is a product of the continuous and complex interaction of heredity and environment" (James M. Tanner, *Foetus into Man, Physical Growth from Conception to Maturity* [Cambridge, MA: Harvard University Press, 1978], 117); "Two fenotypes which produce the same adult height under optimal environmental circumstances may produce different heights under circumstances of privation. . . . Statements about the relative contribution of heredity and environment to adult size and shape must therefore always specify the circumstances with some exactness" (Eveleth and Tanner, *Worldwide Variation*, 176).

7. Floud, Watcher, and Gregory, *Height, Health and History*, 163–75.

8. Steckel, "Stature and the Standard of Living," 1916; Komlos, "Shrinking," 794.

9. "The interest generated by the anthropometric research program since the pioneering publications of the late 1970s has been predicated to a considerable degree on the discovery of previously unknown cycles in human physical stature since the Industrial Revolution in both Europe and North America. . . . That Europeans were not exempt from such anthropometric cycles was discovered two years later" (Komlos, "Shrinking," 779). The case of Sweden is an exception to this rule. But then the timing was different. See Sandberg, "Was Industrialization Hazardous."

10. González Navarro, *La pobreza*, 188.

11. "Newcomers to the idea that stature measures important aspects of the standard of living should not be sidetracked by genetic issues. Genes are important determinants of individual height, but genetic differences approximately cancel in comparisons of averages across most populations, and in these

situations heights accurately reflect health status" (Steckel, "Stature and the Standard of Living," 1903). "Statements such as 'Height is an inherited characteristic' or 'Intelligence is a product of social forces' (or vice versa of course) are intellectual rubbish to be consigned to the trash can of propaganda" (Tanner, *Foetus*, 109).

12. This section is based on Tanner, *Foetus*; Steckel, "Stature and the Standard of Living"; and Komlos, "Shrinking."

13. "The infancy stage occupies the first three years of human postnatal life. Infancy is characterized by the most rapid velocity of growth of any of the postnatal stages. . . . The transition from the juvenile to the adolescent stage of growth and development is signaled in the rate of growth, from deceleration to acceleration" (Barry Bogin, *The Growth of Humanity* [New York: Wiley-Liss, 2001], 77, 87).

14. McCaa, "Peopling of Mexico," 241, 295.

15. "The newer biocultural model posits that there is recurring interaction between human biology and the sociocultural environment. Not only does the latter influence the former, but human biological variation modifies social and cultural processes as well. It is now understood, for example, that environmental forces, including the social, economic, and political environment, regulate the expression of DNA as much, or more so, than DNA regulates human biology" (Bogin, *Growth of Humanity*, 15).

16. All these tests will be done with regression analysis techniques. The Appendix will cover the more technical aspects of regression analysis methodology as well as calculations. The accuracy of the analysis corresponds to the quality of the data, as all anthropometric history literature explains; there will always be inaccuracies in the estimations due to data quality when compared to studies of the contemporary period. Notwithstanding, it has to be kept in mind that this is a common risk in all historical research. By determining the extent and direction of the biases inherent in the data by the use of standard techniques we can reach a higher level of accuracy.

17. Anthropometric history literature defines a "secular trend" in heights as an increasing trend in average heights over time during periods of economic growth.

18. Most of the anecdotal evidence on the living standards of the working classes during this time period constantly refers to alcoholism as one of the main problems of this segment of society.

19. I decided to use this division based on the population distribution across the national territory.

20. R. Douglas Cope, *The Limits of Racial Domination: Plebeian Society in Colonial Mexico City, 1660–1720* (Madison: University of Wisconsin Press, 1994), 161.

21. Eveleth and Tanner, *Worldwide Variation*, 179.

22. Komlos, "How To," 165.

23. Vanderwood, *Disorder and Progress*, 108–9.

24. Keesing, "Structural Change in Early Development," 723.

25. Alan Knight, *The Mexican Revolution*, vol. 1, *Porfirians, Liberals and Peasants* (Cambridge: Cambridge University Press, 1986), 79–80.

26. "Although information about these postindependence agrarian transformations remains limited, it appears that social changes after 1821 often benefited rancheros and the agrarian poor at the expense of the struggling elite. The years following independence brought economic decline to landed power holders and an expansion of peasant and ranchero production" (John Tutino, *From Insurrection to Revolution, Social Bases of Agrarian Violence, 1750–1940* [Princeton, NJ: Princeton University Press, 1988], 228–29).

27. Vanderwood, *Disorder and Progress*, 108.

28. Richard Salvucci, "Mexican National Income in the Independent Era, 1800–40," in *How Latin America Fell Behind: Essays on the Economic Histories of Mexico and Brazil*, ed. Stephen Haber (Stanford, CA: Stanford University Press, 1997), 223.

29. "Liberal leaders appeared more concerned with mobilizing community properties than with insuring that the villages obtained payments owed to them. The resulting loss of community wealth no doubt confirmed many villagers' opposition to the privatization program" (Tutino, *From Insurrection*, 272).

30. "Many villagers remained determined, and often violent, opponents throughout the years after independence. Ultimately they did not object to owning the subsistence plots they had long cultivated. But they resented deeply the loss of village pastures and woodlands. And they objected strongly to the alienation of community income properties—the bases of local government and religious life" (ibid., 274).

31. Justo Sierra, *The Political Evolution of the Mexican People*, trans. Charlen Ramsdell (Austin: University of Texas Press, 1969), 367–68.

32. Steckel, "Stature and the Standard of Living"; Komlos, "Shrinking."

33. See Enrique Krauze, *Biography of Power: A History of Modern Mexico, 1810–1996* (New York: HarperCollins Publishers, 1997), 343.

34. Let us not forget that there is an undercount of people from border states in this sample.

35. Bogin, *Growth of Humanity*, 131.

36. J. M. Prince and Richard H. Steckel, "Tallest in the World: Native Americans of the Great Plains in Nineteenth Century" (National Bureau of Economic Research Working Paper Series, Historical Paper No. 112, 1998), 10.

37. Tanner, *Foetus*, 166.

38. "Obregón instituted educational and cultural policies to channel the energy unleashed by ten years of revolution. The Department of Public Education was established and charged with enormous tasks in a country 72 percent illiterate" (Hernández Chávez, *Mexico*, 240).

39. Héctor Aguilar Camín and Lorenzo Meyer, *A la sombra de la Revolución Mexicana* (Mexico City: Editorial Cal y Arena, 2008), 89; Hernández Chávez, *Mexico*, 266.

40. "Hygienic education was promoted in books, magazines, fliers, and through free public and popular conferences, and certain reputable doctors and hygienists wrote about medical practice or domestic hygiene in books in which they gave detailed information of what every member of society would have to do to preserve health and prevent diseases. According to the medical profession, women were natural allies to the hygienist's endeavors, mothers in particular since they had the mission of motherhood and children's education" (Claudia Agostoni, "Discurso médico, cultura higiénica y la mujer en la ciudad de México al cambio del siglo [XIX–XX]," *Mexican Studies/Estudios Mexicanos* 18, no. 1 [2002]: 22).

41. Steckel, "Stature and the Standard of Living," 1909.

42. This gap in heights between Mexicans and Spaniards grew larger over the second half of the twentieth century.

43. Steckel and Floud, *Health and Welfare*, 427.

44. Ibid., 425.

45. Hennock, *Origin of the Welfare State*, 338.

46. Coatsworth and Tortella Casares, "Instituciones y desempeño económico," 47; Moramay López-Alonso, "La alfabetización en el crecimiento económico de México (1930–1970)" (Tesis de Licenciatura, Mexico City, ITAM, 1994), 151–52.

47. Steckel, "Percentiles of Modern Height Standards," 157.

48. Ibid., 158.

49. "The Mexican Family Survey 2002 (MxFLS-1), a multipurpose household survey that is representative at the national, urban-rural and regional level and was carried out from April to July 2002" (Luis Rubalcava and Graciela Teruel, "The Role of Maternal Cognitive Ability on Child Health," *Economics and Human Biology* 2, no. 3 [December 2004]: 441).

50. "With some notable exceptions, preindustrial life was characterized by poverty, slow growth, poor health, widespread illiteracy, and rural habitation" (Steckel and Floud, *Health and Welfare*, 428).

Section 3

1. James C. Riley, *Low Income, Social Growth and Good Health: A History of Twelve Countries* (Berkeley: University of California Press/Milbank Memorial Fund, 2008), 2.

2. Ibid., 9.

3. Ibid., 2.

4. Ibid., 3.

5. Ibid., 133–41.

6. Ibid., 137, 139.

7. Ibid., 138.

Section 3, Chapter 1

1. Márquez Morfin, *La desigualdad ante la muerte*, 189.

2. "Around the middle of the nineteenth century, life expectancy at birth for both sexes combined in the major regions of the world fell in a band extending from the low 20s to the lows 40s" (Easterlin, *Reluctant Economist*, 86). Massimo Livi-Bacci, *The Population of Europe: A History*, trans. Cynthia de Nardi Ipsen and Carl Ipsen (Oxford: Blackwell Publisher, 2000), 135.

3. Márquez Morfin, *La desigualdad ante la muerte*, 203.

4. Harry F. Dowling, *Fighting Infection: Conquests of the Twentieth Century*, 2nd ed. (Cambridge, MA: Harvard University Press, 2000), 1–2.

5. "William Oster, the leading teacher of medicine at the turn of the (twentieth) century wrote in 1905 that more had been accomplished for the health of the human race in the nineteenth century than at any period in the past" (Dowling, *Fighting Infection*, 10); Livi-Bacci, *Population*, 126.

6. Joel Mokyr, "Review: Three Centuries of Population Change," *Economic Development and Cultural Change* 32, no. 1 (October 1983): 187.

7. Livi-Bacci, *Population*, 126.

8. "The conflict between vigorous economic growth and very limited improvements or reversals in the nutritional status and health of the majority of the population suggests that the modernization of the nineteenth century was a mixed blessing all through it. However, the industrial scientific achievements of the nineteenth century were a precondition for the remarkable achievements of the twentieth century, including the unprecedented improvements in the conditions of life experienced by ordinary people" (Robert Fogel, *The Escape from Hunger and Premature Death (1700–2100): Europe, America and the Third World* [Cambridge: Cambridge University Press, 2004], 19).

9. "Edwin Chadwick based his proposals for cleaning up cities on epidemiological evidence of the association of 'filth' and disease that he interpreted in term of the miasmatic theory of disease" (Easterlin, *Reluctant Economist*, 93); Dowling, *Fighting Infection*, 7; Roy Porter, *Disease, Medicine and Society in England, 1550–1860*, 2nd ed. (Cambridge: Cambridge University Press, 1993), 57.

10. Dowling, *Fighting Infection*, chap. 1.

11. Easterlin, *Reluctant Economist*, 33; Porter, *Disease*, 58.

12. Dowling, *Fighting Infection*, 22.

13. Porter, *Disease*, 60.

14. Dowling, *Fighting Infection*, 11.

15. "By 1920, the Rockefeller Foundation was already playing a leading role in the planning and administration of public health programs, research, and education in dozens of locales around the globe, including every Latin

American country" (Anne-Emmanuelle Birn, *A Marriage of Convenience: Rockefeller International Health and Revolutionary Mexico* [Rochester, NY: Rochester University Press, 2007], 2).

16. "As is recognized in the health literature, the control of infectious diseases involves serious issues of market failure such as information failure, externalities, public goods, free-rider problems, and so forth. . . . Because of market failure, public intervention has been essential to achieve major reduction of mortality of the type experienced in the last century" (Easterlin, *Reluctant Economist*, 136).

17. Livi-Bacci, *Population*, 142.

18. Ibid., 140.

19. Porter, *Disease*, 60.

20. Steven Cherry, *Medical Services and the Hospital in Britain, 1860–1939* (Cambridge: Cambridge University Press, 1996), 12.

21. Ibid.

22. Ibid., 27; Porter, *Disease*, 47.

23. Hennock, *Origin of the Welfare State*, 87.

24. Ibid., 143.

25. Ibid., 341.

26. Cherry, *Medical Services*, 6.

27. Bernard Harris, *The Origins of British Welfare: Society, State, and Social Welfare in England and Wales, 1800–1945* (New York: Palgrave Macmillan, 2004), 1.

28. There are other works on the topic such as Jared Diamond's *Guns, Germs and Steel: The Fates of Human Societies* (New York: W. W. Norton, 1998) and Gregory Clark's *A Farewell to Alms: A Brief Economic History of the World* (Princeton, NJ: Princeton University Press, 2007). I do not elaborate on these works because they are not relevant to explain and/or understand the case of Mexico.

29. "Even the poorest recorded hunter-gatherer group enjoys a caloric intake superior to that of impoverished contemporary urban populations" (Mark N. Cohen, *Health and Rise of Civilization* [New Haven, CT: Yale University Press, 1989], 132).

30. "Modern civilizations are clearly successful in the sense that they provide for increasing numbers of people, even if they have added little to the health and nutrition of the individuals involved until quite recently" (ibid., 141).

31. "The world's poor clearly did not share in the recent improvements in life expectancy until the past 150 years or less and still share only to a substantially reduced degree" (ibid., 140).

32. Ibid., 141.

33. "We have built our images of human history too exclusively from the experiences of the privileged classes and populations, and we have assumed too close a fit between technological advances and progress for individual lives" (ibid., 140).

34. "We live today in the midst of two great revolutions that are sweeping the world and have changed human life forever. The Industrial Revolution of the late eighteenth century marked the onset of modern economic growth, a phenomenon that has raised material living levels by tenfold or more among the leaders in the process. The Mortality Revolution that started in the late nineteenth century has already more than doubled life expectancy at birth in many parts of the world" (Easterlin, *Reluctant Economist*, 19).

35. Ibid., 97.

36. Ibid., 111.

37. The Tribunal del Protomedicato was established in New Spain in 1646.

38. From the beginnings of the colonial period, the Church and state collaborated to provide care for the sick and place for burial. The powers of the Church and state were intertwined in such a way that the state could not dismiss the common belief that illnesses and epidemics were a divine punishment. Hence, the state authorities did not oppose ecclesiastic activities, such as pilgrimages and promises, as an additional way to fight diseases.

39. "Since 1541 the Crown ordered that in every Spanish and Indian town hospitals be funded to cure the poor. In general this initiative to build hospitals was successful in Indian towns, although the works of clergy were behind them. . . . In the seventeenth century, almost every Indian town of any importance established hospitals that were almost always supported by the caciques" (González Navarro, *La pobreza*, 82).

40. Ibid., 110.

41. Ibid., 109.

42. Spaniards believed that the practice of frequent bathing was due to a lack of cleanliness in their souls; see Díaz del Castillo, *Conquest of New Spain*, 225.

43. América Molina del Villar, *Por voluntad divina: Escasez, epidemias y otras calamidades en la ciudad de México (1700–1762)* (Mexico City: CIESAS, 1996), 57.

44. One novelty of this period was the opening of new routes of disease expansion. During the colonial period, most of the diseases came to Mexico by ship from the Old World, even if they were from other places. The nineteenth century inaugurated the route of the north. Cholera, a new pandemic, came by foot from the Texas border in the 1830s. Elsa Malvido Miranda and Miguel Ángel Cuenya, *El cólera de 1833: Una nueva patología en México. Causas y efectos* (Mexico City: Instituto Nacional de Antropología e Historia, 1992), 13.

45. Ordenanzas municipales de 1841. La salud es el más importante objeto de la institución de los ayuntamientos. Fernando Martínez Cortés, *De los miasmas y efluvios al descubrimiento de las bacterias patógenas. Los primeros cincuenta años del Consejo Superior de Salubridad* (Mexico City: Bristol-Myers Squibb de México, 1993), 41.

46. Ibid., 41–42.

47. Ibid., 47.

48. "By contrast, diseases such as typhus, cholera and typhoid, associated with poor hygiene, are usually more prevalent among low income groups whose hygienic conditions are bad" (Márquez Morfin, *La desigualdad ante la muerte*, 77).

49. "Conditions in this part of the city (first section) worsened and, by the early twentieth century, especially in the city-center, sanitary conditions were disastrous; out of the total surface, only a fifth had some form of paving while the rest was in a very different state of preservation. Only paved streets had a public service to clean the streets" (ibid., 331).

50. For a thorough explanation on the intellectual origins of the public health initiatives during the Díaz administration, see Mauricio Tenorio-Trillo, *Mexico at the World's Fairs: Crafting of a Modern Nation* (Berkeley: University of California Press, 1996), chap. 9. Agostoni, "Discurso médico," provides a clear and extensive explanation of the efforts made by government agencies to disseminate public health information in Porfirian Mexico City.

51. Tenorio-Trillo, *Mexico*, 157.

52. Ibid., 147.

53. Miguel E. Bustamante, "La situación epidemiológica de México en el siglo XIX," in *Ensayos sobre la historia de las epidemias en México*, ed. Enrique Florescano and Elsa Malvido, Colección Salud y Seguridad Social, Serie Histórica (Mexico City: Instituto Mexicano del Seguro Social, 1982), 431.

54. Agostoni, "Discurso médico," 12.

55. Moisés González Navarro, "El Porfiriato: Vida social," in *Historia moderna de México*, 2nd ed., ed. Daniel Cosío Villegas (Mexico City: Editorial Hermes, 1970), 4:43.

56. There was a debate on whether indigenous peoples had or did not have higher mortality rates than mestizos. On the one hand, Dr. Orvaña-nos stated that the indigenous population had higher mortality rates because they had a lack of hygienic habits. On the other hand, *El Observador Médico*, a medical journal, stated a completely opposite opinion, showing that indigenous people did not suffer from high-altitude anemia or any disease caused by undernutrition that people from other races did have. Along the same lines, the Mexico City journal showed that mortality rates were lower in the Indian sectors of the city; see González Navarro, *Porfiriato*, 43–45.

57. Mortality rates were different in other regions of Mexico; the south and north had higher life expectancies, but some states of the center, like Morelos, had even lower life expectancies than Mexico City.

58. "Early towns were generally crowded and unsanitary, so that infectious diseases such as plague, typhus, dysentery, and smallpox spread quickly. Life expectancy at birth in London in the late eighteenth century, a mere 23 years, was thus lower than for most preindustrial societies, even though London then was perhaps the richest city in the world" (Clark, *Farewell to Alms*, 93).

59. Nutrition-related diseases were also referred to as constitutional dominant diseases (*enfermedades constitucionales dominantes*); see González Navarro, *Porfiriato*, 54.

60. "Analysis of mortality trends is based on information compiled by the Registrars General for England and Wales from 1837 and from Scotland from 1855" (Cherry, *Medical Services*, 12).

61. "America lagged behind England in the collection of such data [vital statistics], partly because of its widely scattered population and partly because, to a practical people, collecting statistics did not seem as important as tilling the soil, mining coal, and building houses and factories. . . . At the turn of the century the functions of the only federal agency, the Marine Hospital Service, but not until 1912 did Congress stress its major role by calling it the Public Health Service" (Dowling, *Fighting Infection*, 8).

62. Sánchez Santos, *Obras*, 145; González Navarro, *Porfiriato*, 80–82.

63. Martínez Cortés, *De los miasmas*, 26.

64. For more information on the members of the *Científico* group that made up part of the hygienists, see appendix 1 of Tenorio-Trillo, *Mexico*, 255–61.

65. Laura Cházaro García, "Medir y valorar los cuerpos de una nación: Un ensayo sobre la estadística médica del siglo XIX en México" (PhD diss., Universidad Nacional Autónoma de México, 2000), 147.

66. For example, the cure for yellow fever was discovered by Carlos J. Finlay, a Cuban doctor in the 1880s, but it was not until twenty years later that Mexican doctors decided to try it on their patients, even though yellow fever was a serious threat to public health.

67. Tenorio-Trillo, *Mexico*, chap. 9.

68. "Article 73, Fraction XV. Congress has the faculty to dictate laws on nationality, legal condition of foreigners, citizenship, naturalization, colonization, emigration and immigration and Public Health in the Republic" (Tena Ramírez, *Leyes fundamentales de México*, 848).

69. Birn, *Marriage of Convenience*.

70. Ibid., 2.

71. Ibid., 3.

72. Ibid., 181.

73. Tenorio-Trillo, *Mexico*, 92.

74. Manuel Gamio, *Algunas consideraciones sobre la salubridad rural: Contribución de la Secretaría de Gobernación a la Conferencia Inter-Americana de Higiene Rural* (Mexico City: DAPP, 1939), 11–14.

75. Ibid., 15.

76. Ibid., 27–28.

77. Ibid., 29.

78. John Scott, "The Social Failure of the Mexican Revolution: Redistributive Constraints Under High Inequality" (paper presented at the UCLA-CIDE conference on Latin America and Globalization, April 2009), 20, 32.

79. "The demography of northwestern Europe before has been intensively researched. Parish records of baptisms, and marriage in both England and France allow historical demographers to establish fertility rates back to 1540" (Clark, *Farewell to Alms*, 71).

80. "Nonetheless, we know that there was a high number of free unions: people living in consensual unions. . . . Apparently these unions among low income Mexicans prevailed in the nineteenth century" (Márquez Morfin, *La desigualdad ante la muerte*, 89). "Family reconstitutions provide valuable clues about legitimate fertility, but methodological limitations do not permit measurement of extramarital fertility; where non-marital fertility is common but invariable, as in Mexico, other methods are required" (McCaa, "Peopling of Mexico," 270).

81. "There is a consensus among historians that smallpox struck central Mexico in 1520, the first of a series of devastating multiyear epidemics that erupted in the sixteenth century. . . . Recovery of the native population began, nonetheless, by the middle of the seventeenth century according to most accounts" (ibid., 258, 262).

82. Robert McCaa, "Paleodemography of the Americas: From Ancient Times to Colonialism and Beyond," in *The Backbone of History: Health and Nutrition in the Western Hemisphere*, ed. Richard H. Steckel and Jerome C. Rose (Cambridge: Cambridge University Press, 2002), 94.

83. "Hunger was certainly not absent from Mexico in the nineteenth century as in the twentieth century either but frequency and intensity of famine seem to have lessened following the end of Spanish colonialism" (McCaa, "Peopling of Mexico," 287–88).

84. "Cholera found virgin soil in Mexico in 1833 following outbreaks in Western Europe and North America" (ibid., 290).

85. "The old demographic regime persisted into the nineteenth century, if the picture developed here from the osteological evidence is trustworthy" (McCaa, "Paleodemography," 94).

86. Livi-Bacci, *Population*, 35; Willem Jongman, "Beneficial Symbols: Alimenta and the Infantilization of the Roman Citizen," in *After the Past. Essays in Ancient History in Honour of H. W. Pleket*, ed. Willem Jongman and Marc Kleijwegt (Leiden: Brill, 2002), 49; Willem Jongman, "Hunger and Power: Theories, Models and Methods in Roman Economic History," in *Interdependency of Institution and Private Entrepreneurs (MOS STUDIES 2) Proceedings of the Second MOS Symposium (Leiden 1998)*, ed. A.C.V.M. Bongenaar (Leiden: Nederlands Historisch-Archaeologisch Instituut te Istanbul, 2000), 261.

87. "Since population can change only slowly, the short-run effect of a technological improvement was an increase in real incomes. But the increased income reduced the death rate, birth exceeds deaths, and population grew. The growth of population only ended when income returned to subsistence. At the new equilibrium the only effect of the technological change was to

increase the population. There was no lasting gain in living standards" (Clark, *Farewell to Alms*, 28).

88. Alejandro Tortolero Villaseñor, *De la coa a la máquina de vapor: Actividad agrícola e innovación tecnólogica en las haciendas mexicanas: 1880–1914* (Mexico City: Editorial Siglo XXI, 1995), 48; Beatty, *Institutions and Investment*, 114.

89. Tortolero Villaseñor, *De la coa*, 46, 355, 357.

90. "Land exploitation continued to be extensive; this is based in the opening up of new land, old forms of labor division and the use of rudimentary agricultural tools, with the exception of foreign plows that were widely used in Morelos" (ibid., 360).

91. "Compared to recent decades, food production for domestic consumption during the Porfiriato grew generously, even at a faster pace than population growth. Mexicans did not eat better in 1907 than in 1877, but on the average, they certainly did not eat less" (Coatsworth, *Los orígenes del atraso*, 177).

92. "Immigration was an even greater disappointment. In 1900, after decades of promoting European immigration, 99.5% of the resident population of Mexico was also born in Mexico" (McCaa, "Peopling of Mexico," 277).

93. González Navarro, *Porfiriato*, 153.

94. Ibid., 183.

95. McCaa, "Missing Millions: The Demographic Cost of the Mexican Revolution," *Mexican Studies/Estudios Mexicanos* 19, no. 2 (Summer 2003): 367.

96. Ibid., 396.

97. "Indeed, the rapid growth of Mexico City in the late nineteenth century was due in part to an unrelenting campaign in which twenty to fifty thousand children were treated annually, and smallpox deaths were reduced to a few hundred" (McCaa, "Peopling of Mexico," 290).

98. Scott, "Social Failure," 20.

99. Clark, *Farewell to Alms*, 72.

100. McCaa, "Peopling of Mexico," 292.

101. González Navarro, *Porfiriato*, 385; Elena Poniatowska, *Hasta no verte, Jesus mío* (Mexico City: Era, 1978).

102. See observations on fruits in Ethel Alec-Tweedie, *Mexico as I Saw It* (London: Hurst and Blackett), 253; Fanny Calderón de la Barca, *Life in Mexico* (Berkeley: University of California Press, 1982), 29; Carl Sartorius, *Mexico About 1850* (Stuttgart: Antiquarium, 1961), 75; Brantz Mayer, *Mexico as It Was and as It Is* (New York: J. Winchester, 1844), 21.

103. William Bullock, *Six Months' Residence and Travels in Mexico; Containing Remarks on the Present State of New Spain, Its Natural Productions, State of Society, Manufactures, Trade, Agriculture, and Antiquities* (Port Washington, NY: Kennikat Press, 1971), 195.

104. Calderón de la Barca, *Life*, 23.

105. Ibid., 95.

106. Alec-Tweedie, *Mexico*, 144.

107. Calderón de la Barca, *Life*, 30.

108. Ibid., 102.

109. Ibid., 66.

110. Sartorius, *Mexico*, 49.

111. Ibid., 75.

112. Ibid, 59.

113. Ibid., 29.

114. Ibid., 62.

115. Ibid., 71.

116. See Birn, *Marriage of Convenience*, chap. 1.

117. Tserverkoi in William Richardson, *Mexico Through Russian Eyes, 1806–1940* (Pittsburgh, PA: University of Pittsburgh Press, 1988), 91.

118. "With the great mass of Mexicans there is no such thing as domestic cookery. The laborer sallies forth with his *clacos* in his pocket, and two or three of them will purchase his cakes from an Indian woman. A few steps further on, another Indian woman has a pan boiling over a portable furnace, and containing the required *beans* and *chilé*. The hungry man squats down beside the seller—makes a breakfast or dinner table of his knees—holds out his *tortilla* spread flat on his hand for a ladle of *chilé* and a lump of meat" (Mayer, *Mexico as It Was*, 16–17).

119. Martín González de la Vara, *La cocina mexicana a través de los siglos*, vol. 5, *Tiempos de guerra* (Mexico City: Clío, 1997), 9.

120. González Navarro, *Porfiriato*, 399.

121. A "fonda" is a sort of small diner.

122. Antonio García Cubas, "Dinner in the Conejo Blanco Fonda," in *El libro de mis recuerdos: Narraciones anecdóticas y de costumbres mexicanas anteriores al actual estado social, ilustrado con más de trescientos fotograbados* (Mexico City: Imprenta de Arturo García Cubas, Hermanos Sucesores, 1904), 164.

123. Salvador Novo, *Cocina mexicana o historia gastronómica de la ciudad de México*, 9th ed. (Mexico City: Editorial Porrúa, 2007), 45.

124. Gamio, *Algunas consideraciones*, 29.

125. González Navarro, *Porfiriato*, 396.

Section 3, Chapter 2

1. "But unlike height, measure of average weight and Body Mass Index, can reflect nutritional status in adulthood after the cessation of growth in stature" (Roderick Floud, "Height, Weight and Body Mass of the British Population Since 1820" [Working Paper Series on Historical Factors in Long Run Growth, Historical Paper No. 108, October 1998], 4).

2. Several scholars and specialists on anthropometric history (R. Steckel and John Komlos, among others) use the results of the Bellagio Conference as a guideline.

3. The basic features of the military sample (social class, region of birth). The sample for which we have information on the health status of the soldiers contains 1,463 soldiers born between 1880 and 1910. Because this subsample was drawn from the Personal Extinto files, it does not contain members from the upper strata of the population or soldiers from the poorest backgrounds.

4. Deserters are not included because their files do not have information on health history.

5. BMI is useful to assess nutrition and health after reaching adulthood.

6. Thomas McKeown, *The Modern Rise in Population* (New York: Academic Press, 1976), 128.

7. Let us remember that average age of recruitment for the sample is twenty-six years.

8. Life expectancy may change whether it is measured at birth, at age five, or at age twenty-five, especially if public health improves. Unfortunately, historical statistics of Mexico only provide life expectancy at birth.

9. McKeown, *Modern Rise*, 129.

10. Prince and Steckel, "Tallest in the World," 4.

11. Sherburne F. Cook and Woodrow Borah, *Essays in Population History: Mexico and California* (Berkeley: University of California Press, 1979), vol. 3, chap. 2.

12. Ibid., 129.

13. Ibid., 138.

14. Ibid., 139.

15. Ibid., 176.

16. Ibid., 142.

17. This refers to the number of times in a week that people ate meat, chicken, fish, and eggs.

18. "Proteins serve the body as building blocks in the growth and repair of tissues, as enzymes in the metabolism, as hormones; as regulators of the body's fluid balances; as transporters; as antibodies; and in many other ways. When people are deprived of protein, energy or both, the result is protein energy malnutrition (PEM). Although (PEM) touches many adult lives, it most often strikes early in childhood. It is the most widespread form of malnutrition in the world today, afflicting over 500 million children" (Eleanor Noss Whitney and Sharon Rady Rolfes, *Understanding Nutrition*, 7th ed. [Minneapolis/St. Paul, MN: West Publishing Company, 1996], 212.

19. "Inadequate food intake leads to poor growth in children and to weight loss and wasting in adults. Children who are thin for their height may be suffering from acute PEM (recent severe food deprivation), whereas children who are short for their age have experienced chronic PEM (long term food deprivation)" (ibid., 216).

20. The question in the 1940 population census provided information on people who did or did not eat wheat bread *and* slept in a bed (*población que*

come y población que no come pan de trigo y duerme en el suelo, cama, etc.). The
1950 population census asked if people habitually (a) ate or (b) did not eat
wheat bread (*personas que habitualmente: a) comen pan de trigo; b) no comen pan de
trigo*).

21. Instituto Nacional de Nutrición Salvador Zubirán, *Encuestas nutricionales de México* (Mexico City: INNSZ, 1965), 334.

22. The BMI is calculated with following formula:

$$BMI = \frac{weight}{height^2}$$

Weight is expressed in kilograms and height in meters. According to medical
conventions, the normal ranges of BMI are 19–25. An individual with a BMI
lower than 19 is considered underweight, and someone with a BMI above 25
is considered overweight.

23. Novo, *Cocina mexicana*, 146–48.

24. McCaa, "Peopling of Mexico," 294.

25. Gamio, *Algunas consideraciones*, 14.

26. "The salubriousness problems are horrific. The majority of the population lacks sewerage systems and drinking water; this increases mortality numbers impressively, especially among children under age two. The lower tropical
zones have a great potential to create wealth. The problem lies in the need to
clean those zones and that costs hundreds of million pesos. The works done
on this area will inevitably be a project taking several years" (Silva Herzog,
"Meditaciones sobre México," 25).

Overview and Final Conclusions

1. "Ample research opportunities remain. Several additional countries
could be added to the data base—Norway, Austria, Hungary, Spain, and Italy
come readily to mind in Europe, while in the Western Hemisphere, Canada
and several Latin American countries have considerable potential for developing data bases on living standards" (Steckel and Floud, *Health and Welfare*,
437).

2. Richard H. Steckel, "Heights and Human Welfare: Recent Developments and New Dimensions," *Explorations in Economic History* 46 (2009): 14.

3. Jared Diamond and James A. Robinson, "Afterword: Using Comparative
Methods in Studies in Human History," in *Natural Experiments of History*, ed.
Jared Diamond and James A. Robinson (Cambridge, MA: Harvard University
Press, 2010), 272.

4. Richard H. Steckel, "What Can Be Learned from Skeletons That Might
Interest Economists, Historians and Other Social Scientists?" (National Bureau of Economic Research, Working Paper 9519, February 2003), 1.

5. Lourdes Márquez and Andrés del Ángel, "Height Among Prehispanic Maya of the Yucatán Peninsula: A Reconsideration," in *Bones of the Maya: Studies of Ancient Skeletons*, ed. Stephen L. Whittington and David M. Reed (Washington, DC: Smithsonian Institution Press, 1997), 60.

6. Kuntz Ficker, *Historia económica general de México*, 16.

7. Steckel, "Heights and Human Welfare," 14.

8. David B. Ryden, "Perhaps We *Can* Talk: Discussant Comments for 'Taking Stock and Moving Ahead: The Past, Present, and Future of Economics for History,'" *Social Science History* 35, no. 2 (Summer 2011): 211.

9. Easterlin, *Reluctant Economist*, 11.

Major Archival Sources

Archivo General de la Nación, Mexico City (AGN).
Ramos:
Guerra y Marina
Legajos de Gobernación 1821–1920

Secretaría de la Defensa Nacional, Mexico City (SDN).
Dirección General de Archivo e Historia
Sección de Cancelados
Sección de Personal Extinto de Caballería, Infantería y Artillería
Personal de Sanidad

Secretaría de Relaciones Exteriores, Mexico City (SRE).
Archivo de Pasaportes años 1918–1942

Government Sources

Censo Nacional de Población, 1950, 1960, 1970.
Consejo Superior de Salubridad. *Ordenanzas municipales de junio de 1841. La salud pública es el más importante objeto de la institución de los ayuntamientos.*
Decretos y reglamentos a que se refiere el estatuto provisional del Imperio Mexicano. Primera parte. Mexico City: Imprenta de Andrade y Escalante, 1865.
Diario Oficial de la Federación, Acuerdo de Creación de la Comisión del Programa Nacional de Solidaridad, 6/12/1988.
Estadística de la República Mexicana, 1888.
Instituto Nacional de Geografía Estadística, Geografía e Informática. *Encuesta nacional de ingresos y gastos de los hogarares.* Mexico City: INEGI, 1984, 1992, 1994.
———. *Estadísticas históricas de México,* 2 vols. Mexico City: INEGI, 1994.
Instituto Nacional de la Nutrición Salvador Zubirán. *Encuestas nutricionales de México, División de Nutrición L1–2da.* Mexico City: Instituto Nacional de la Nutrición, 1965.

Memoria de las obras de las conferencias de la Sociedad de San Vicente de Paul, dependientes del Consejo Superior de la República Mexicana durante el año de 1871.
Mexico City: Imprenta de la V. e Hijos de Murguía, Portal del Águila
de Oro, 1872.

Secretaría de la Defensa Nacional. Memoria de la Secretaría de Guerra y Marina,
1896–1899, vol. 1.

Secondary Sources

Adler de Lomnitz, Larissa. Cómo sobreviven los marginados. 10th ed. Mexico
City: Siglo XXI, 1991.

Agostoni, Claudia. "Discurso médico, cultura higiénica y la mujer en la ciudad de México al cambio del siglo (XIX–XX)." Mexican Studies/Estu-
dios Mexicanos 18, no. 1 (2002): 1–22.

———. Monuments of Progress. Modernization and Public Health in Mexico City,
1876–1910. Calgary: University of Calgary Press, 2003.

Aguilar Camín, Héctor, and Lorenzo Meyer. A la sombra de la Revolución Mexicana. 39th ed. Mexico City: Editorial Cal y Arena, 2008.

Alec-Tweedie, Ethel. Mexico as I Saw It. London: Hurst and Blackett, 1901.

Alessio Robles, Miguel. La filantropía en México. Mexico City: Editorial Botas,
1944.

Andrade, José María. Informe sobre los establecimientos de beneficencias y corrección de esta capital. Escrito póstumo de Don Joaquín García Icazbalceta.
Mexico City: Moderna Librería Religiosa, 1907.

Arrom, Silvia Marina. Containing the Poor: The Mexico City Poor House, 1774–
1871. Durham, NC: Duke University Press, 2000.

Attack, Jeremy, and Peter Passell. A New Economic View of American History
from Colonial Times to 1940. 2nd ed. New York: W. W. Norton and
Company, 1994.

Bazant, Jan. Los bienes de la Iglesia en México, 1856–1875: Aspectos económicos y sociales de la revolución liberal. 2nd ed. Mexico City: El Colegio de
México, 1995.

Beatty, Edward. Institutions and Investment: The Political Basis of Industrialization
in Mexico Before 1911. Stanford, CA: Stanford University Press, 2001.

Bellagio Conference. "The Relationship of Nutrition, Disease, and Social
Conditions: A Graphical Presentation." Journal of Interdisciplinary History
14 (Autumn 1983): 503–6.

Birn, Anne-Emmanuelle. A Marriage of Convenience: Rockefeller International
Health and Revolutionary Mexico. Rochester, NY: Rochester University
Press, 2007.

Blinder, Alan S. "The Level and Distribution of Economic Well-Being." In
The American Economy in Transition, edited by Martin Feldstein, 415–79.
Chicago: University of Chicago Press/NBER, 1980.

Bliss, Katherine. *Compromised Positions: Prostitution, Public Health and Gender Politics in Revolutionary Mexico City.* University Park: Pennsylvania State University Press, 2001.

Blum, Ann S. "Conspicuous Benevolence: Liberalism, Public Welfare, and Private Charity in Porfirian Mexico, 1877–1910." *The Americas* 58, no. 1 (2001): 7–38.

———. *Domestic Economies: Families, Work, and Welfare in Mexico City, 1884–1943.* Lincoln: University of Nebraska Press, 2009.

Bogin, Barry. *The Growth of Humanity.* New York: Wiley-Liss, 2001.

———. *Patterns of Human Growth.* 2nd ed. Cambridge: Cambridge University Press, 1999.

Bortz, Jeffrey Lawrence. *Los salarios industriales en la ciudad de México, 1939–1975.* Translated by Eduardo L. Suárez. Mexico City: Fondo de Cultura Económica, Economía Latinoamericana, 1988.

Bortz, Jeffrey Lawrence, and Marco Antonio Aguila. "Earning a Living." *Latin American Research Review* 42, no. 2 (2006): 112–38.

Brundage, Anthony. *The English Poor Laws, 1700–1930.* New York: Palgrave, 2002.

Bullock, William. *Six Months' Residence and Travels in Mexico; Containing Remarks on the Present State of New Spain, Its Natural Productions, State of Society, Manufactures, Trade, Agriculture, and Antiquities and c.* Port Washington, NY: Kennikat Press, 1971.

Bustamante, Miguel E. "La situación epidemiológica de México en el siglo XIX." In *Ensayos sobre la historia de las epidemias en México,* edited by Enrique Florescano and Elsa Malvido, 425–76. Mexico City: Colección Salud y Seguridad Social, Serie Historia, Instituto Mexicano del Seguro Social, 1982.

Calderón de la Barca, Madame (Frances Erskine Inglis). *Life in Mexico.* 1st California ed. Berkeley: University of California Press, 1982.

Cámara Hueso, Antonio David. "Living Standards in Rural Eastern Andalusia (1750–1950)." PhD diss., Universidad de Granada, 2006.

Carmagnani, Marcello. *Estado y mercado: La economía pública del liberalismo mexicano, 1850–1911.* Mexico City: Fondo de Cultura Económica, Fideicomiso de las Américas, Serie Hacienda, 1994.

Carmagnani, Marcello, Alicia Hernández Chávez, and Ruggiero Romano, eds. *Para una historia de América II. Los nudos (1).* Mexico City: Fideicomiso Historia de las Américas, Serie Américas, Fondo de Cultura Económica, 1999.

Challu, Amilcar E. "Living Standards and the Great Decline: Biological Well-Being in Mexico, 1730–1840." In *Living Standards in Latin American History,* edited by Ricardo D. Salvatore, John H. Coatsworth, and Amílcar E. Challú, 23–68. Cambridge, MA: David Rockefeller Center for Latin American Studies/Harvard University, 2010.

Chávez, Adolfo, Miriam M. de Chávez, J. Antonio Roldán, and Abelardo Ávila. *La nutrición en México y la transición epidemiológica.* Mexico City: Instituto Nacional de Nutrición Salvador Zubirán, 1993.

Cházaro García, Laura. "Medir y valorar los cuerpos de una nación: Un ensayo sobre la estadística médica del siglo XIX en México." PhD diss.,
Universidad Nacional Autónoma de México, 2000.

Cherry, Steve. *Medical Services and the Hospital in Britain, 1860–1939.* Cambridge: Cambridge University Press, 1996.

Clark, Gregory. *A Farewell to Alms: A Brief Economic History of the World.*
Princeton, NJ: Princeton University Press, 2007.

Clark, Marjorie Ruth. *Organized Labor in Mexico.* Chapel Hill: University of
North Carolina Press, 1934.

Coatsworth, John. "Indispensable Railroads in a Backward Economy: The
Case of Mexico." *Journal of Economic History* 39, no. 4 (December 1979):
939–60.

———. *Los orígenes del atraso: Nueve ensayos de historia económica de México en los
siglos XVIII y XIX.* Mexico City: Alianza Editorial Mexicana, 1990.

———. "Structures, Endowments, and Institutions in the Economic History of Latin America." *Latin American Research Review* 40, no. 3 (2005):
126–44.

———. "Welfare." *American Historical Review* 101, no. 1 (February 1996): 1–12.

Coatsworth, John H., and Alan Taylor, eds. *Latin America and the World Economy Since 1800.* Cambridge, MA: Harvard University Press, 1998.

Coatsworth, John H., and Gabriel Tortella Casares. "Instituciones y desem-
peño económico a largo plazo en México y España (1800–2000)." In
México y España ¿historias económicas paralelas?, edited by Rafael Dobado,
Aurora Gómez Galvarriato, and Graciela Márquez, 47–76. Mexico
City: Fondo de Cultura Económica, 2007.

Cohen, Mark Nathan. *Health and the Rise of Civilization.* New Haven, CT:
Yale University Press, 1989.

Cook, Sherburne F., and Woodrow Borah. *Essays in Population History: Mexico
and California, Volume III.* Berkeley: University of California Press, 1979.

Cope, Douglas. *The Limits of Racial Domination: Plebeian Society in Colonial
Mexico City, 1600–1720.* Madison: University of Wisconsin Press, 1994.

Cosío Villegas, Daniel. *Historia moderna de México: El Porfiriato y vida social.* 3rd
ed. Mexico City: Editorial Hermes, 1973.

———. "Mexico's Crisis." In *The Mexico Reader*, edited by Gilbert Joseph and
Timothy Henderson, 470–81. Durham, NC: Duke University Press,
2002.

Costa, Dora L., and Richard Steckel. "Long Term Trends in Health, Welfare
and Economic Growth in the United States." In *Health and Welfare During Industrialization*, edited by Richard H. Steckel and Roderick Floud,
172. Chicago: University of Chicago Press, 1998.

Crosby, Alfred W., Jr. *The Columbian Exchange: Biological and Cultural Consequences of 1492.* Contributions in American Studies Number 2. West-
port, CT: Greenwood Press, 1972.

Cuff, Timothy. *The Hidden Cost of Economic Development: The Biological Standard of Living in Antebellum Pennsylvania.* Burlington, VT: Ashgate Publishing Company, 2004.

Cumberland, Charles. *Mexican Revolution: Genesis Under Madero.* Austin: University of Texas Press, 1952.

David, Paul A., and Mark Thomas, eds. *The Economic Future in Historical Perspective.* Oxford: Oxford University Press, 2006.

De la Cueva, Mario. *El nuevo derecho mexicano del trabajo.* 6th ed. Mexico City: Editorial Porrúa, 1984.

Diamond, Jared. *Guns, Germs and Steel: The Fates of Human Societies.* New York: W. W. Norton, 1998.

Diamond, Jared, and James A. Robinson. "Afterword: Using Comparative Methods in Studies in Human History." In *Natural Experiments of History,* edited by Jared Diamond and James A. Robinson, 257–76. Cambridge, MA: Harvard University Press, 2010.

———. eds. *Natural Experiments of History.* Cambridge, MA: Harvard University Press, 2010.

Díaz del Castillo, Bernal. *The Conquest of New Spain.* Translated with an introduction by J. M. Cohen. London: Penguin Books, 1963.

Dowling, Harry F. *Fighting Infection: Conquests of the Twentieth Century.* 2nd ed. Cambridge, MA: Harvard University Press, 2000.

Drukker, J. W., and Vincent Tassenaar. "Paradoxes of Modernization and Material Well-Being in the Netherlands During the Nineteenth Century." In *Health and Welfare During Industrialization,* edited by Richard H. Steckel and Roderick Floud, 331–78. Chicago: University of Chicago Press, 1997.

Easterlin, Richard. *The Reluctant Economist: Perspectives on Economics, Economic History, and Demography.* Cambridge: Cambridge University Press, 2004.

El Colegio de México. *Estadísticas históricas del Porfiriato, fuerza de trabajo y actividad económica por sectores.* Mexico City: El Colegio de México, 1961.

———. *Historia general de México, versión 2000.* Mexico City: El Colegio de México, 2000.

Eveleth, Phyllis B., and James M. Tanner. *Worldwide Variation in Human Growth.* 2nd ed. Cambridge: Cambridge University Press, 1990.

Falcón, Romana, ed. *Culturas de resistencia y pobreza: Estudios de marginados, proscritos y descontentos México 1084–1910.* Mexico City: El Colegio de México/Universidad Autónoma de Querétaro, 2005.

Florescano, Enrique. *Precios del maíz y crisis agrícolas en México (1708–1810).* Mexico City: El Colegio de México, 1969.

Florescano, Enrique, and Elsa Malvido, eds. *Ensayos sobre la historia de las epidemias en México.* Vols. 1 and 2. Mexico City: Colección Salud y Seguridad Social, Serie Historia, Instituto Mexicano del Seguro Social, 1982.

Florescano, Enrique, and Margarita Menegus. "La época de las reformas borbónicas y el crecimiento económico, 1750–1808." In *Historia general*

de México, edited by El Colegio de México, 363–430. Mexico City: El
Colegio de México, 2000.

Floud, Roderick. "Height, Weight and Body Mass of the British Population
Since 1820." Working Paper Series on Historical Factors in Long Run
Growth, Historical Paper 108, October 1998.

———. "The Human Body in Britain." In *The Economic Future in Historical
Perspective*, edited by Paul A. David and Mark Thomas, 401–18. Oxford:
Oxford University Press, 2006.

Floud, Roderick, Kenneth Watcher, and Annabel Gregory. *Height, Health
and History: Nutritional Status in the United Kingdom, 1750–1980*. Cambridge: Cambridge University Press, 1990.

Fogel, Robert W. "Economic Growth, Population Theory and Physiology:
The Bearing of Long-Term Processes on the Making of Economic
Policy." NBER, Working Paper No. 4638, February 1994.

———. *The Escape from Hunger and Premature Death (1700–2100): Europe,
America and the Third World*. Cambridge: Cambridge University Press,
2004.

Galeana, Patricia, ed. *Los siglos de México*. Mexico City: Nueva Imagen, 1991.

Gamio, Manuel. *Algunas consideraciones sobre la salubridad rural: Contribución de la
Secretaría de Gobernación a la Conferencia Inter-Americana de Higiene Rural*.
Mexico City: DAPP, 1939.

———. *Antología*. Mexico City: Biblioteca del Estudiante Universitario, Universidad Nacional Autónoma de México, 1975.

García Cubas, Antonio. *El libro de mis recuerdos: Narraciones anecdóticas y de
costumbres mexicanas anteriores al actual estado social, ilustrados con más de
trescientos fotograbados*. Mexico City: Imprenta de Arturo García Cubas,
Hermanos Sucesores, 1904.

Gilly, Adolfo. *The Mexican Revolution*. New York: The New Press, 2005.

Gómez-Galvarriato, Aurora. "The Evolution of Prices and Real Wages in
Mexico." In *Latin America and the World Economy Since 1800*, edited by
John H. Coatsworth and Alan Taylor, 347–78. Cambridge, MA: Har-
vard University Press, 1998.

Gómez-Galvarriato, Aurora, and Aldo Musacchio. "Un nuevo índice de precios para México 1886–1929." Working Paper CIDE No.113, 1998.

González, Luis. "El liberalismo triunfante." In *Historia general de México*, edited by El Colegio de México, 633–706. Mexico City: El Colegio de
México, 2000.

González de la Vara, Martín. *La cocina mexicana a través de los siglos*, vol. 5,
Tiempos de guerra. Mexico City: Clío, 1997.

González Navarro, Moisés. *Anatomía del poder (1848–1853)*. Mexico City: El
Colegio de México, 1977.

———. *La pobreza en México*. Mexico City: Fondo de Cultura Económica, 1985.

————. *Porfiriato: Vida social.* In *Historia moderna de México,* 2nd ed., vol. 4, edited by Daniel Cosío Villegas. Mexico City: Editorial Hermes, 1970.

Gujarati, Damodar. *Basic Econometrics.* 3rd ed. New York: McGraw-Hill, 1995.

Haber, Stephen, ed. *How Latin America Fell Behind: Essays on the Economic Histories of Brazil and Mexico, 1800–1914.* Stanford, CA: Stanford University Press, 1997.

Haber, Stephen, Armando Razo, and Noel Maurer. *The Politics of Property Rights: Political Instability, Credible Commitment, and Economic Growth in Mexico, 1876–1929.* Cambridge: Cambridge University Press, 2003.

Haines, Michael A., and Richard H. Steckel. *A Population History of North America.* Cambridge: Cambridge University Press, 2000.

Hale, Charles. "Political and Social Ideas in Latin America, 1870–1930." In *Cambridge History of Latin America,* vol. 4, edited by Leslie Bethell, 367–441. Cambridge: Cambridge University Press, 1986.

Harris, Bernard. *The Origins of British Welfare: Society, State, and Social Welfare in England and Wales, 1800–1945.* New York: Palgrave Macmillan, 2004.

Hennock, E. P. *The Origin of the Welfare State in England and Germany, 1850–1914: Social Policies Compared.* Cambridge: Cambridge University Press, 2007.

Hernández Chávez, Alicia. *Mexico: A Brief History.* Translated by Andy Klatt. Berkeley: University of California Press, 2006.

Jongman, Willem. "Beneficial Symbols: Alimenta and the Infantilization of the Roman Citizen." In *After the Past. Essays in Ancient History in Honour of H. W. Pleket,* edited by Willem Jongman and Marc Kleijwegt, 47–80. Leiden: Brill, 2002.

————. "Hunger and Power: Theories, Models and Methods in Roman Economic History." In *Interdependency of Institutions and Private Entrepreneurs (MOS STUDIES 2) Proceedings of the Second MOS Symposium (Leiden 1998),* edited by A.C.V.M. Bongenaar, 259–84: Leiden Netherlands Historisch-Archaelogisch Instituut te Istanbul, 2000.

Jongman, Willem, and Marc Kleijwegt, eds. *After the Past. Essays in Ancient History in Honour of H. W. Pleket.* Leiden: Brill, 2002.

Katz, Friedrich. "Labor Conditions on Haciendas in Porfirian Mexico: Some Trends and Tendencies." *Hispanic American Historical Review* 54, no. 1 (1974): 1–47.

————. "The Liberal Republic and the Porfiriato." In *Mexico Since Independence,* edited by Leslie Bethell, 49–124. Cambridge: Cambridge University Press, 1991.

————. *The Secret War in Mexico: Europe, the United States, and the Mexican Revolution.* Chicago: University of Chicago Press, 1981.

Keen, Benjamin, and Keith Hayes. *A History of Latin America.* 6th ed. Boston: Wadsworth Publishing, 2000.

Keesing, Donald B. "Structural Change in Early Development: Mexico's Changing Industrial and Occupational Structures from 1895 to 1950." *Journal of Economic History* 29, no. 4 (1969): 716–38.

Knight, Alan. *The Mexican Revolution*, vol. 1, *Porfirians, Liberals and Peasants*. Cambridge: Cambridge University Press, 1986.

———. *The Mexican Revolution*, vol. 2, *Counter-Revolution and Reconstruction*. Cambridge: Cambridge University Press, 1986.

———. "The Rise and Fall of Cardenismo, c. 1930–c. 1946." In *Mexico Since Independence*, edited by Leslie Bethell, 241–320. Cambridge: Cambridge University Press, 1991.

Komlos, John, ed. *The Biological Standard of Living on Three Continents: Further Explorations in Anthropometric History*. Boulder, CO: Westview Press, 1995.

———. "How to (and How Not to) Analyze Deficient Height Samples, an Introduction." *Historical Methods* 37, no. 4 (Fall 2004): 160–73.

———. "Shrinking in a Growing Economy? The Mystery of Physical Stature During the Industrial Revolution." *Journal of Economic History* 58, no. 3 (September 1998): 779–802.

———. "Stature and Nutrition in the Habsburg Monarchy: The Standard of Living and Economic Development." *American Historical Review* 90, no. 5 (December 1985): 1140–61.

Komlos, John, and Joo Han Kim. "Estimating Trends in Historical Heights." *Historical Methods* 23, no. 3 (Summer 1990): 116–21.

Kourí, Emilio, ed. *En busca de Molina Enríquez: Cien años de los grandes problemas nacionales*. Mexico City: El Colegio de México and Centro Katz, 2009.

———. *A Pueblo Divided: Business, Property, and Community in Papantla, Mexico*. Stanford, CA: Stanford University Press, 2004.

Krauze, Enrique. *Biography of Power: A History of Modern Mexico, 1810–1996*. New York: HarperCollins Publishers, 1997.

Kuntz Ficker, Sandra. *Empresa extranjera y mercado interno: El ferrocarril central mexicano, 1880–1907*. Mexico City: El Colegio de México, 1995.

———, ed. *Historia económica general de México: De la colonia a nuestros días*. Mexico City: El Colegio de México/Secretaría de Economía/Comisión Organizadora de las Celebraciones del Bicentenario, 2010.

Laurell, Asa Cristina. "Pronasol o la pobreza de los programas contra la pobreza." *Nueva Sociedad* 31 (May–June 1994): 156–70.

Leunig, Timothy, and Hans-Joachim Voth. "Height and the High Life." In *The Economic Future in Historical Perspective*, edited by Paul A. David and Mark Thomas, 419–38. Oxford: Oxford University Press, 2006.

Lewis, Oscar. *Five Families: Mexican Case Studies in the Culture of Poverty*. New York: Basic Books, 1959.

Lindert, Peter H., and Jeffrey G. Williamson. "English Workers' Living Standards During the Industrial Revolution: A New Look." *Economic History Review* 36, no. 1 (February 1983): 1–25.

Livi-Bacci, Massimo. *The Population of Europe: A History.* Translated by Cynthia de Nardi Ipsen and Carl Ipsen. Oxford: Blackwell Publishers, 2000.

López-Alonso, Moramay. "La alfabetización en el crecimiento económico de México (1930–1970)." Tesis de Licenciatura, ITAM, 1994.

———. "Growth with Inequality: Living Standards in Mexico, 1850–1950." *Journal of Latin American Studies* 39, no. 1 (2007): 81–105.

López-Alonso, Moramay, Lourdes Márquez Morfin, and Laura Gómez Santana. "Living Standards in Pre-Industrial Mexico." Paper presented at "Biological Welfare and Inequality in Pre-Industrial Times: A Political Economy Workshop," Yale University, 2005.

López-Alonso, Moramay, and Raul Porras Condey. "The Ups and Downs of Mexican Economic Growth: The Biological Standard of Living and Inequality, 1870–1950." *Economics and Human Biology* 1 (2003): 169–86.

Malthus, T. R. *An Essay on the Principle of Population; or, a View of Its Past and Present Effects on Human Happiness; with an Inquiry into Our Prospects Respecting the Future Removal or Mitigation of the Evils Which It Occasions.* Selected and introduced by Ronald Winch using the text of the 1803 edition and prepared by Patricia James for the Royal Economic Society, 1990, showing the additions and corrections made in the 1806, 1807, 1817, and 1826 editions. Cambridge: Cambridge University Press, 1992.

Malvido Miranda, Elsa, and Miguel Ángel Cuenya. *El cólera de 1833: Una nueva patología en México. Causas y efectos.* Mexico City: Instituto Nacional de Antropología e Historia, 1992.

Márquez Morfin, Lourdes. *La desigualdad ante la muerte en la ciudad de México: El tifo y el cólera (1813 y 1833).* Mexico City: Editorial Siglo XXI, 1994.

Márquez, Lourdes, and Andrés del Angel. "Height Among Prehispanic Maya of the Yucatán Peninsula: A Reconsideration." In *Bones of the Maya: Studies of Ancient Skeletons,* edited by Stephen L. Whittington and David M. Reed, 51–61. Washington, DC: Smithsonian Institution Press, 1997.

Martínez, José Luis, ed. *Clásicos de la literatura mexicana: Selección de ensayos de los siglos XIX y XX: De Justo Sierra a Carlos Monsiváis.* 2nd ed. Mexico City: Editorial PROMEXA, 1992.

Martínez Carrión, José Miguel. "Estatura, salud y bienestar en las primeras etapas de crecimiento económico español. Una perspectiva comparada de los niveles de vida." Documento de Trabajo de la Asociación de Historia Económica, No. 0102, Murcia, 2001.

———. "Estaturas, desigualdad regional y desarrollo económico en Italia y España durante el siglo XX." *Mediterráneo Económico* 7 (2005): 206–28.

———, ed. *El nivel de vida en la España rural, siglos XVIII–XX.* San Vicente del Raspeig: Publicaciones de la Universidad de Alicante, 2002.

Martínez Carrión, José Miguel, and Juan José Pérez Castejón. "Creciendo con desigualdad. Niveles de vida biológicos en la España rural mediterránea desde 1840." In *El nivel de vida en la España rural,* edited by José Miguel

Martínez Carrión, 405–60. San Vicente del Raspeig: Publicaciones de la Universidad de Alicante, 2005.

Martínez Cortés, Fernando. *De los miasmas y efluvios al descubrimiento de las bacterias patogenas. Los primeros cincuenta años del Consejo Superior de Salubridad.* Mexico City: Bristol-Myers Squibb de Mexico, 1993.

Marx, Karl. *Capital,* vol. 1. New World Edition, 10th ed. New York: International Publishers, 1983.

Mayer, Brantz. *Mexico as It Was and as It Is.* New York: J. Winchester, 1844.

McCaa, Robert. "Missing Millions: The Demographic Cost of the Mexican Revolution." *Mexican Studies/Estudios Mexicanos* 19, no. 2 (Summer 2003): 367–400.

———. "Paleodemography of the Americas: From Ancient Times to Colonialism and Beyond." In *The Backbone of History: Health and Nutrition in the Western Hemisphere,* edited by Richard H. Steckel and Jerome C. Rose, 94–124. Cambridge: Cambridge University Press, 2002.

———. "The Peopling of Mexico from Origins to Revolution." In *The Population History of North America,* edited by Michael Haines and Richard H. Steckel, 241–304. Cambridge: Cambridge University Press, 2000.

McCaa, Robert, Lourdes Márquez Morfin, Rebecca Storey, and Andrés Del Angel. "Health and Nutrition in Prehispanic Mesoamerica." In *The Backbone of History: Health and Nutrition in the Western Hemisphere,* edited by Richard H. Steckel and Jerome C. Rose, 307–38. Cambridge: Cambridge University Press, 2002.

McKeown, Thomas. *The Modern Rise in Population.* New York: Academic Press, 1976.

Meyer, Jean. *La Cristiada,* vol. 2, *2, El conflicto entre la iglesia y el estado, 1926–1929.* 19th ed. Mexico City: Editorial Siglo XXI, 2005.

———. "Mexico in the 1920s." In *Mexico Since Independence,* edited by Leslie Bethell, 201–40. Cambridge: Cambridge University Press, 1991.

Mokyr, Joel. "Review: Three Centuries of Population Change." *Economic Development and Cultural Change* 32, no. 1 (October 1983): 183–92.

Mokyr, Joel, and Cormac O'Gráda. "Poor Getting Poorer? Living Standards in Ireland Before the Famine." *Economic History Review* 41, no. 2 (1988): 209–35.

Molina del Villar, América. *Por voluntad divina: Escasez, epidemias y otras calamidades en la ciudad de México (1760–62).* Mexico City: CIESAS, 1996.

Molina Enríquez, Andrés. *Los grandes problemas de nacionales.* Mexico City: Instituto Nacional de la Juventud Mexicana, 1964.

Moreno-Brid, Juan Carlos, and Jaime Ros. *Development and Growth in the Mexican Economy: A Historical Perspective.* Oxford: Oxford University Press, 2009.

Murray, Paul V. *The Catholic Church in Mexico: Historical Essays for the General Reader, Vol. I (1519–1910).* Mexico City: Editorial E. P. M., 1965.

Nicholas, Stephen, and Richard H. Steckel. "Tall but Poor: Nutrition and the Living Standards in Pre-Famine Ireland." NBER Historical Working Paper No. 39, August 1992.

North, Douglass. *Institutions, Institutional Change and Economic Performance.* Cambridge: Cambridge University Press, 1990.

Noss Whitney, Eleanor, and Sharon Rady Rolfes. *Understanding Nutrition.* 7th ed. Minneapolis/St. Paul, MN: West Publishing Company, 1996.

Novo, Salvador. *Cocina mexicana o historia gastronómica de la ciudad de México.* 9th ed. Mexico City: Editorial Porrúa, 2007.

Piccato, Pablo. *City of Suspects: Crime in Mexico City, 1900–1931.* Durham, NC: Duke University Press, 2001.

Pilcher, Jeffrey M. *Que vivan los tamales! Food and the Making of Mexican Identity.* Albuquerque: University of New Mexico Press, 1998.

Poniatowska, Elena. *Hasta no verte, Jesús mío.* 16th ed. Mexico City: Era, 1978.

Porter, Roy. *Disease, Medicine and Society in England, 1550–1860.* 2nd ed. Cambridge: Cambridge University Press, 1993.

Prince, J. M., and Richard H. Steckel. "Tallest in the World: Native Americans of the Great Plains in the Nineteenth Century." National Bureau of Economic Research Working Paper Series, Historical Paper No. 112, 1998.

Quiroga Valle, Gloria. "Estatura y condiciones materiales de vida en el mundo rural español (1893–1954)." In *El nivel de vida en la España rural, siglos XVIII–XX,* edited by José Miguel Martínez Carrión, 461–96. San Vicente del Raspeig: Publicaciones de la Universidad de Alicante, 2002.

Reyes Heroles, Jesús. *El liberalismo mexicano, vols. I, II and III.* 3rd ed. Mexico City: Fondo de Cultura Económica, 1994.

Ricardo, David. *On the Principles of Political Economy and Taxation.* In *The Works and Correspondence of David Ricardo,* vol. 1, edited by Piero Sraffa, with the collaboration of M. H. Dobb. Cambridge: University Press of the Royal Economic Society, 1951.

Richardson, William. *Mexico Through Russian Eyes, 1806–1940.* Pittsburgh, PA: University of Pittsburgh Press, 1988.

Riley, James C. *Low Income, Social Growth, and Good Health: A History of Twelve Countries.* Berkeley: University of California Press/Milbank Memorial Fund, 2008.

Rondfelt, David F. "Atencingo and the Politics of Agrarian Struggle." PhD diss., Stanford University, 1971.

Rosenzweig Hernández, Fernando. *El desarrollo económico de México 1800–1910.* Mexico City: Colegio Mexiquense A.C.-ITAM, 1989.

Rosner, David. *A Once Charitable Enterprise: Hospitals and Health Care in Brooklyn and New York 1885–1915.* Interdisciplinary Perspectives in Modern History. Cambridge: Cambridge University Press, 1982.

Rubalcava, Luis, and Graciela Teruel. "The Role of Maternal Cognitive Abil-
    ity on Child Health." *Economics and Human Biology* 2, no. 3 (December
    2004): 439–55.
Ryden, David B. "Perhaps We *Can* Talk: Discussant Comments for 'Taking
    Stock and Moving Ahead: The Past, Present, and Future of Economics
    for History.'" *Social Science History* 35, no. 2 (Summer 2011): 209–12.
Salvatore, Ricardo D., John H. Coatsworth, and Amílcar E. Challú, eds. *Liv-
    ing Standards in Latin American History: Height, Welfare, and Development,
    1750–2000.* Cambridge, MA: David Rockefeller Center for Latin
    American Studies/Harvard University, 2010.
Salvucci, Richard. "Mexican National Income in the Era of Independence,
    1800–40." In *How Latin America Fell Behind*, edited by Stephen H.
    Haber, 216–42. Stanford, CA: Stanford University Press, 1997.
Sánchez Santos, Trinidad. *Obras selectas*, vol. 1. Puebla: Linotipografía, 1945.
Sandberg, Lars. "Was Industrialization Hazardous to Your Health? Not in
    Sweden." In *Health and Welfare During Industrialization*, edited by Rich-
    ard H. Steckel and Roderick Floud, 127–60. Chicago: University of
    Chicago Press, 1997.
Sartorius, Carl. *Mexico About 1850.* Stuttgart: Antiquarium, 1961.
Schneider, Ronald. *Latin American Political History: Patterns and Personalities.*
    Boulder, CO: Westview Press, 2006.
Sciulli, Paul W., and Richard M. Gramly. "Analysis of the Ft. Laurens, Ohio,
    Skeletal Sample." *American Journal of Physical Anthropology* 80 (1989):
    11–24.
Scott, John. "The Social Failure of the Mexican Revolution: Redistributive
    Constraints Under High Inequality." Paper presented at the UCLA-
    CIDE conference on Latin America and Globalization, April 2009.
Segura-Ubiergo, Alex. *The Political Economy of the Welfare State in Latin Amer-
    ica: Globalization, Democracy and Development.* Cambridge: Cambridge
    University Press, 2007.
Sierra, Justo. *The Political Evolution of the Mexican People.* Translated by Charles
    Ramsdell. Austin: University of Texas Press, 1969.
Silva Herzog, Jesús. "Meditaciones sobre México, ensayos y notas." *Ediciones
    Cuadernos Americanos* 14 (1947): 9–46.
———. *El pensamiento económico, social y político de México, 1810–1964.* Mex-
    ico City: Instituto Mexicano de Investigaciones Económicas, 1967.
Slack, Paul. *The English Poor Law, 1531–1782.* New Studies in Economic and
    Social History. Cambridge: Cambridge University Press, 1990.
Sledzik, Paul S., and Peer H. Moore-Jansen. "Dental Disease in Nineteenth
    Century Military Skeletal Samples." In *Advances in Dental Anthropology*,
    edited by Marc Kelley and Clark Spencer Larsen, 215–24. New York:
    Wiley-Liss, 1991.

Smith, Adam. *An Inquiry into the Nature and Causes of the Wealth of Nations.* 5th ed., 2 vols. Chicago: Cannan, 1976.

Smith, Peter. "Mexico Since 1946: Dynamics of an Authoritarian Regime." In *Mexico Since Independence*, edited by Leslie Bethel, 321–96. Cambridge: Cambridge University Press, 1991.

Sokoloff, Kenneth L. "The Heights of Americans in Three Centuries: Some Economic and Demographic Implications." In *The Biological Standard of Living on Three Continents: Further Explorations in Anthropometric History*, edited by John Komlos, 133–50. Boulder, CO: Westview Press, 1995.

Sokoloff, Kenneth, and Georgia Villaflor. "The Early Achievement of Modern Stature in America." *Social Science History* 6, no. 4 (Autumn 1982): 453–81.

———. "Migration in Colonial America: Evidence from the Militia Muster Rolls." *Social Science History* 6, no. 4 (Fall 1982): 539–70.

Speckman Guerra, Elisa. *Crimen y castigo: Legislación penal, interpretaciones de la criminalidad y administración de justicia (ciudad de México, 1872–1910).* Mexico City: El Colegio de México/Universidad Nacional Autónoma de México, 2002.

Steckel, Richard H. "Height and Per Capita Income." *Historical Methods* 16, no. 1 (Winter 1983): 1–7.

———. "Heights and Human Welfare: Recent Developments and New Directions." *Explorations in Economic History* 46 (2009): 1–23.

———. "Percentiles of Modern Height Standards for Use in Historical Research." *Historical Methods* 29, no. 4 (Fall 1996): 157–65.

———. "Stature and the Standard of Living." *Journal of Economic Literature* 33, no. 4 (December 1995): 1903–40.

———. "What Can Be Learned from Skeletons That Might Interest Economists, Historians and Other Social Scientists?" National Bureau of Economic Research, Working Paper 9519, February 2003.

Steckel, Richard H., and Roderick Floud, eds. *Health and Welfare During Industrialization.* Chicago: University of Chicago Press, 1998.

Steckel, Richard H., and Jerome Rose, eds. *The Backbone of History: Health and Nutrition in the Western Hemisphere.* Cambridge: Cambridge University Press, 2002.

Steegman, A. Theodore, Jr. "18th Century British Military Stature: Growth Cessation, Selective Recruiting, Secular Trends, Nutrition at Birth, Cold and Occupation." *Human Biology* 57, no. 1 (February 1985): 77–95.

Steegman, A. Theodore, Jr. and P. A. Haseley. "Stature Variation in the British American Colonies: French and Indian War Records, 1755–1763." *American Journal of Physical Anthropology* 75, no. 3 (March 1988): 413–21.

Suárez-Potts, William J. "The Making of Labor Law in Mexico, 1875–1931." PhD diss., Harvard University, 2005.

Tannenbaum, Frank. *The Mexican Agrarian Revolution.* Reprint from the 1928 edition unaltered unabridged. Hamden: Archon Books, 1968.

Tanner, James M. *Foetus into Man.* Cambridge, MA: Harvard University Press, 1978.

Teja Zabre, Alfonso. *Historia de México. Una moderna interpretación.* Mexico City: Imprenta de la Secretaría de Relaciones Exteriores, 1935.

Tena Ramírez, Felipe. *Leyes fundamentales de México, 1808–2005.* Mexico City: Editorial Porrúa, 2005.

Tenorio-Trillo, Mauricio. *Mexico at the World's Fairs: Crafting a Modern Nation.* Berkeley: University of California Press, 1996.

Tenorio-Trillo, Mauricio, and Aurora Gómez Galvarriato. *El Porfiriato.* Mexico City: Centro de Investigación y Docencia Económicas / El Fondo de Cultura Económica, 2006.

Thorp, Rosemary. *Progress, Poverty and Exclusion: An Economic History of Latin America in the 20th Century.* Baltimore, MD: Johns Hopkins University Press / Inter-American Development Bank, 1998.

Tortolero Villaseñor, Alejandro. *De la coa a la máquina de vapor: Actividad agrícola e innovación tecnológica en las haciendas mexicanas: 1880–1914.* Mexico City: Editorial Siglo XXI, 1995.

Turner, Joseph Kenneth. *Barbarous Mexico.* 2nd ed. Austin: University of Texas Press, 1970.

Tutino, John. *From Insurrection to Revolution, Social Bases of Agrarian Violence, 1750–1940.* Princeton, NJ: Princeton University Press, 1988.

Van Young, Eric. "The Age of Paradox: Mexican Agriculture at the End of the Colonial Period, 1750–1810." In *The Economies of Mexico and Peru During the Late Colonial Period, 1760–1810,* edited by Nils Jacobsen and H. J. Phule, 64–90. Berlin: Colloquium Verlag, 1986.

Vanderwood, Paul. *Disorder and Progress, Bandits, Police and Development.* Lincoln: University of Nebraska Press, 1981.

Waaler, H. T. "Height, Weight and Mortality: The Norwegian Experience." *Acta Medica Scandinavica* 679 (1984): S1–S56.

Warman, Arturo. *"We Come to Object": The Peasants of Morelos and the National State.* Translated by Stephen K. Ault. Baltimore, MD: Johns Hopkins University Press, 1980.

Watcher, Kenneth, and James Trusell. "Estimating Historical Heights." *Journal of the American Statistical Association* 77, no. 378 (June 1982): 279–95.

Weir, David R. "Economic Welfare and Physical Well-Being in France, 1750–1990." In *Health and Welfare During Industrialization,* edited by Richard H. Steckel and Roderick Floud, 191. Chicago: University of Chicago Press, 1998.

Wilkie, James W. *The Mexican Revolution: Federal Change and Social Change Since 1910.* Berkeley: University of California Press, 1967.

Wilkie, James W., and Albert L. Michaels, eds. *Revolution in Mexico: Years of Upheaval, 1910–1940.* New York: Knopf, 1969.

Wrigley, E. A. *Poverty, Progress and Population.* Cambridge: Cambridge University Press, 2004.

INDEX

Italic page numbers indicate material in tables or figures.

SOCIAL SCIENCE HISTORY

Jeffrey Bortz and Stephen Haber, *The Mexican Economy, 1870–1930: Essays on the Economic History of Institutions, Revolution, and Growth*

Edward Beatty, *Institutions and Investment: The Political Basis of Industrialization in Mexico Before 1911*

Jeremy Baskes, *Indians, Merchants, and Markets: A Reinterpretation of the* Repartimiento *and Spanish–Indian Economic Relations in Colonial Oaxaca, 1750–1821*